Booze for Babes

BOOZE FOR BABES
The Smart Woman's Guide to Drinking Spirits Right by Kayleigh Kulp

Hundred Proof Publishing Co., Washington, D.C.
Nonprofits, corporations and retailers may purchase this book in bulk at discounts. For more information, please email orders@boozeforbabes.com.
www.BoozeforBabes.com

Paperback ISBN: 978-0-9857731-0-6

Printed in the United States of America

Book design by Lan Truong
Cover photo by Vanessa K. Rees; styled by Lauren LaPenna; lettering by Tuesday Bassen
Illustrations by Rebecca Pry
Edited by Lisa Butterworth

The contents of this book are for informational and entertainment purposes only. No parts should be interpreted as professional medical advice or as encouragement to drink alcohol. Readers should consult a physician with matters relating to their health and drink responsibly. Never drink and drive.

Although the author, editor, and publisher have made every effort to ensure that the information in this book was correct at press time, they do not assume and hereby disclaim any liability to any party for any loss, damage, or disruption caused by errors or omissions, whether such errors or omissions result from negligence, accident, or any other cause.

Library of Congress Cataloging-in-Publication Data 2013913641

Kulp, Kayleigh, 1986-
Booze for Babes: The Smart Woman's Guide to Drinking Spirits Right/by Kayleigh Kulp
- 1st ed.
Includes bibliographical references and index.
ISBN 978-0-9857731-0-6

For Jay

Table of Contents

CHAPTER 4:

Home Is Where the Booze Is:
How to Build Your Very Own Bar

CHAPTER 5:

Gin for the Win........110

CHAPTER 6:

Whiskey a Go-Go........134

Foreword

I came to New York City to be a Broadway star and I stayed for cocktails.

Good booze, in its complex and romantic way, does that to you. To fully "get it," though, you have to be adventurous and curious. Once exposed to its vast world, you're staying in it.

Let me explain: When I began working as a waitress in a Gramercy Park cocktail bar in 2003, the hot drinks of the day ended with 'tini— key lime pie martinis, chocolate martinis, even a Flirtini (raspberry vodka, Cointreau, and pineapple, cranberry, and lime juices).

If not overly sweet and oversized cocktails like those, I was serving—and drinking—candy-colored tipples made with store-bought mixes and cutesy names aimed at attracting women (think Sex on the Beach, Kamikazes, Cosmopolitans, and Fuzzy Navels). But after practice sessions, my mentor, Amber Tinsley, and I began going for nightcaps after closing across town to a beautiful new place on 19th Street called the Flatiron Lounge. It was like being transported to the gilded age of cocktails. You could imagine Ingrid Bergman drinking there at the long wooden bar under the Art Deco arch that was both inviting and mysterious. The Flatiron Lounge was run by three women: Julie Reiner, Susan Fedroff, and Michelle Connolly—a rarity, even though ladies had a long and storied history in America as tavern owners and formidable cocktail party hostesses.

Bye bye 'tinis; hello romantically named and completely fresh concoctions like the Geisha and Persephone. A martini here was a beautiful stirred (not shaken) blend of gin (holy cow! No vodka?), and vermouth (why did theirs not taste like rancid wine?)! This was the high-end lounge lifestyle as we knew it, and, as a 20-something bartender in training, I wanted to be a part of it. There was something glamorous about the atmosphere, about the curvaceous shapes of the glasses.

Call it my epiphany. I stalked the bar for over a year, and in 2004 landed a job there among barkeeps Katie Stipe and Phil Ward. Julie Reiner, who is one of our modern day female bartending pioneers, rewarded hard work sans gender preferences. My experiences there drove my transition from traveling musical theater minstrel to a serious cocktail bartender with a passion for creating liquid art.

At the same time, I saw my own preference evolve from sugary drinks to balanced cocktails with fresh ingredients as my palate grew with each flight of new cocktails I got to taste nightly. Once you go fresh you never go back. There was nothing more exciting than sharing my knowledge and preferences with other young ladies who wanted to try something new but were intimidated to reach beyond the billboards and marketing that had shackled

2

them.

In 2009, I began to parlay my experiences into a platform—a movement of sorts—for smart, spirited, and sassy women. I launched the New York City chapter of Ladies United for the Preservation of Endangered Cocktails, an organization that honors the cocktails, hospitality, and spirits traditions of our forebroads and encourages women to embrace them. Our goal is to constantly educate ourselves and to give back to charities. Then in 2010, I co-founded Speed Rack, an all ladies bartending competition, with another awesome bartender, Ivy Mix. All of the proceeds are donated to breast cancer research. We've met some incredible women who are behind some of the best cocktail bars, decked out in bandannas, a fearless attitude, and with endless support for the cause.

Women have come a long way in solidifying our place in the workforce, honing our tastes in gourmet food and wine, and overall kicking butt in life. But there is still work to be done when it comes to being completely comfortable drinking a scotch neat or a bourbon and branch the way men have for decades. But the tides are changing. I have recently seen several "old man" whiskey brands making an active effort to include women in the brown and aged spirits conversation, and more and more young women are choosing brown spirits over the flavored vodkas that were once their go-tos.

It goes without saying that it is time for *Booze for Babes,* a smartly written starter guide for women who want to be spirits-savvy, but don't know where to begin. Don't worry, you'll get there. Just like with food, there are so many opportunities to access quality products, with micro-distilleries popping up like breweries and more bartenders who won't settle for less than fresh citrus. So arm yourself with the knowledge in the subsequent pages and if you *do* want a "pink" drink, make it a Pink Lady.

Here's to you, drinking better. Cheers!

LYNNETTE MARRERO
Owner of DrinksAt6 Cocktail Consulting, President of Ladies United for the Preservation of Endangered Cocktails New York City, and Co-Founder of Speed Rack

PINK LADY
1 1/2 ounces gin
1/2 ounce lemon
1/4 ounce simple
1/2 ounce grenadine
1/2 ounce applejack bonded apple whiskey
1 egg white

Add all ingredients to a shaker. Shake and strain into a coupe glass and garnish with a cherry.

Introduction

If there's one overarching lesson you will take away from *Booze for Babes*, it's to never let anything intimidate you. If you bought this book, you are a babe and a force to be reckoned with. That's not to mention you want to learn how to appreciate booze. Not just any kind, but the kind that reflects refinement, the kind that takes a lot of time, care, and expertise to produce.

Even the most well educated and independent gal can make mistakes at the bar, and I don't mean taking home the wrong kind of man or getting tipsy in front of the boss. I'm talking about bigger disgraces, like giving bartenders the vaguest of drink criteria or letting a guy buy you something mixed with soda or pre-made sour mix. Both are surefire ways to lower a girl's badass factor and generally perpetuate the stereotype that women don't know Jack Daniels about booze.

I know because that was me! I used to be the sort of girl who generally knew what I wanted in life but managed to instantly lose my way at a bar. When people came over, I'd grab a no-fuss bottle of wine or six-pack of beer. I was guilty of blindly asking bartenders for drinks ("I don't know. Give me something fruity and not too strong, please!"). Rather than savoring a cocktail, I considered it an accessory. I often chose drinks that overpowered the main spirit, rather than enhanced its flavor. I also didn't know enough to choose a booze that didn't *need* the cover-up help.

Crucial mistake! After all, I was a woman who appreciated the finer things in life, enjoyed good food, wine, traveling, learning. It wasn't until a trip to the heart of whiskey and bourbon country that I learned to appreciate what the wide world of liquor and specifically, brown spirits, could offer the refined palate. I went to America's heartland a wimpy girl and came back a whiskey girl, garnering newfound respect at the bar. Soon enough, I was teaching my husband and his friends about booze. I ordered bourbon Manhattans and neat scotches at the bar, much to the staff's surprise. Despite the sometimes jolted looks I'd receive when asking exactly which Japanese whiskies were available and oh – can please give me a side of room temperature water? – most everyone found a young woman knowing her brown booze was incredibly sexy, and more importantly, I felt sexy too. Though I enjoyed cooking and entertaining at home, I finally felt I had graduated to a new level of culinary refinement.

Since then, I have become dedicated to empowering babes everywhere to embrace, learn about, and consume various fine spirits—from whiskey to brandy to tequila—the way they should be (responsibly, of course). Once I began researching the on-again, off-again relationship between women and booze throughout history—history largely dominated by men—it was easy to see why we have been in the dark about liquor all these years. The liquor companies are also partly to blame for our ignorance about liquor. If you look at contemporary ad campaigns, you'd think only men drink booze that isn't clear and that women won't touch a drink if it's not candy-colored. You'd think that women only want to drink what they are told to drink, and not what their husbands or boyfriends like. Spirits companies assume you won't like the good stuff, introducing sweeter, crossover blends and bottled cocktails meant to entice females (think skinny this, skinny that, or black cherry flavored bourbon). But these aren't necessary and we don't need stepping stones. Once babes are exposed to the beauty of sipping a well made spirit by itself or simply accented with quality ingredients, you won't wanna drink anything but the good stuff, and I'll teach you how to find it.

This book sheds some light in a succinct overview, with special shout outs to particular women who have staked their claim in the world of booze. There is one disclaimer: I am not a professional bartender, and I do not claim to have all the answers when it comes to all things booze. However, I know what it is like to feel lost when it comes to liquor. And when I wanted to learn more, there were no resources that spoke to me. It seemed there were only cocktail recipe books that dumbed it all down, niche books honing in on one element of cocktails, or those written for the experts. I just needed a quick reference guide for drinking better. You do too!

I wrote this book in a way that I would have found amply useful when starting my cocktail and spirits self-education—by breaking down tidbits about entertaining, bar etiquette, health, and basic types of booze in ways that will actually come in handy on an average Friday night. As a bonus, these tidbits might even make for titillating cocktail conversation. I also include information that helps us become better, more responsible, and more educated drinkers. Did you know, for example, that women actually get drunker faster than men because we produce less of an enzyme that breaks down alcohol? Or that after menopause we begin to break down alcohol at a similar pace as men? Did you know that coffee and bread are the absolute last things you should eat while drinking? Disseminating these insightful truths, while also highlighting amazing women who are working in the liquor industry as distillers, professional tasters, bartenders, and enthusiasts, are two more good reasons why I wrote this starter guide for women everywhere who want to be savvy about spirits and be able to confidently assert themselves in any boozy situation.

Throughout this book, I will also make a few recommendations and offer tips based on these situations and moods. Whether you are looking for a fun and approachable go-to, an easy drink to sip over conversation with girlfriends, a practical and crowd-pleasing way to serve a spirit to guests, assertive power happy hour suggestions, or an adventurous drink outside of your comfort zone, there is a gateway drink for you, as well as tons of useful information for drinking better and having a blast while doing so.

I hope *Booze for Babes* will help you understand and strengthen your relationship with the hard stuff, and will encourage you to pursue the finer things we women have formerly held outside of our comfort zone. It's amazing what a little historical context, engaging education, and, oh yeah, plenty of tasting can do!

CHAPTER 1

Why Every Lady Should Know Her Liquor

Before we get started, it's important to determine what, for all intents and purposes here, defines a babe. Technically, the term is a 14th-century Welsh derivative of the word *baban*, which referred to the sound babies make. In the last century or so, babe has been used simply to describe attractive women.

And if you consult the articulate, insightful users of UrbanDictionary.com, the word ranges in definition from "a famous pig" or a nickname given by someone who hasn't bothered to learn a person's name, to a woman who is "pleasantly proportioned," or that the word is simply an "incredibly patronizing, supposedly 'endearing' term."

Obviously the word babe is loaded with stereotypes that generally don't reflect a woman's intellectual and independent qualities. A babe is *actually* a balanced woman who maintains a sense of her own identity. She's authentic, bold and not fearful of others' disapproval. She's independent but feminine. She's straightforward and classy. She's refined and enjoys the finer things in life. She's hot—not just on the outside, but on the inside, too. Babes are women who are admired by other women and men alike.

It's time we channel our inner babes via the art of drink, too. After all, times have changed since drinking liquor was neither ladylike nor appropriate for us. Women now make up half of the workforce and consequently, the happy hour crowd. We have more disposable income than ever to spend on those Sazeracs. Combine that with the comeback of classic cocktail culture, which emulates a time when stiff, fresh, no-frills drinks like Manhattans and gin gimlets reigned, and you'd think women would know their booze. But we still don't drink on an equal playing field as men.

I'll never forget the night I spent talking with a stranger in a Nashville honkytonk. It was the night before I would begin a tour of whiskey distilleries, in an effort to learn about bourbon and Tennessee whiskey. The nice, middle-aged man was fascinated by my career as

THE SAZERAC
This boozy New Orleans classic cocktail is similar to an old-fashioned, but the addition of absinthe gives it an extra kick. Some make the drink with a sugar cube, but I sub in simple syrup for mixability.

3 ounces rye whiskey
$1/2$ ounce simple syrup
Few drops of absinthe
dash of Peychaud's bitters
lemon peel

Roll a few drops of absinthe around in a rocks glass. In a separate glass, combine the rye whiskey, simple syrup and bitters with ice and stir well. Strain into the glass with the absinthe in it. Twist the lemon peel over the glass to release its essential oils, and then drop it in the glass and enjoy!

a travel and booze writer, my fancy college education in New York City, and my enjoyment of cocktails. Attempting to discern my tastes, he mentioned that his favorite whiskey was Johnnie Walker. "Oh, I don't think I'm going to visit Johnnie Walker on this trip," I replied innocently. He chuckled. "I guess not," he replied. "It's in Scotland."

Ouch. Turns out Johnnie Walker is a scotch whiskey and this guy had taken me to school about it. I'm not afraid to admit that at that point, I didn't even know because I hadn't bothered to learn. Despite my enjoyment of good food and drink, I couldn't tell my backside from a bourbon. I'd like to say this man was a tad shocked, since I portrayed myself as an educated and refined young woman, but I played right into a common assumption that ladies know squat about libations. Well, I've since boned up, and I'm here to kick down some knowledge. I'm not saying you need to know about every single brand of whiskey and exactly where it comes from, but you should know the difference between scotch and bourbon, and that's just the beginning.

Why? Aside from the fact that a woman who can knowingly appreciate everything from a single malt scotch to a simple, well-made sidecar is damn sexy, you should be able to confidently make, ask for, and receive good drinks. Not only will this infinitely increase your enjoyment of imbibing, but it will also help us blow the lid off of the women-don't-know-Jack-about-liquor stereo-type. Still not convinced? Here are a few more reasons women should brush up on their booze.

1. *Learning about booze is fun.* On the aforementioned trip to American whiskey country, which inspired this book and jump-started my libation learning quest, I distinctly remember sit-

ting in front of Jack Daniels' master distiller Jeff Arnett as he coached our tour group through a whiskey tasting. I held the whiskey to my nose to get a true sense of the deep vanilla and oak aromas. I winced as the strong flavor tingled my tongue for several seconds, which, I learned, is not unusual for 80 proof liquor. I wasn't accustomed to drinking whiskey, especially straight. But what the hell? I became determined to properly savor it. After all, this stuff had been aged and tended to with care for four years—longer than most wines on the market—and I was on the stomping grounds of a brand that proudly serves its typical customer "from LDA to DND" (Legal Drinking Age to Damn Near Dead). By the end of the trip, and several boozy tastings later at small and large distilleries, I knew enough to hone my tastes and determine a favorite. Plus, the experience had been a blast! I had tasted so many new spirits with new friends I'd made along the way. It sparked a lifelong, enjoyable pastime of tasting and learning I'd share with family and friends over plenty of laughs, stories and meals.

Plus, having spent several years as a travel writer, I can't tell you how much the love—and knowledge—of booze unites people of all ages and backgrounds. Anywhere you go in the world, with a little digging you can find a local spirit you've never heard of, and will probably never be able to try or buy again; each one will likely have a storied tradition behind it with hometown history woven in.

Pair that with a city's drinking customs, and you have one surefire way of having a hell of a good time while learning about a new culture. Befriend a local at a bar and you will have the time of your life on any vacation. I try a new booze everywhere I go, and I love to collect bottles of one-of-a-kind liquors, spirits, and mixers to display on my bar at home.

2. **We should drink like we eat.** Think about it: these days we obsess over chefs, farm-to-table ingredients and the presentation of our food. However, many of us give hardly a thought to the quality of spirits we imbibe, what's in our drinks, the accolades of the bartender who makes them, or how they look when they reach your table. Why can some foodies distinguish between merlots from Italy, Mexico, Spain, or California, but not between a single malt scotch and a bourbon? Why is eating out of season or un-local fruits and vegetables a culinary catastrophe, but purchasing pre-made sour and Bloody Mary mixes still de rigueur? It's time we change that, especially among women. If you like to know the cuts of your steak, you should also know—or at least be curious about—the mash of your bourbon.

3. **Babes have extraordinary palates.** Being unknowledgeable about booze is a shame, because women generally have fantastic palates for identifying the complex characteristics and nuances of aged spirits. Many of us just don't realize how good our instincts and senses are . . . yet. Whiskey, for example, arguably offers more aroma compounds than any other spirit. It engages the senses and is meant to be savored, much like a delicious meal. If you love to enjoy the finer things in life, good booze is an affordable luxury.

4. **Good booze is good for you (in moderation).** In the world of booze, wine gets all the credit for being the healthy choice, but

did you know that one ounce of a spirit has the same cholesterol-lowering effect as a serving of vino? A standard liquor serving has about 97 calories, similar to a typical glass of wine. A fall 2010 study in the *British Medical Journal* indicated that a daily drink for women resulted in lower risk of heart disease and healthy cholesterol levels. That's not to mention that a shot of whiskey has the same antioxidant benefits as the recommended daily intake of vitamin C (according to researchers at Australia's Monash University), or that Angostura bitters—herb- and spice-infused alcohol created to treat fevers and digestive disorders—can cure hiccups (so says the *New England Journal of Medicine*).

And contrary to popular belief, moderate alcohol consumption helps stymie weight gain over time, particularly in females (more on that later). The truth is that the real culprits to your waistline are yucky cocktail juices, mixes and spirits fortified with fake sugars. When you learn to drink a spirit straight with no additives, or mix simple drinks from quality ingredients, your body will thank you and you can enjoy a moderate amount of spirits and cocktails without guilt.

5. ***You'll dispel the "girlie drink" myth.*** We've all heard the phrase "girlie drink" come out of a man's mouth at least once. If a cocktail is pink, topped with an umbrella, or looks otherwise "traditionally" feminine, many men won't be caught dead with it. And in the past, thanks to marketing and the socialization of gender roles that stretch beyond the bar, women who ordered an añejo tequila neat or an extra dry martini might have seemed gruff. But now, drinking that tequila or martini makes a woman appear

powerful and determined. You might even get an approving nod or "hell yeah!" from a bartender when you order it. Dark spirits, especially, are becoming more appealing to ladies because the definitions of what is womanly and what's manly are starting to blur. Societal norms are changing, and our drink preferences are following suit. Let's force bar-goers to ask, "What *is* a girlie drink or manly drink, anyway?" Because guess what? Girls drink whiskey and cognac, and men drink daiquiris!

6. ***Drinking decent booze shows good taste.*** In 1879, G. L., the author of the *Science of Taste: A Treatise on its Principles*, wrote, "Taste may be concisely defined as the capability of appreciating the beautiful; and the beautiful is, primarily, that which, by attracting the eye, satisfies and elevates the mind." This fine 19th-century gentleman was talking about great taste in the style sense, but his insight applies easily to booze as well. And since you are a babe, you already have good taste, so why not show it off in your glass? Women who show they can drink a strong spirit, and step outside their comfort zone with classics like rye whiskey, bourbon, or gin show they care about what they ingest while earning respect at the bar and in life. Drinking well exhibits confidence, sexiness, and adventurousness. Make your drink of choice aged and brown and you will practically knock the pants off any man (not that we are doing so for the enjoyment of anyone but ourselves).

Got your attention? Let's get started.

CHAPTER 2

The Herstory of Liquor

I'd venture to assume that most women—including me before writing this book—are not aware of the impact our fellow broads have had on the world of booze throughout history, and how this informs our current relationship with the hard stuff today.

Alcohol, and especially liquor, have spent the better part of civilization's existence in the realm of men. When women were able to wrangle a foothold in the booze business—like the tavern-running ladies of America's colonial era—they faced a double standard. Men allowed us to help produce and serve booze, sure, but a gal couldn't drink it in public without being dubbed a floozy.

Today, women drink freely with men, there are stellar female bartenders elevating the craft, and more women are running distilleries and working as master tasters and blenders, proving they know their stuff and can hang with the boys. But many women remain in the dark about spirits, particularly the brown categories. Women make up just 25 percent of whiskey drinkers even though whiskey is the second bestselling booze, making up 24 percent of industry revenues in 2011 (just behind vodka, which made up 32 percent), according to the Distilled Spirits Council of the United States. So why is it we don't know how to pick a proper scotch, how gin is made, or feel natural ordering a boozy and stirred cocktail, rather than a vodka soda? Let's get some context.

Since it would take an entire book to cover the history of women's involvement in booze around the world, let's narrow it down. Upon colonizing America, our English ancestors brought their drinking experiences, traditions, and societal norms with them, and alcohol trends and movements in both countries continued to echo each other for two hundred years. So here's a crash course in the break-up-and-make-up relationship we've had with booze in the United States and the United Kingdom.

WE LOVE IT . . .

I'll begin in late medieval England, when women dominated the drink trade. Ballads extolled how valuable an attractive wife could be for business at taverns as she welcomed guests, plied them with liquor, and kept them entertained. It's safe to assume this mentality continued for a couple hundred years, even overseas. That's because the history books show that in colonial America, women could not legally own or acquire property, enter into a contract, or write a will, but they were offered liquor licenses when widowed as an alternative to public assistance. By 1696, women held almost half of the liquor licenses in Boston and managed a third of its 75 taverns.

In Charleston, South Carolina, women outnumbered male barkeeps in all but one year of the 15 preceding the American Revolution. Ladies weren't just making a living off of liquor; several colonial women made big waves in the industry. Deborah Man was the most successful liquor retailer in Boston in the 1710s, and Rebecca Holmes presided over Bunch of Grapes, the renowned Boston tavern that became a Revolutionist hangout for the Sons of Liberty.

But despite their role behind the bar, ladies looking to imbibe faced a double standard. Though women were expected to use their sex appeal to sell drinks, and display motherly and hospitable sensibilities to make guests feel at home at the bar, it was considered unladylike to drink booze or hang out in taverns. Female patrons earned bad reputations and were accused of using the establishments to engage in illicit sex.

GIN SINS

Across the pond in England, where gin was incredibly popular, women were facing the same double standard. Society believed that ladies' gin drinking threatened families thanks in part to one particularly high profile case in 1734, when a woman named Judith Dufour strangled her two year-old child and sold his new clothes to buy gin. Society even blamed gin-drinking women—but not men— for the spread of syphilis and adultery. Part of this is attributed to the fact that gin shops, which operated like taverns, happened to be hangouts for prostitutes seeking tipsy male customers.

By the time the Gin Act of 1736 was enacted, which increased licensing fees and taxes on gin while authorizing rewards for snitching on petty, illegal gin hawkers in London, women were several times more likely than men to be charged, convicted, and sent to prison because of a belief that women did not belong in the business even though they were excluded from many other occupations. Though women accounted for less than 20 percent of all known gin retailers in East London and the City of London, they accounted for nearly 70 percent of the individuals charged under the Gin Act of 1736.

In folklore, female gin drinkers were characterized as witches—the ultimate diss. Take Madam Geneva, an unholy creature described as "part whore and part witch," who is the star of William Hogarth's "Gin Lane" illustration, which was published in 1751 and depicts the evil caused by gin. The star of the photo – a woman, of course – has got a baby falling from her lap off of a staircase, an open blouse and syphilis sores on her legs. The image makes the story's moral clear: gin drinking ages and destroys women, and consequently wreaks havoc on society. This is how gin got the nicknames "Ladies' Delight" and "Mothers' Ruin."

WIDESPREAD DISCRIMINATION IN THE 19TH CENTURY

The double standard didn't end there. Women continued to face libation discrimination into the 19th century, which also saw ladies experiencing a roller coaster–like struggle with their feelings about booze.

Around the world, saloons were old boys' clubs where men could escape home, down drinks, wage bets, make loans, and exchange stories among other men. After all, slouching against the bar with one foot on the rail would have been unthinkable behavior for most "respectable" women. Bars were decorated with artwork depicting cockfights, horse races, and battleships, and the whole culture revolved around the "regular" customer who told dirty jokes at women's expense. As Catherine Gilbert Murdock writes in *Domesticating Drink: Women, Men, and Alcohol 1870-1940*: "From the workplace to the blue-collar saloon and blue-chip private club, alcohol promoted male bonhomie. The drink he chose, and where he chose to drink it, defined a man's profession, his ethnicity, his community standing."

In the early part of the century, American women were getting particularly fed up, having to deal with all the responsibilities of a home and family while their men were getting good and drunk. United States women organized temperance groups to put pressure on their husbands, fathers, and sons to quit drinking. In fact, their hatred of booze really brought them together—the Daughters of Temperance boasted 20,000 members in the first half of the 19th century, making it the largest women's organization of any kind prior to the Civil War. It was this controversy over alcohol that inspired women's political participation in a variety of issues—such as the right to vote.

Not all women were on board with this movement, however, whether at home or overseas. Saloon back rooms were frequently used for coed parties or vaudeville shows, and women often came in to purchase carryout growlers of whiskey or beer. Of course they were allowed in through a ladies-only side entrance, which minimized their public appearance at the tavern and kept women from entering the barroom proper. If women drank in public, they were expected to do so moderately.

Instead of facing scrutiny, some women drank alone in the privacy of their homes, while others sought the company of female neighbors. Men had their taverns, and women would sometimes gather on stoops and in courtyards to drink together. Outside of taverns, men and women did not always drink separately, particularly among the working class. In the evenings and on Sundays, men and women might participate in growler fests (drinking parties) on rooftops or in courtyards.

But around the late 19th century, with social politics in mind, drinkers began to move the party from taverns to hotel bars where ladies were welcome, though they remained segregated in different rooms so as not to impose on male bonding. Slowly men and women began to drink together in dance halls, cabarets, and restaurants, sparking a heated public debate. Keeping women from drink-

THE FREE LUNCH

Paid for by brewery subsidies in the late 1880s, taverns began to offer free hot lunches with the purchase of a five-cent drink. Since these lunches were, by far, a better value than what could be bought anywhere else in town, and were actually tasty, many female workers were lured into saloons, though they entered through side doors and ate in their back rooms.

ing was consistent with society's insistence that good wives fulfill their duties to husbands and children by remaining at their labors rather than squandering time drinking. And people were plenty vocal about it!

However, it was completely socially acceptable for men to get housed on the regular. Most, but not all, men still loved alcohol and wanted the pastime of drinking to remain their own. They loved the saloons and fraternal societies where they imbibed. Women felt their husbands spent too much time drinking and not enough time at home with their families. Many women and children were also suffering abuse at the hands of drunken fathers and husbands. Some ladies tried to woo their husbands away from the saloon by keeping themselves attractive and their homes comfortable, while other wives tried to beat the saloon by drinking with their husbands at home.

WE LEAVE IT . . .

At the same time and into the start of the 20th century, other women were leading a charge for alcohol temperance. Perhaps the most famous and influential female temperance leader, instrumental in eventually enacting Prohibition, was Carry Nation. Nation, a strong and somewhat scary woman—she dressed in black and carried a hatchet—was a member of the Women's Christian Temperance Union, which backed legislation to restrict or ban the sale of alcohol in local communities. The group labeled drunkenness "a national curse," and by holding nonviolent protests was able to close over 25,000 drinking establishments. So why was Nation such a buzz kill? Blame it on her first husband, Dr. Charles Glloyd, who hid in his local Masonic lodge during irresponsible drinking binges and allowed fellow Masons to shelter him from his wife's reckoning (Nation would later attack fraternal organizations as vigorously as saloons). In an uncommon move for the time, Nation separated from him while pregnant. Six months after the child's birth, Glloyd drank himself to death. In Nation's eyes, alcohol was responsible for ruining her marriage and those of countless others, which is why she worked tirelessly to ban booze. In response to her efforts, Maine became the first state to outlaw the sale and manufacture of alcoholic beverages in 1851. By 1855, 13 other territories and states followed suit.

In 1877, she married pastor David Nation and the two settled in Medicine Lodge, Kansas. When she learned local saloon owners were violating the Kansas constitutional amendment prohibiting the manufacture and sale of intoxicating beverages, she organized a local chapter of the WCTU. Entering bars, the group sang hymns and prayed for the souls of the patrons. She began attacking illegal saloons and liquor proprietors with stones and hatchets. Eventually, these demonstrations drove the saloons out of business, and though she won that battle, her violent behavior caused her second husband to divorce her.

Carry Nation's campaign of destruction, which she called "hatchetation," resulted in her being arrested 30 times. Before her crusade ended, Nation came to Miami in 1908 to support locals in drying up the "wicked little city." While in Miami, a city that banned the sale of alcohol on Sundays, Nation went on an unannounced inner city tour, noting an abundance of crime and corruption.

BALLSY BABES OF THE PROHIBITION ERA

Temperance groups like Nation's finally got their way, and Prohibition, which banned the production, sale, and consumption of alcohol in the United States, was enacted in 1919. In fact, women supported Prohibition more than any other single issue at the time, including suffrage (women got the right to vote a year later in 1920). Furthermore, in supporting Prohibition, women were dismantling society's strongest link to masculinity at the time. But not all women supported the alcohol ban, feeling liberated by the ability to not only drink freely among men in speakeasies and other illegal watering holes, but to capitalize on illicit booze profits. During Prohibition, a few women played crucial roles on both sides of the booze battle.

Spanish Marie

I love the story of Mary Waite, a six-foot-tall broad with a fiery temper who made a name for herself in the rumrunning biz, one of the most popular and easy ways to get booze into the United States. Rumrunners would load up ships and boats in the Caribbean, where  rum was being produced, and sneak rum into Florida ports, where it was then distributed to the state's speakeasies and beyond. And it didn't take long for rumrunners to also smuggle Canadian whiskey, English gin, and French champagne to New York and Boston.

Mary Waite's husband, Charlie, was a top dog in the rumrunning business. But when he died in a 1926 Coast Guard shootout, Mary took over the empire, keeping a home base in Havana. With part Mexican heritage and part Swedish, she was nicknamed "Spanish Marie" and became controller of the booze trade from Cuba to

South Florida, operating several speedboats and becoming incredibly wealthy as a result of her business savvy. She had several partners in the bedroom and led a generally risque life.

Her demise came during a routine run. One of her boats, which was loaded with firepower but not with booze, was meant to lure the Coast Guard and attract their attention so that her other booze-laden boats could skate by them unnoticed. The Coast Guard finally caught Waite by intercepting and breaking her radio codes during this scheme, and they arrested her while she unloaded liquor from her boat in Miami on March 12, 1928. The boat had 5,526 bottles of whiskey, rum, gin, wine, champagne, and beer.

Because Mary had left her sleeping children at home that day, she retained an attorney and pleaded with law enforcement to let her return to them, promising to show up for a court hearing the next day. They conceded, but Mary never showed up. In fact, she disappeared, along with her money and boats, forever.

Gertrude Lythgoe

Gertrude Lythgoe grew up a smart orphan who, during Prohibition, worked for a London liquor exporter. Her employer saw an opportunity in supplying liquor to the United States through the Bahamas.

Needing a savvy businessperson to oversee their affairs, the company tapped the likable Lythgoe for the assignment. In Nassau, she set up the company's wholesale liquor business on Market Street, initiated sales transactions with potential buyers, and oversaw the shipments.

Buyers in the male-dominated business were wary of her, but her smarts overcame their skepticism and she became known as "The Bahama Queen." Lythgoe sailed on the schooner of notorious rum-runner Bill McCoy from New York to Rum Row, a line of anchored boats just outside United States waters on the Atlantic Coast. Like Spanish Marie, this babe meant business and she was known to threaten members of Nassau rum mobs with pistols.

Lythgoe was arrested in 1925 and charged with smuggling 1,000 cases of whiskey into New Orleans. At the time, *The St. Petersburg Times* newspaper called her "Queen of the Booze Buccaneers of the Bahamas." But because Lythgoe had left the shipment with a subordinate who had shadily arranged the deal to make himself the beneficiary, she got off the hook, became a celebrity, and wrote a memoir (*The Bahama Queen: the Autobiography of Gertrude "Cleo" Lythgoe*, published in 1965). She died in Los Angeles in 1974, at the age of 86.

Mabel Walker Willebrandt

On the flipside of the Prohibition debate, one of the most hard-nosed enforcers happened to be a lady—Mabel Walker Willebrandt. In 1921, Willebrandt was appointed assistant attorney general and took up the enforcement of Prohibition. Since women had just been granted the right to vote, the fact that she was given so much power and authority is pretty remarkable. When she came in, liquor laws were openly being defied; law enforcement had been corrupted by smugglers. Willebrandt had $11 million appropriated by Congress so that the Coast Guard could fight rum runners like Mary Waite by expanding the fleet with 203 large patrol boats, advanced radio technology, and officers. Her determination eventually led to the curtailing of smuggling, resulting in boats being confiscated and hundreds of arrests and convictions.

CHANGING OUR MINDS AGAIN

Shortly after they helped instate Prohibition in 1919, women soon became a part of the movement to repeal it, thanks to the negative effects the booze ban had on their lives. Instead of drinking in plain sight, legally, their loved ones were drinking under wraps. As a result, some found themselves tangled up in criminal business ventures, bootlegging and chugging alcohol in sultry, mixed-sex speakeasies. Plus, Prohibition had facilitated the entry of drink into the sacred home for illegal cocktail parties, exposing families to the detriments of liquor. So the "gentler sex" rallied once again, this time forming the Women's Organization of National Prohibition Reform—the most popular repeal organization in the country.

The 1933 repeal of Prohibition made it legal once again for Americans to imbibe, but men were still finding ways to keep women out of their drinking scene. Afraid that barmaids were encroaching on their jobs, bartenders in New York City in 1936 sought to legally ban women from drinking booze *and* pouring it. But with the start of World War II, more and more women began to take places behind the bar, filling in for the men who went off to fight. These women began forming unions, and by 1953, were gaining serious ground, defeating potential laws that would ban them from running barrooms.

By the beginning of the 1960s, cocktail culture of the *Mad Men* variety became a part of the high life and women were again expected to serve, and allowed to partake in moderation. Ladies drank and served stiff whiskey, gin, and rum drinks and could down a Manhattan with the best of them. But even with all that progress, in 1971, laws still existed in California that prohibited women from serving whiskey. After that, it had become socially acceptable for women to indulge in drink alongside men, but with unspoken boundaries (such as men drank "manly" drinks like whiskey and women did not touch them).

BARTENDER BABES

We can't begin to understand the complex relationship between women and bars without also honoring the women *behind* bars throughout history. These bottle-slingin' babes have brought some serious cred to the male-dominated industry, proving that women have the wherewithal and booze savvy to drink and serve spirits right.

Alice Guest

After her husband died in 1685, this widow received a tavern license and ran her public house from a cave along the Delaware River in colonial Philadelphia. Her location gave her prime access to mariners and ship workers, and she earned an extraordinary amount of revenue. By the time she passed in 1693, Guest had constructed an entire compound along the river and was revered as a fine businesswoman.

Ada Coleman

A leading lady of London's regal and famous Savoy Hotel in the late 20th century, Coleman mentored Harry Craddock, an underling at the Savoy who eventually wrote the home bar staple, *The Savoy Cocktail Book.* She was well-known among prestigious authors, politicians, and celebrities at a time when few women earned such high-browed clients' respect in the service sector. Coley—as Coleman was nicknamed—became known as the world's most famous barmaid.

Helen David

David was still bartending at the Brass Rail in Port Huron, Michigan, when she died in 2008 at 91. David was born above an ice cream parlor owned by her family; in 1937, her mother converted it to a bar when her father died and times got tough.

According to a published interview with David's cousin, Tony Abou-Ganim, a bartender and author of *The Modern Mixologist,* David was startled by her mother's decision, telling her that proper ladies didn't run saloons. David's mother said something to the effect of, "A lady is a lady no matter where you put her, but she needs to have a buck in her pocket!" David was a modern lady pioneer of bar hospitality, providing her employees with sick leave, paid holiday, and health insurance. And her life is still honored in the industry—every year at Tales of the Cocktail, the country's premier annual spirits conference, a bartender is given the Helen David Lifetime Achievement Award.

THE NEW GUARD

Acclaimed bartender and author gaz regan wrote this in his 2003 book *The Joy of Mixology*:

"In 1973, when I started tending bar in New York, there were very few female bartenders in the city. Bar owners justified their hiring practices by claiming they needed men to carry cases of beer, heave garbage pails full of ice, and deal with unruly customers, but times have changed. I would venture to guess that there are now just as many women as men behind the stick in Manhattan: they carry cases, heave garbage pails full of ice, and deal with unruly customers just as successfully as any man—as long as they are cut out to be bartenders. And of course, the same applies to men—if bartending isn't in their hearts, they won't do a good job. The rule of thumb is this: A good bartender, male or female, can handle any given situation at any given time in any given bar."

Thankfully, that sentiment is being heeded, and there are a number of women making names for themselves in today's booze biz, like *Aisha Sharpe* who is revered in the industry for her cocktail consulting work with her firm Contemporary Cocktails Inc. and has had recipes featured in *The New York Times* and *New York Magazine*. *Julie Reiner* is another. After an apprenticeship under "King Cocktail" Dale DeGroff in the late 1990s, Reiner made her mark with innovative drinks before opening revered New York City bars Flatiron Lounge and Clover Club. Reiner's recipes have been featured in *The New York Times, Wall Street Journal, Playboy, Food & Wine*, and more. *Audrey Saunders* also worked under Dale DeGroff in the late 1990s before opening two successful

MEET LADIES UNITED FOR THE PRESERVATION OF ENDANGERED COCKTAILS (LUPEC)

In addition to the libation-loving ladies we discussed earlier, who are elevating women in the business and exposing female imbibers to the world of drink through the craft of bartending, there is a nationwide organization that is doing the same. With a twinkle in their eyes and swizzle sticks in their glasses, the Ladies United for the Preservation of Cocktails (LUPEC) are hell-bent on creating an atmosphere in which classy broads can honor the spirits of the past, while continuing the "150-year American tradition of dangerous women calling themselves ladies while they chip away at the patriarchy." The organization also encourages the collection of throwback cocktail recipes and the use of vintage barware as a nod to women's mark on the barroom tradition. Over the past couple of years, LUPEC has thrown a Macallan scotch party during New York Fashion Week, a whiskey cocktail soiree honoring International Women's Day, and more.

Check LUPEC.org for more details on upcoming events and how you might be able to become a member.

bars focusing on fresh, classic cocktails called Blackbird and Pegu Club, both in New York City. And *Charlotte Voisey* was recognized by the James Beard Foundation in 2009 for her contribution to the trade, is a brand ambassador for Hendrick's gin, and has even appeared as a contestant on *Top Chef.* Her acclaim started back in 2002 when she opened a classic cocktail bar in London called Apartment 195 and subsequently became U.K. Bartender of the Year—quite a feat in Britain's male-dominated scene. *Lynnette Marrero*, who wrote the foreword for this book, is not only a celebrated bartending queen in New York, but she also cofounded Speed Rack—the first national cocktail competition to honor and engage top female bartenders—with colleague Ivy Mix in 2011.

In addition to those slinging drinks behind the bar, there are also plenty of entrepreneurial ladies following their bliss in the booze business now. A few that come to mind include Ana Lorena Vásquez Ampié and Joy Spence, the master blenders of Zacapa and Appleton rums, respectively, Maribel Garcia, the master distiller of Don Diego Santa tequila, Lesley Gracie, the master distiller of Solerno blood orange liqueur, Melanie Asher, master distiller of Macchu Pisco, and Erin Brophy and Mhairi Voelsgen, founders of BroVo Spirits. You'll find interviews with several others throughout this book. They are pioneers, inspired by a select few before them like Bessie Williamson, who ran the Laphroaig scotch distillery from 1954 to 1967, or Marjorie Samuels, who built a renowned brand when she gave Maker's Mark bourbon its name, designed its distinctive label, and came up with its signature wax seal in 1959.

Despite their progress, many of these bartenders, representatives and businesswomen admit they've experienced gender discrimination during their tenures. Heather Greene, a former brand ambassador for Glenfiddich scotch, said when she began marketing the spirit she'd spend a half hour explaining to a room full of men that she knew her stuff so she could earn their respect. When Lisa Laird Dunn, vice president of Laird's Applejack brandy, took her post, she was told by a client that he wouldn't buy his whiskey from a woman. But those instances are luckily getting fewer and farther between.

The bottom line is that there is countless female talent out there, ladies who are masterfully pouring drinks and producing liquor like a boss, all representing just how badass booze-loving babes can be. So next time you order a drink, raise a glass to the ladies who've raised the bar!

CHAPTER 3

The Right Way to Drink

By now you babes have learned how to drink. But have you learned how to drink *well?* How we drink is as important as how we eat, dress, speak or pretty much do anything in life. It helps paint a picture of our personalities, priorities, and moods. Furthermore, how you drink sends a message about you to the company you keep. The right drink at the right time feels good in your bones. It hits the spot. You see, the ritual of drinking is as important as the drink itself. When you drink, it should be meaningful, and you should feel *good* about it.

In this chapter, I will discuss what a cocktail is, what makes good booze and how to shop for it, how to taste booze and the science behind why you like what you like, how to mix a drink properly, how booze affects women's health, and how to be a babe at a bar – the kind of knowledge that is sure to sure to turn you into the savvy, sophisticated drinker we know you can be!

COME CORRECT: WHAT *IS* A COCKTAIL?

According to *The Balance, and Columbian Repository*, a 1806

New York newspaper, a cocktail is "a stimulating liquor, composed of spirits of any kind, sugar, water, and bitters." It was the first known documentation of the cocktail's definition in print and continues to be the gospel in the industry today.

A general rule of thumb is that a cocktail contains *strong, sweet, sour* and *weak* ingredients, but the ratio of each is different depending on what you're going for, flavor-wise. *Strong* refers to the base spirit, such as gin, whiskey, brandy or vodka. *Sweet* refers to the sugar, such as liqueurs, syrups or fruit. *Sour* includes tart ingredients like cranberries or apples but also covers citrus, vermouths and bitters. *Weak* means water, and this usually comes in the form of ice. All cocktails need *weak*. In fact, about 25 percent of a drink consists of water, usually via ice melting while shaking or while sitting in your glass.

And while all of this means, for lack of specificity, that a cocktail could technically contain an infinite number of sweet, bitter, and boozy ingredients, it's best to keep the ingredient total to no more than five. Any ingredients you add should be high quality and enhance the flavors and attributes of the other ingredients, rather than mask or overwhelm them. A simple drink is a classy drink.

It's also important to remember that the key to a good drink is balance. Remember, the goal is not to get immensely trashed, either. Knowing your tastes and honing your palate will help you determine the right balance in a particular drink. For example, ryes are generally drier than bourbons. If you're using a rye to make a Manhattan, you'll probably want to pair it with a sweet, rather than dry vermouth.

That being said, there are thousands of recipes available

out there so that you – or your bartender – don't have to do the guesswork. When I asked Philip Duff, a well-known bartender and cocktail consultant about how home bartenders can ensure they make a good drink any time, he said, "If you did not know anything about computers you would not start building one from scratch. There's a misconception that you're not a proper cocktail maker if you can't come up with your own. You might screw [a recipe] up a little bit but cocktail recipes are incredibly robust."

If you want to experiment, use these tried and true recipes as a base for tweaking to your own tastes.

STIR IT UP: HOW BOOZE IS SERVED

When a server or bartender asks how you'd like your hooch, know the answer. Here are a few terms you should know.

When drinking booze straight, you can order it:

Neat: In a glass without ice
On the rocks: In a glass with ice

Cocktails are served several ways:

Shaken: Rattled with ice in a cocktail shaker. Reserved for drinks with fruit and citrus juices to wake up and evenly distribute flavors.

Stirred: Poured into a glass and stirred with a spoon or swizzle stick. Best when all ingredients are alcoholic.

Straight up or up: Shaken or stirred with ice, then strained and served without ice, usually in a stemmed glass (so your hands don't warm it up).

With a twist: A citrus peel is squeezed over the drink, which gives it a nice aroma and releases the peel's essential oils. Yes, that garnish *does* serve a purpose!

Rinse: You would not likely specify ordering a drink this way, per se, but I included it here because you will occasionally see it on a cocktail menu or find the technique helpful at home. Rinsing means taking about a quarter ounce of a spirit—for just a hint of its flavor—and rolling it around to coat the inside of the glass before discarding the excess liquid.

Though "cocktail" is generally used to describe all alcoholic concoctions, there are terms that distinguish certain styles of drinks, including:

Fizz: Contains sugar, citrus, sometimes egg, and carbonated water.

Sour: Contains equal parts citrus and sugar, along with a liquor and/or liqueur.

Flip: Contains sherry, egg and sugar, making for a light and creamy consistency.

Aperitif (ah-pear-ah-teef): A light alcoholic drink served before dinner, usually a liqueur, vermouth or other fortified wine.

Digestive (dee-jest-teev): A heavier alcoholic drink served after dinner with the intention of aiding digestion; usually a liqueur or brown spirit served straight.

Pousse-cafe: A drink made with multiple liqueurs layered by density.

Toddy: A cocktail with alcohol, spice, and hot water.

Long or tall: A drink with more liquid volume, basically, in the form of a mixer. Usually served in a Collins or highball glass, and consisting of a liquor and non-alcoholic mixer(s), such as a gin and tonic. You could ask a bartender if he or she had any suggestions for long tequila drinks, for example.

Short: A drink with less liquid volume and non-alcoholic mixer, and therefore higher alcohol content. Usually served in rocks or coupe glasses, for example, like an old-fashioned.

TOP SHELF: WHAT MAKES GOOD BOOZE

Good cocktails are defined by good ingredients, and the same goes for each individual spirit that goes into a drink. Over time and the more you taste, your palate will develop and you'll be able to distinguish each ingredient in a drink. Better yet, you'll prefer your best spirits neat or with minimal mixers. But in the meantime, how do you know if a booze is good enough to drink on its own?

They say the only bad wine is wine that's turned to vinegar. The rest is subjective. The same generally holds true with spirits. If you like something, you like it. But you only *really* like it if you can drink it straight. Don't worry if you're not there yet. Practice makes perfect!

The qualities that make a spirit good largely vary by category, which we'll get into later. The same reason a cognac is extraordinary is not necessarily the same reason that makes a tequila great.

There are plenty of large brands that put out good, reliable products, but small batch labels offer greater variety and, sometimes, more complexity. There is more flexibility to experiment with small batches, and the end result is usually more unique. Since there's a wide array available, you're more likely to discover something you love because it has been tweaked with just the right hints of herbs, florals, fruits, grain, or wood.

For the sake of consolidation, there are a few general guidelines that determine whether a liquor is worth its glass. A good spirit:

- Contains flavors that change or develop depending on how you taste or mix it.

- Contains no additives or artificial sugars.

- Does not contain hints of wet hay, rotten apples, sulfur, or soapiness, which indicate distillation and fermentation flaws and occur more often in craft spirits, which are artisanal and/or independent spirits produced in relatively small batches. The spirit should also not taste or smell like astringent or ethyl alcohol. This indicates a high level of phenols and tannins.

- Tastes balanced. No one ingredient or flavor should dominate a spirit, unless it is purposeful (like anise, artichoke, orange, or cherry liqueur).

- Should feel clean and light in your mouth, rather than thick and heavy.

SHOP GIRL: HOW TO SHOP FOR GOOD BOOZE

When shopping for your sauce, how can you tell whether a bottle will disappoint you or not once you crack it open? The truth is you can't—not without doing your research, and especially not without tasting it. Sure, the bottle may prominently display accolades from *Tasting Panel* magazine, which is always a good sign, but labels from the Beverage Testing Institute, on the other hand, are pay-for-play and do not indicate the quality of a spirit. I know, I know—how the heck can you decipher all of this?

Ivy Mix, a bartender at the venerable Clover Club in New York City and co-founder of Speed Rack, says she simply goes for what her grandmother drank, which includes staples of Beefeater or Absolut. She also never buys spirits in plastic bottles, since those containers can leak carcinogens.

If you truly want to learn what you like and what is good quality, read as many reviews as you can before grabbing a shopping cart. After all, if you are going to spend upwards of $30, $40, and even $50 or more, it is worth the effort. Perhaps the most venerable spirits reviewer in the country is F. Paul Pacult, who writes a quarterly *Spirits Journal* with reviews on every new and established product across every category imaginable. He's also published two volumes of reviews in book form, *Kindred Spirits* and *Kindred Spirits 2*. Pacult has been tasting booze professionally since 1997, and his reviews are notoriously, brutally honest. Magazines with primarily male audiences (big surprise!) cover booze really well—*GQ*, *Esquire*, *Private Clubs*, and *Wine & Spirits* come to mind. Check blogs and websites like Liquor.com or DrinkoftheWeek.com.

But just because a reviewer says a product is good or not good does not mean that you will or will not like it. Be adventurous, and taste whatever intrigues you because everyone's palate is different. Taste as much as you can. Comparison is key. You'll probably have little memory of how a Woodford Reserve bourbon tastes two days later when you go to taste a Knob Creek bourbon, for instance, but if you put them side by side at the same time, you'll be better able to distinguish between their characteristics. You'll develop a preference and that's what it is all about.

PRINCIPLES OF PALATE:
THE SCIENCE OF TASTING BOOZE

Taste—whether literal or figurative—is *so* subjective and personal.

The *American Heritage Dictionary* tells us that taste is "the sense that distinguishes the sweet, sour, salty, umami (savory, meaty, or brothy), and bitter qualities of dissolved substances in contact with the taste buds on the tongue and that this sense, in combination with the senses of smell and touch, receives a sensation of a substance in the mouth."

There are many factors affecting our taste preferences. While research shows that everyone likes sweet, a person's salt preference could be affected by whether their mother lost electrolytes and sodium during pregnancy through morning sickness. If that is the case, children are more likely to prefer salty foods. In fact, flavors pass from a mother to her baby via amniotic fluid near the end of the first trimester, so our natural preferences come from our mother's diet at the time of pregnancy, according to sommelier François Chartier's book, *Taste Buds and Molecules: the Art and Science of Food, Wine, and Flavor.*

Another factor affecting your preference is that your taste buds turn every few days, so it's also possible something could taste awry one day and great the next. Your booze tastes will naturally change over time, and that means, ladies, that your tastes can also be trained! All it takes is an open mind and practice.

THE NOSE KNOWS: HOW SMELL AFFECTS TASTE

While different regions of the tongue can recognize several tastes at once, bitter receptors are documented as being mostly on the back of the tongue and in the cheek of the mouth. The tip of the tongue is responsive to all five tastes, but is particularly sensitive to sweet and salty. The sides of your tongue are most responsive to sour or acidic tastes. Your whole tongue is receptive to umami.

But tasting is about so much more than just buds in your mouth. Flavors are the nuances of food and booze. Something that tastes like raspberry, pepper, coffee, or pineapple, is actually identified through the nose. Your tongue does not recognize these! Your tongue only recognizes that raspberry is sweet or that coffee is bitter. Nancy Fraley, a professional taster and whiskey and rum blender who owns a sensory analysis consultancy called Nosing Services, hardly relies on her tongue to taste for her. It's all about the nose and its 50,000 receptors that identify characteristics and associate them with those you've smelled before. Those receptors also connect those smells with sounds, like a crunch, or an appearance. If you want to know how important your nose is to tasting, just bite into an apple while holding your nose. If you were blindfolded, you might not be able to detect what it is because the flavors would be nearly nonexistent, though you may be able to figure it out from texture, taste (i.e., acidic), and temperature.

THE SUPERTASTERS

Some people are physically and genetically more adept at tasting booze. They can identify aromas and flavors that no one else can, and they can identify consistencies in a batch of booze the way only few can.

I am incredibly impressed by cognac and scotch blenders, especially for big brands. Every bottle of Hennessy VSOP or Glenfiddich 18 you buy has been personally approved by a company's master blender, and their sole job is to make sure it tastes the same—and awesome—every time you buy it.

They do this despite variables beyond their control, like the quality of the grain, grape, agave, or other harvest or climate changes in a warehouse where barrels are stored for aging. This takes a special nose and a lot of practice.

THE "BITTER" TRUTH: HOW YOUR TONGUE TASTES IT

Bitter is a taste commonly found in a spirit or cocktail and there is a lot at play in determining how we may feel about them.

For starters, bitter compounds exist in just about all foods and drinks, from cider apples to broccoli, coffee, tea, and zucchini. They exist in spirits like Campari, Cynar (an artichoke aperitif), and other cocktail ingredients. When you taste something bitter, your mouth and brain perceive it as a danger signal. In fact, the cavemen did not initially eat bitter foods because they thought them to be harmful. That is one reason many bitter foods are

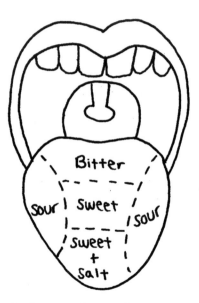

not essential to the human diet and why some people are more sensitive to bitter booze. Alternatively, some bitter compounds have been used in healing recipes (hence: flavored bitters used in cocktails). On average, humans are 1,250 times more sensitive to quinine, a bitter compound found in tonic water, than to sucrose, which is why some adore gin and tonics while others despise them.

STRESS AND TASTE
According to research reported by François Chartier, a renowned sommelier who wrote *Taste Buds and Molecules: the Art and Science of Food, Wine, and Flavor*, people who are stressed or nervous have more trouble distinguishing bitter and salty tastes than do other tasters. So next time you go to taste new booze, relax!

But on the flipside, women who are pregnant, menstruating, are on some types of birth control, or who smoke, can't perceive bitterness as well as others, according to research by Russell L. Rouseff, the editor of *Bitterness in Foods and Beverages*. As we grow older, particularly after the age of 50, we begin to lose taste buds. The salty and sweet go first, while the bitter and sour taste buds stick around longer. These taste buds deteriorate sooner for women than for men. Wisdom tooth extraction can damage the chorda tympani taste nerve, which affects one's ability to taste bitterness. Head injuries, Alzheimer's, and Parkinson's also affect bitter-sensing nerves.

If you come to love bitter items, though, and drink or eat a lot of them, you will tire out your taste buds. That means it will be harder and harder to distinguish between tastes. It's better enjoy bitter flavors integrated in a balanced drink.

WHY WE LOVE SWEETNESS

As you get older, you lose taste buds that are more sensitive to sweet, making bitter tastes more appealing. But the opposite is true of our younger years. Did you know that a mother's milk tastes like vanilla to a baby? It's one of the reasons sweet appeals to us as children.

But aside from our natural penchant for sweetness that stems from our wee years, science suggests that alcohol satisfies the same craving that sugar does, making their combination a physiological dream. In fact, sugar consumption in the United States skyrocketed following the enactment of Prohibition.

While you may be more apt to enjoy sweet drinks as a novice taster, you can teach yourself to like things that are less sweet by swapping the sweet ingredient for something that simply *smells* sweet. When it comes to manufacturers of foods and spirits, making things sweet is a lazy way of making products more palatable, says Barb Stuckey in her book, *Taste What You're Missing: the Passionate Eater's Guide to Why Good Food Tastes Good.* When you want to add the perception of sweet without an actual sweet ingredient, combine spirits with ingredients like nutmeg, vanilla, cocoa, and cinnamon. Though they are inherently bitter-tasting, their use in sweet recipes tricks our olfactory system into associating them with such, making a cocktail or drink you'd otherwise despise easier to drink.

HOW TO FIGURE OUT WHAT YOU LIKE

Do upscale cocktail bars give you anxiety? Do you fear ordering a new drink because you're scared you'll hate it? Want to begin exploring the world of brown spirits but you're not sure how? Maybe you enjoy tasting new spirits but aren't sure how to describe them?

Making sure you'll get something you like is dependent on your ability to describe your tastes. The more specific you can be, the more likely a server, liquor retailer, or bartender will be able to hook you up with the perfect product. Part of it comes from flavors you've tasted and know you like, as we discussed before, such as caramels, cherries, oak, or citrus.

Once these are determined, you can use these characteristics to find similar traits in new drinks and spirits. For example, if you usually enjoy a whiskey sour, you probably enjoy lemon or citrus combined with the robust nature of a grain-based spirit. Use this as a jumping off point to try more citrus-forward gins, for example.

QUICK TIP
Vanilla has an intensity-calming effect on other overwhelming tastes. A very spicy drink or dish can be softened by its presence.

TRAINING YOUR TASTEBUDS: HONING GOOD TASTE

The more spirits and cocktails you try, the better taste you'll acquire. I'm not talking about the physical kind here, but rather in the stylish sense. Becoming a drinker with good taste is not natural or automatic. It is the result of research and experience.

It's knowing there are only 3,000 Pappy Van Winkle 23-year-old bourbons in the country, and ordering one to see how its coveted characteristics dance on the palate. It's having read that Casa Dragones' joven tequila made Oprah's Favorite Things and ordering it to see if it's worth its salt.

HOW SPIRITS GET THEIR AROMAS

The rum and bourbon you taste do not actually have caramel or coffee in them, so why do they smell like they do?

Several factors during production determine a spirit's aromas. Most of them come from the type of wood barrels in which a spirit is aged, but also from compounds exposed through distillation, fermentation, and aging.

For example, the firing and toasting of barrels in which a spirit is aged creates a phenol compound called vanillin, a major source of vanilla aromas. Other scents from barrels could include roasted almonds, sawdust, maple syrup, toast, caramel, and toasted licorice. Volatile compounds that signify flaws in distillation or aging could include coffee, burnt sugar, walnuts, curry, bread, green apples, and smoke.

When professionals put together pairings, they pair the compound causing the flavor in booze with a food that contains the same compound. They don't taste the same on the surface, but this compound link makes them subtly harmonious. Neat, right?

**SAY ANYTHING: HOW TO DESCRIBE A DRINK WITH
WORDS OTHER THAN "I LIKE IT"**

Here are a few adjectives that can help you describe what you're
tasting and understand why you do or do not like something:

Acidic	Full-bodied	Sharp
Acrid	Harsh	Spicy
Aftertaste	Intense	Sour
Aromatic	Mellow	Strong
Astringent	Mouthwatering	Sugary or sweet
Biting	Peppery	Tangy
Candied	Piquant	Tart
Caustic	Robust	Tasteless
Complex	Salty	Velvety
Fruity	Savory	Zesty

Once you've had the best, you won't look back, and the key to getting the best is getting educated. Taste everything. Some spirits will be good, some will be bad. Some of them will be amazing but they're just not your thing. It's almost like going through a bunch of bum boyfriends before finding "the one" that has all of the qualities you like. Don't be intimidated. If you see a $22 or $32 glass of something on a cocktail menu, ask the bartenders about it. Why is it expensive? Who makes it? If you can afford to order it, do so and ask yourself and the bartender why it tastes the way it does. If you can't afford it, write down the name and see if you can purchase the bottle in a store, maybe even splitting the cost with a friend to taste. I keep a tasting log—just a compact Moleskine notebook will do—to record notes about each new liquor I taste. It is difficult to remember them for future reference and comparison if you don't. Besides, it's also fun to record the date, the names of people you're with, and the setting or place at which you tried it for reminiscing down the road, particularly if it's an extra special product.

That being said, the best liquor isn't always the most expensive. Define the qualities that make a product unique, and determine its dollar-to-goodness ratio based on your comparisons of it to other products. Soon enough, you will have honed good taste.

FLAVOR SAVERS: TRICKS FOR MAXIMIZING THE TASTE OF YOUR TIPPLES

Now that you've learned how to taste, let's learn how to put those skills to work. For starters, you'll want to prepare booze correctly so that its natural flavors are best exhibited. This is how to do it:

Don't freeze your spirits: Freezing dulls flavors, so taste at room temperature. When serving cocktails, freeze your glasses instead of the booze to achieve the chilling effect without sacrificing quality.

Garnish is important: A twist isn't just for show; the peel adds essential oils to the top of the drink. Add them when a recipe calls for it, and skip them when it doesn't. When creating your own drinks, keep this in mind and choose to garnish or not based on your desired outcome for aroma and taste.

Shake vs. stir: If the recipe calls for citrus or fruit juice, eggs, or cream, the general rule is to shake it to extract the best flavors and properly integrate the juices. So when it is time to shake, shake, shake, do it horizontally, vigorously. The contents don't mix as well when shaken vertically, top to bottom. Use both hands. If all of the cocktail ingredients are alcoholic, stir your drink instead.

Don't make it too hot: When making hot cocktails, be careful. The alcohol will evaporate if too hot and the drink will lose its aromas. You should be able to hold the glass comfortably.

TEMPERATURE AND TASTE

To further emphasize how much the temperature at which you serve booze impacts the flavors you'll taste in it, here are a few tidbits, which also apply to wine, to keep in mind for getting the most out of your drinking experience, and help you adjust to new flavors and textures as you learn to booze:

- A sweet spirit served cold will seem less sweet than it really is.
- A dry spirit will seem more acidic if served cold.
- When booze is served at a warmer temperature, you will inherently taste the sweet more, and bitter and acidic less.

ALL TOGETHER NOW: TO MIX, OR NOT TO MIX?

The point of this book is to teach you how to be the ultimate babe you are by appreciating fine spirits with minimal coverup. With so many great craft spirits coming out across the board, it's worth giving "neat" a try, especially when it's a fine (usually read: expensive) spirit.

There's a place for spirits in cocktails, of course! What would a cocktail be without a good base? But what we never want is a mixer that is artificial, processed (yes, that takes store-bought OJ out of the picture), or that masks the taste of the spirit. Mixing spirit with Coke is what you do in college when you just want to get drunk. When you have a carefully crafted, high-quality spirit, less is more. In my opinion, the worst store-bought mixer is sour mix. Lord knows what's in that stuff, but it's the biggest culprit of headaches I have ever experienced. And the sad part is, it's so easy to make it fresh.

MAKE HOMEMADE SOUR MIX
Sour mix is easy and when homemade, is fresh and sweet.

1 oz water
1 oz sugar
2 parts fresh squeezed lemon juice

Simmer water and sugar on the stove until the sugar is dissolved. Let cool. Combine the simple syrup and lemon juice.

A mixer can make or break a drink, because the entire cocktail is only as good as the weakest ingredient in it. Take a margarita, for example. Make a margarita using fresh lime juice and agave nectar, and you'll never touch a store-bought mix again. The more natural and fresh your ingredients are, the fewer hangovers you'll have, the more flavor you'll taste, and the more enjoyable it will be.

Think twice about mixing when:
1. You paid more than $40 for a 750 ml bottle of spirit
2. You have never tried the spirit
3. The spirit is rare

Mix when:
1. Your bottle is cheap (or cheaper)

2. You want to steadily and more easily sip a drink

3. You like the spirit, and want to see its flavors enhanced

Here are a few mixing ingredients to keep on hand for making the healthiest, tastiest, all-natural cocktails at home:

Citrus and fruit juices: Citrus is a great way to counter sweet in a cocktail. Grapefruit, lemon, orange, and lime juices, as well as juices from other fruits, are delectable mixers and should always be fresh squeezed, pureed or muddled.

Grenadine: A variation of a simple syrup that uses pomegranate juice. Never use store-bought grenadine, instead use the recipe on page 86 to make your own.

Olive juice brine: This juice, which is produced while packaging olives, adds a subtle complexity to a martini or other savory cocktail.

Soda water: A dash of soda water adds texture and dilution to any drink, and mixes particularly well with citrus and fruits. When possible, carbonate filtered water yourself with a CO_2 charger or SodaStream. This way, you can prepare the soda water as needed and eliminate preservatives found in store-bought options. You can flavor it too.

Egg whites: When I first started learning about booze and drinking new cocktails, I was totally grossed out by the idea of an egg in my drink. But there's no need to be. An egg white used properly in a drink adds frothiness and depth to a cocktail, and you can barely taste it.

Simple syrup: Simple syrup is a cocktail staple, so experiment with it! To make a strong simple syrup, bring one part water to a boil, and dissolve two parts sugar into it. You can also do a one-to-one ratio for a less dense version. Remove from heat; let cool and thicken. Then store it in the fridge for up to two months.

THE BIG SQUEEZE: MAKE YOUR OWN JUICE

I don't care what anyone says—fresh-squeezed juice in a cocktail is worth the extra time it takes to make it. It's the difference between the "ahhh" after a first sip, and the "eh."

To do this, you'll need a hand juicer or citrus press, which is one of those ones with a pulley and stand so you can pack more power behind it. Better yet, get an electric juicer. If you have one of those, you can juice items that would otherwise be extremely difficult like ginger, wheatgrass, celery, and apples. Imagine the cocktails you could concoct!

To easily extract the most and sweetest juice from fruits:

1. Don't refrigerate fruits meant for juicing because the juice will not come out as easily. Instead, allow them to sit on the kitchen counter for a half hour or more until they become room temperature.

2. Roll citrus before juicing to loosen the juices. A friend of mine swears by popping a whole lime in the microwave for about 20 seconds, which warms the juices and makes them easier to extract.

3. Once you have extracted your juice, store it in the fridge to safeguard against bacteria for up to a week, no longer.

GUIDELINES FOR CITRUS JUICE MEASUREMENTS
It took me a while of winging it before I realized that precision in the measurements for citrus juice matters (you mean all fruits aren't the same size?!). While each fruit will yield a slightly different amount of juice, here's a general guide:

1 lime = 1 ounce juice
1 lemon = 1 1/4 ounces juice
1 orange = 3 1/2 ounces juice
1 grapefruit = 6 – 7 ounces juice

FANTASTIC JUICERS

A few excellent choices for getting your squeeze on:

Hurom Slow Juicer, $359.99

This juicer works flawlessly, even offering a "reverse" option for when fruits and vegetables get backed up. It can handle everything from ginger, beets, limes, lemons, and apples to you name it. It's called a slow juicer because of the way the motor works; the actual juicing is quick and easy.

Jack LaLanne's Power Juicer Pro, $149.97

This machine is quiet and efficient, and is one of the more affordable electric juicers on the market.

Breville Juice Fountain Elite, $299

This juicer is sleek and easy to take apart, and is particularly great at filtering pulp from the juice. Breville has another nifty model called the Juice & Blend with a blender attachment that allows you to make smoothies and other juice-based concoctions.

DRINK TO YOUR HEALTH:
HOW BOOZE AFFECTS YOUR BODY

In order to get the most fulfillment and enjoyment from amazingly made cocktails and spirits, it's important to know their effects on your body and respect your limits.

First of all, women are at a bit of a disadvantage to men when it comes to drinking. Not only are we often smaller, but a greater proportion of our weight is fat compared to muscle. Since fat is poorly supplied with blood vessels, the alcohol that reaches them gets distributed to organs faster. That means babes with more body fat will get drunker than muscular ones.

Women are also more vulnerable to the long-term effects of alcohol abuse. *Heavy* drinking – say, four or more servings daily – wreaks physiological havoc, including weight gain, high blood pressure, spider veins on the face, abdomen, or chest, and liver problems. It also raises estrogen levels that cause red palms and have been linked to breast cancer. In fact, several dozen studies and reports by organizations like the American Cancer Society, Kaiser Permanente, and the National Institutes of Health have concluded that women who indulge in one or two drinks per day appeared to have an increased risk of breast cancer compared to non-drinkers by roughly 10 percent. This is certainly a serious factor to consider. Research found in a 2013 study by the Journal of Clinical Oncology concluded that moderate drinking has little effect on survival after breast cancer diagnosis, and may reduce deaths from cardiovascular disease, which is a top cause of mortality among breast cancer survivors.

Since drinking alcohol also reduces levels of folic acid, which copies and repairs DNA in your blood, it is important that you take in plenty of folate-full oranges, greens and fortified grains if and when you drink to help reduce the risk of your body producing incorrectly copied blood cells that could become cancerous.

And, while the livers of most men can make a full recovery right before cirrhosis (when the liver becomes laden with fat and damaged by scarring) hits if they stop drinking, women usually can't. Don't worry—you'd have to drink several drinks every day for at least 15 years, which is definitely not advised.

A MARTINI A DAY KEEPS THE DOCTOR AWAY?

It may sound that like the deck is stacked against women in the booze department, but in actuality, there's no reason to panic. According to several more studies, drinking moderate amounts of alcohol can be good, too.

Beginning in the 1970s, the Nurses' Health Study followed nearly 100,000 female nurses throughout their lifetimes. It showed that all causes of death were reduced through light and moderate drinking. Social drinkers lived longer, whether male or female, but people who ingested more than six alcoholic drinks a day died younger.

Moderate or light drinkers have up to half the risk of getting heart disease than nondrinkers. Even when moderate drinkers do have a heart attack, they have a lower risk of dying than teetotalers or heavy drinkers, and older people who drink moderately have a lower risk of heart failure. Even as little as one drink a week may protect against ischemic stroke and could cut the risk of developing dementia and Alzheimer's disease, according to the National Institute on Alcohol Abuse and Alcoholism.

Moderate drinking also makes osteoporosis less likely, particularly after age 65. And, contrary to popular belief, moderate alcohol consumption helps stymie weight gain over time, particularly in females. Nearly 19,220 healthy women over the age of 39 were examined over 13 years in a study released in the spring 2011 issue of *Archives of Internal Medicine*. Those who didn't drink gained about eight pounds while women who drank about 12 ounces of alcohol daily gained about three pounds. Of course, that doesn't mean you should overindulge—those who drank heavily in both studies experienced opposite, detrimental effects.

So what is moderation, anyway? It's about 1¼ ounces of 80-proof spirit, 4 to 5 ounces of wine, or 12 ounces of beer, per day. So, enjoy that daily nightcap while toasting to your health! Just don't go overboard.

THE SKINNY: HOW TO CUT COCKTAIL CALORIES

Calorie-conscious babes should not rule out cocktails. Two ounces of 80- to 100-proof spirit (a normal pour in a mixed drink) actually contains about the same number of calories as 12 ounces of beer or a six-ounce pour of wine. Of course, that doesn't count the calories in your mixers. That's why I have put together a few pointers on how to indulge in the pastime while keeping your waistline trim:

- *Avoid processed and sugary mixers.* Not only do most store-bought mixers provide enough sugars to up your likeliness of developing gallstones, you could ingest 1,000 liquid calories in one big night alone. Thinking about a rum and Coke? The average can of soda sweetened with sugar contains 150 calories, according to the Harvard School of Public Health. Chalk that rum and processed cola up to 220 calories.

- *Eat a meal or a few healthy snacks before happy hour.* Most bar snacks and bar menus are calorie dense. Beef up your pre-drink tummy with high-proteins and natural fats like nuts, raisins, quinoa, and avocado, which not only slow the absorption of alcohol, but will also lessen your cravings for quesadillas and potato skins while you drink.

- *Drink smaller portions.* Do you really need that jumbo daiquiri? Not only does ordering big drinks make you feel like you need to drink it all, potentially leading to rapid drunkenness and consequently, poor decision-making, but they are also double the calories. When you're out, go with the smaller portion. When at home, serve drinks in smaller glasses. You can always reach for seconds, but you might not want them. I keep two-ounce cordial glasses, four-ounce cocktail glasses, one-ounce snifters, five-ounce coupe glasses, and five-ounce rocks glasses on hand. Try not to serve or be served drinks in eight- or ten-ounce glasses. Besides, our fore-broads of the cocktail world would have never done so: they cause drinks to get watered down and warm before we have a chance to finish them.

- *Switch out an ingredient for a lower-calorie alternative with the same flavor.* Take a margarita, with one ounce of pure agave tequila, one ounce of Cointreau or Grand Marnier, fresh-squeezed lime, and a squeeze of agave nectar, and you are looking at a drink with about 180 calories. Substitute that Cointreau or Grand Marnier with a similar flavor, such as fresh-squeezed orange, and you can cut that to about 120.

AVERAGE CALORIES BY DRINK
- 2 ounces of brandy, bourbon, gin, rum, tequila, scotch, or vodka = 165 calories
- 6 ounces of wine = 155 calories
- 12 ounces beer = 150 calories, on average

RULES FOR IMBIBING: HOW TO SIDESTEP SLOPPINESS

Nobody likes a sloppy drunk. Overindulging in alcohol leads to lower inhibitions, and that opens the possibility of making many regrettable mistakes. And making regrettable mistakes is not babe-like.

To keep the kind of composure and class necessary to garner respect at the bar, while entertaining, or anywhere alcohol is served, remember the following:

- *Drink slowly.* Let your metabolism work. If you are anxious or nervous and sipping the cocktail or drink helps calm you because it's something to do, alternate your sips with a glass of water.

- *You will be tempted to say things you shouldn't, but don't.* It's important to tame that uninhibited voice inside your head that wants to reveal your deepest secrets to strangers. Be aware of when it stops in for a visit, and train yourself to ignore it.

- *Know your limits and alcohol's effect on you.* Be aware of how your personality shifts while under the influence. Make a mental note of how much you can drink and still feel good the next day. Imbibing should be fun, but over-indulging leads to drama, disaster, and sickness.

SOBER UP SCHEMES THAT DON'T WORK

Another reason to keep your composure while drinking is that once you've gone over the drunken edge, you can't turn back.

Need to sober up? Forget the late-night snacks and coffee. The *only* thing you can do to sober up is to let your body ride it out and allow the alcohol to leave your system on its own through

CALORIE CONSCIOUS COCKTAILS

Think cocktails kill your waistline? Think again! Using fresh ingredients and quality booze limits sugars and carbs that turn to fat. Here, a few low-cal cocktails from the Royalton Hotel in New York City:

Agave Royale *(142 calories)*
A sweet and sour cocktail that is a refreshing and fruity alternative to the standard margarita.
Created by the Royalton Hotel

1 1/4 ounces silver tequila
1/4 ounce maraschino liqueur (such as Luxardo)
3/4 ounce fresh-squeezed lemon juice
3/4 ounce ginger syrup
    (see recipe below)
2 blackberries,
    one for garnish

Muddle one fresh blackberry, add all liquid ingredients, shake with one ice cube, strain into a chilled double rocks glass, and top with crushed ice. Garnish with blackberry.

Gin Lantern *(139 calories)*
The herbal qualities in this spritzer add interest and balance to the dry gin.
Created by Enid Cortes

1 1/4 ounces London Dry gin
1/4 ounce aromatic herbal liqueur (such as Benedictine)
1/2 ounce yuzu juice (available in Asian grocery stores; if you
    can't find this Japanese citrus juice, an equal mixture of
    lemon and lime juice will do)
1/4 ounce honey syrup (3 parts honey to 1 part water)
Splash of club soda
1 rosemary stalk, for garnish

Combine all ingredients sans club soda in a shaker with ice. Shake and pour all contents into a frosted pilsner glass. Top with club soda and garnish with a rosemary stalk.

Ginger Julep *(131 calories)*
The ginger puts a little spice in this traditionally sweet concoction.
Created by Justin Delasko

1 1/2 ounces bourbon
2 mint leaves
2 lemon wedges
2 ginger coins (1/8-inch across-the-grain slices)
3/4 ounce simple syrup
1 mint leaf for garnish

In a cocktail shaker, muddle ginger and lemon wedges; add lightly bruised mint. Add liquid ingredients, shake with one ice cube, and strain over crushed ice into a julep mug. Garnish with mint leaf.

Two If By Sea *(140 calories)*
The dark rum's sweetness is balanced by the bitters and lemon, making for a dynamic and interesting medley of flavors.
Created by Joshua Brandenburg

1 1/2 ounces dark rum
3/4 ounce chai tea syrup*
3/4 ounce lemon juice
2 blackberries
Splash of Fee Brothers whiskey bitters
1 cinnamon stick

In a cocktail shaker, muddle blackberries, add all other ingredients, shake with ice, and pour directly into a single rocks glass. Garnish with a cinnamon stick.

*Add ½ cup sugar to ½ cup chai tea and dissolve over medium heat. Remove from heat, strain, and let cool.

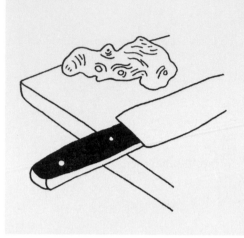

Make your own ginger syrup
Mix one part water to one part raw sugar in a pot over medium heat. Add a knob of whole, peeled ginger cut into three one-inch pieces. Allow the sugar to dissolve then remove from heat and let cool. Remove the ginger knobs.

oxidation. Drinking water won't sober you up, but it's still beneficial, replacing some of the fluids lost from alcohol's dehydrating effects.

Bread also won't sober you up. Alcohol causes your pancreas to produce large quantities of insulin so that a person's blood-sugar level is dramatically lowered (this causes those god-awful, waking-up-in-the-middle-of-the-night-sweating episodes). This is why you crave carbohydrates, which turn to sugar, but you'll have to let your body take care of its insulin levels on its own.

And to dispel the biggest myth of all: coffee definitely doesn't help, as confirmed by a study by Philadelphia's Temple University that appeared in journal *Behavioral Neuroscience* in 2009. Not only will the brew's acid probably irritate your stomach, it will also dehydrate you by causing you to pee incessantly.

However, coffee essentially tricks your mind into thinking

you're sobering up because you'll be wired, thanks to the caffeine's stimulating effect, which makes it harder to realize how wasted you are, and could potentially cause you to make some dumb decisions. Avoid it.

THE HANGOVER: PREVENTING IT

Alcohol affects you faster than food does, and just one ounce of spirit is metabolized per hour. When you drink more than your body can metabolize, the alcohol lingers and temporarily paralyzes your organs, causing the dreaded hangover.

A hangover is like the devil. We all know how it feels to be lying in bed the morning after, wishing you could sleep. Wishing your headache would just go away. Wishing you could just do *something*. Even scientists acknowledge they know little about why exactly alcohol wreaks so much havoc on our systems the next day, and find it puzzling that alcohol is so toxic once it leaves the body.

And here's the bad news: women suffer hangovers worse than men because our bodies have less of the good enzymes (acetaldehyde dehydrogenase, and glutathione) that break down alcohol in the liver. As a result, we not only get inebriated faster, but we also retain the alcohol in our systems longer. That is until after menopause, when women's good enzyme levels rival men's.

The speed at which we metabolize alcohol and reduce blood alcohol level is also determined by our menstrual cycles. When your period is coming, you will likely become drunk faster and have a worse hangover the next day. Way to go, Aunt Flo.

Genes also affect our hangovers. Some Far Eastern and European Jewish populations have a form of acetaldehyde dehydrogenase enzyme that does not easily metabolize alcohol, thus making them more prone to drunkenness and hangovers.

And what exactly causes hangovers (besides more alcohol than your body can metabolize)? Congeners! Congeners, which are impurities produced during the fermentation process and also contribute to a spirit's color and taste, are responsible for the headache, muscle ache and stiffness in your joints. Darker colored spirits have more congeners than white spirits, and as a result, can sometimes cause a worse hangover.

Here's how to avoid the pillow spins:

- *Eat proteins and fats.* Contrary to popular belief, it is proteins and fats you'll want to eat, not carbohydrates. Carbs turn to sugars that are quickly metabolized and burned, while fats will promote slow absorption of alcohol. You could even drink milk, which is high in fat (though it does not actually "coat the stomach" as many people believe).

- *Pace your drinking.* This goes without saying, classy ladies, but try to temper how quickly you put those cocktails down.

Try to drink no more than one drink (two ounces of alcohol) per hour.

WHAT IS THE "HAIR OF THE DOG?" The phrase dates back to Roman times and stems from a superstition that if someone was bitten by a mad dog, they should pluck a hair from the tail of the dog and burn it. The hair was then placed inside the wound to avoid rabies, or crushed into a drink. But now "hair of the dog" means to have some more of what gave you the hangover, i.e. the dog that "bit" you.

- *Sit while drinking.* You'll be more likely to indulge in snacks that temper your drinking, which delay the absorption of alcohol.

- *Avoid sugars.* Sugars are quickly metabolized and burned, adding only calories to your night.

- *Go easy on the fizz.* Fizzy drinks, even if lower in alcohol than others, cause your system to absorb alcohol more quickly. Drink more of them and you get drunker faster, making a nasty hangover more likely.

- *Take vitamins.* Through dehydration and possibly an unwanted upchuck, you will lose electrolytes and vitamins your body needs to feel healthy. Take a multivitamin with magnesium, potassium and calcium before a night of drinking to pad your bod with nutrition.

- *Drink water.* A lot of it. When I'm out for a night of drinking, I have a rule for myself: drink at least one glass of water per glass of alcohol. Do this, and your body will stay hydrated. If your head is spinning by the time you're ready for bed, down 32 ounces with a tablespoon of alkalizing salts, which help regulate your body's pH without irritating your organs, and two aspirin.

THE HANGOVER PART II: CURING IT

Our Roman predecessors may have drunk raw owl eggs or eaten roasted boar's lung to cure a nasty hangover, but we've graduated to more effective (and appetizing) methods these days. Here's how to help your body through a bad day after:

- *Drink coconut water.* A clear liquid extracted from young coconuts, coconut water is high in electrolytes like potassium and sodium, which are great replacements for fluids lost from alcohol.

- *Eat.* I always crave a cheeseburger when I'm hungover, and here's why: eating a high-protein meal will normalize your blood sugar and encourage absorption of lingering alcohol.

- *Take a hot shower.* Hot water will increase your circulation and soothe you.

- **Take a whiff of nigella seeds.** While on a travel assignment in Marrakech, Morocco, I visited a Berber pharmacy that specialized in herbal remedies. They swore by nigella seeds to cure hangovers. Wrap a handful of them, which you can obtain at most natural food stores, in a cloth sack. Inhale from it deeply several times.

- **Wash out your mouth with room temperature water.** Drinking ice water won't necessarily help if your mouth is dry. Washing it out with room temperature water will cure the dryness without upsetting your stomach.

- **Drink carrot-ginger-apple-orange juice.** Carrots are packed with beta-carotene that is converted into vitamin A by your body. Ginger is a natural cure for an upset tummy. The apples, while acidic, cut the carrots' bitterness and ginger's sourness. The orange contains vitamin C, which stimulates the liver to break down alcohol. Peel and juice one cup of carrots, a small piece of ginger root, one orange, and one apple and drink with ice.

- **Avoid coffee.** As mentioned earlier, coffee could upset your stomach and contains caffeine and will make you pee, which will dehydrate you more.

- **Breathe.** Steady, deep breaths of fresh air open up the lungs and allow toxins to escape. Inhale through the nose, out through the mouth. This is a tried and true remedy for me.

- *Drink a small amount of alcohol.* Though I usually find the smell and taste of alcohol repulsive the morning after a night of heavy drinking, others believe all it takes to cure a hangover is to feed your body just a wee bit more of what did it in. I'll let you decide whether that works for you!

TAKE CHARGE: ORDER A DRINK LIKE YOU MEAN IT

Being a babe is not just about looking chic. It's about conducting yourself with class, respect, and the obvious smarts you possess. Doing so redefines your relationship with booze. It shows you can handle yourself, and best of all, it shows you could own the place. Part of building this assertive persona at the bar is the way in which you order. Listen, ladies—in order to be taken seriously, you gotta act like you know your stuff! It's like asking for a raise. When you act like you mean it and you've done your research, you earn the respect of your bartender, who will love to treat you well. You also show bar companions that you not only know what you want to drink, but also what you want in life.

- *Be specific.* How you order a drink is just as important as what you order, so be clear and deliberate. Relaying how you want your drink made shows power and presence.

- *Make ordering a big deal.* Pause your conversation to order your drink. It demonstrates knowledge.

- *If you don't know, just ask—assertively, of course.* Look at the cocktail list first. If something sounds good, try it, and tweak it as necessary. Don't be afraid to ask questions that will help you refine your taste.

- **Do not let your companion pink (ahem, pick) your drink.** Choosing your drink is an opportunity to branch out, try something new, and learn your tastes. Don't leave that up to someone else to decide! Plus, you can show you know what you're doing. Never say you'll have what she or he is having. That is lame and lazy.

- **Don't hesitate.** Hesitation kills confidence. If you have to think about it, it means you're unsure. Before you hesitate while ordering, ask questions. Decide what you're interested in trying silently then voice it definitively.

CLASS ACT: HOW TO BEHAVE IN A BAR

It may go without saying, but it's also important to maintain the utmost professionalism and etiquette while at a bar. A few general guidelines include:

- **Be polite to everyone.** Want your drink quicker, and made with more care? Show good manners, say please and thank you, and tip. Bartenders can also help you out of a sticky situation you might find yourself in, if you are nice to them. And when they are being nice to you, don't automatically assume they are hitting on you.

- **Use your inside voice.** Nothing is worse than a rowdy bar crowd in a chill bar. Keep a mild voice, and please, do not squeal.

- **Don't stand at the bar counter, waving your money at the bartender.** This demonstrates impatience. The bartender will see you and come to you as soon as she or he can.

- **Offer to buy the first round, and make it a quality drink.** Show your appreciation for guests or companions by offering to buy them a quality cocktail. It shows a good faith effort to have a good time, demonstrates excellent taste, and impresses your guest. Now, if you are being courted romantically by a man at the bar, you are his guest. Let him buy the first round, but you pick it.

- **Be gracious to someone who buys you a drink.** You may not be down to meet a romantic interest at the bar, and you should ignore those who approach you in a derogatory or offensive way. However, if someone buys you a drink, always politely thank him but establish your boundaries skillfully. If a man is obviously into you and you're not into him, be clear that you are appreciative but not interested.

- **Buy a guy a drink.** If you *are* interested in someone in a bar, don't wait around for him to invite you to order. It's okay to buy *him* a drink. You can even use your bartender as a wingman or wingwoman!

- **Stay off your phone.** A person who is on their phone appears closed off and not open to conversation. It will also seem like you are not enjoying yourself. Enjoy the experience in the moment.

- **Smile.** Bars can be great places to meet people and enjoy lively conversation, but people will only approach you if you're putting off positive energy. Let's see some teeth.

FLYING SOLO: HOW TO ENJOY A BARSTOOL FOR ONE

In my younger days, and before I became a savvy bar-goer, I was extraordinarily uncomfortable sitting at the bar alone. Would people think I was a loser? And how would it look for a *chick* to be cozying up at the bar by herself? Would they think I was looking for a man? Meanwhile, my husband had no problem patronizing bars solo. "What do you do with no one to talk to?" I'd ask him. "I just talk to the bartender," he'd say, "or make new friends!"

I no longer feel apprehensive about sidling up to a bar by my-self, particularly when I travel. While in a new place, I want to check out the best cocktail and specialty bars. Why would I pass that up just because I'm flying solo? Part of why I enjoy it is the confidence I now have for speaking the bartender's language when it comes to booze. Bartenders can be really fun to talk to about the local flavor, too. Plus, when sitting at the bar by your-self, you're bound to meet some colorful characters that leave you with a cool sense of camaraderie.

I asked Dushan Zaric, owner of popular New York City bars Employees Only and Macau Trading Company and who regular-ly writes about drinks etiquette for Liquor.com, what his advice was for lone women at bars.

"We fortunately live in an age where women are welcomed in bars alone. They can feel safe. The female presence at the bar, regardless of whether she is out to have a couple of drinks or to meet somebody, shifts the whole energy," he says. "The only thing I would advise is to relax and let the bartender guide her through the experience. Open yourself up to the experience of being in that bar. Let your bartender do their job and be your host. Ask them questions. You are the one receiving hospitality."

I agree with him. Of course, you want to make sure you pick a bar with an atmosphere you feel comfortable in. Pool halls may not be your style, or you might not like the ambience of a fancy lounge.

"This is a matter of taste," Zaric adds. "You are basically choosing a bar based on how much it nourishes you. You have to find out for yourself. What works for you? Then go there."

WHAT TO DO IF A BAR SUCKS

The nicest bars and lounges are a joy to behold. You'll be in a comfortable environment—not too quiet, not too loud—and you would never see hundreds of phone numbers written on the bathroom stalls (a big plus). Your cocktail menu will be packaged in a leather compendium, you'll get linen coasters, and some homemade complimentary snacks with your drinks, even. There will be several wines to choose from, signature cocktails, craft beers and a staff who can walk you through it with their eyes closed, helping you find something to drink you'll absolutely love.

But occasionally you'll find yourself in a bar where the head honcho behind the stick doesn't know how to make a classic drink you love, or pours you store-bought sour mix for the same price as a fresh and well-made drink you've had at another bar. Maybe they completely ignore you altogether, even though you are a paying customer. Maybe it's just not your style at all, but hey, you came in here, so you might as well stick it out for a drink. Or do you?

For these dilemmas, I turned to Dave Stolte, author of *Home Bar Basics (and Not-So-Basics)*, who has written about this on his blog:

"The biggest thing is to just manage your expectations. When people get bit by this bug [for good drinks], they think they should be able to get them everywhere," he says. But that just ain't gonna happen all the time. "Besides, if the bartender doesn't already know how to use fresh citrus or make their own simple syrup, even if you coach them—which is not advisable because it comes off as pretentious—the drink probably won't be great anyway" (think: squeezing the pre-cut garnishes behind the bar).

To feel out a place, Stolte recommends watching the bartender make drinks for a little while before ordering to see what kinds of ingredients and spirits they're workin' with. When they don't appeal, Stolte's "safe drinks" are usually a Negroni [page 276] or Old-Fashioned [page 297], since they are simply made and even the worst equipped bars keep their ingredients (such as whiskey, bitters, Campari and gin).

Though Stolte admits he's thought about carrying a mini bottle of Angostura bitters around in case of an emergency, when in a pinch, he orders a a decent liquor served neat, or a beer. When in Rome...

WORKING GIRL: HOW TO MIX BUSINESS WITH BOOZE

A lot of business happens at the bar. That's why it's so important to know what you're doing and how to conduct yourself with a client, co-worker, boss, or potential business partner. When picking a place to conduct business, you'll want to make sure that it has got a wide selection to accommodate your guests' tastes, tables with enough distance from other bar-goers, and that it is not too busy. In addition to the general bar etiquette pointers above, consider the following:

- **Act like you own the place.** This doesn't mean to be bossy. Instead, familiarize yourself with the staff before taking a VIP to a bar. Tell them you would like to bring a business associate. While imbibing with your guest, make the server your friend. It will show your guests you're a take-charge kinda gal with some high-rolling tendencies.

- **Sit at a cocktail table rather than a bar counter.** Sitting at a bar is not conducive to reading or showing body language (there's only one way you can sit, and it's awkward), but it also opens up a private conversation to other bar-goers and the bartenders, who could be distracting. Grab a seat at a cocktail table, where you and your guest can face each other comfortably, and escape crowds.

- **Don't obsess over the menu.** Doing so will show you probably don't know what you want or like, and also wastes time. If you have an idea of what may be offered, you can ask the server more quickly about the choices and decide on the spot.

- ***Don't talk about personal matters.*** Personal problems are distracting. Get the business out of the way first then if there are a couple of moments to talk about how the kids are doing, do it when the check comes.

- ***Sit up straight.*** Sitting up straight subconsciously shows you are confident, alert, and assertive.

- ***Take notes.*** In my work as a travel, food, and spirits writer, details matter. Even one drink can cloud your memory. Write everything down, I mean everything. It also shows that you are paying attention and will follow up.

- ***Only have one.*** See note above: even after one drink, your body becomes relaxed, your memory faded, and your judgment clouded. Keep it tight, have one drink, and stay focused.

- ***Drink something respectable.*** Please, please don't order a vodka soda, apple-tini, or a skinny this or that. Show your knowledge of the finer things in life with a stirred cocktail, or a quality whiskey, gin, rum, tequila, or brandy neat, on the rocks, or with water.

- ***End the meeting promptly after business is taken care of.*** Linger longer and you'll probably have more drinks, which means you might inadvertently say or do something unbecoming of a babe.

- ***Always offer to pay.*** To be treated as an equal in the business world, you've got to share the cost. Even if your companion *really* wants to front the bill, fight for it a little. If you came out of the meeting as the beneficiary of whatever it is you set out to accomplish or discuss, fight for it a lot. It's a small, but symbolic gesture of appreciation and respect.

CHAPTER 4

Home Is Where the Booze Is: How to Build Your Very Own Bar

The best place to get your feet wet with any spirit or drink experiment is in the comfort of your own kitchen. Once you become interested in exploring the wonderful world of liquor and cocktails, you'll likely be excited to test recipes that would cost an arm and a leg at a fancy lounge. Plus, if you enjoy cooking and making DIY gifts, you'll have a ball experimenting with homemade vermouths, bitters, infused liquors, and syrups.

Entertaining is even more fun when your booze house is in order. Unless all of your friends are extremely cocktail savvy, or mixologists themselves, you will likely surprise and impress them with your newfound bartending skills and well-equipped bar goods and liquor selection. People will love coming to your house to try whatever new awesome concoction you're whipping up.

There are many other reasons why learning to booze at home is great:

1. ***No one will judge you.*** You can practice your skills behind

closed doors, and if that drink tastes like dirt, you can just throw it out and move on, without tarnishing your reputation as a master of mixing.

2. *It's cheaper.* Always wanted to try a Martinez (Old Tom Gin, sweet vermouth, maraschino liqueur and orange bitters) but were reluctant to plunk down $12 for it out on the town? If you have stocked your bar with the basics (we get into this below), you can mix it up at home for a much less expensive per-drink price.

3. *You can share your experiences with friends and family in a comfortable environment.* Don't get me wrong: I love a good bar, pub, or lounge. But *everybody* loves a house party. There's nothing better than sharing a drink where you can play your own music, eat your favorite snacks, and take up a seat with your shoes off and your legs curled up in comfy chair.

4. *Bar tools, a pretty bar, and homemade concoctions like bitters, infusions, and liqueurs make wonderful décor accents.* Set up an attractive bar, and it will not only inspire conversation with guests, but will also jazz up your digs in a way you can enjoy every day.

HOME BAR BASICS: WHAT YOU NEED TO GET STARTED

There are times when you may walk into Sur la Table or Williams-Sonoma and are drawn in by all of the cool-looking bar tools. Some of them are the best, most useful tools you can buy. But let's be honest, most are totally unnecessary. Minimize clutter and up your bar game with these staples:

Oversized, square ice cube trays: Bigger ice cubes create less surface area in the glass, which means they melt more slowly. These are perfect for solo spirits or simple rocks cocktails. I buy rubber molds from Tovolo, which can be purchased for less than $10 on Amazon.com.

Muddler: Necessary for drinks that call for herbs (e.g. mojito), and some muddled fruits. Purchase a durable one and it will do right by you forever. I like a muddler with grates on the bottom, almost like a soccer cleat. It won't slip around in the glass like a wooden muddler does.

Cocktail shaker: Invest in a metal shaker and have fun with the kind you buy. I have an extra large vintage metal shaker with a handle and strainer spout that I found at a thrift store. Prices run the gamut from $10 at Target to $500 sterling silver antiques. I've even seen shakers that look like penguins with top hats and frosted glass shakers. Beware: it's easy to get obsessed with collecting these, but they make great displays!

11-inch stirring spoon or barspoon: This long
spoon allows you to mix a drink in a Collins glass
without sticking your fingers down in there, as
my dad used to do in a pinch. It provides optimal
stirring in a cocktail shaker as well and thanks to
its often decorative handle looks cool in your bar
toolbox.

Paring knife: A paring knife is the best tool to
use for easily peeling strips of zest and garnish,
the essential oils of which add subtle flavors and
aromas to a drink.

Funnel set: A set of three funnels of various sizes will be useful
once you learn how to make your own vermouths or bitters (we
will get to that later), or if you are decanting liquids into decorative bottles.

Jigger: A good drink is
all about balance, which
you'll get when you mea-
sure its ingredients with
a jigger. A typical jigger
looks like an hourglass
and usually has a one-
ounce measure at one end
and a half-ounce measure
on the other. Use this, and
use it faithfully.

Ice bucket: Pick up one of these to store on your bar, so you don't have to run to the fridge when you need ice for your shaker. When serving made-ahead cocktail batches at parties, you'll want to serve ice separately in the bucket so as not to water the beverage down.

Cutting board: Keep one near your bar for cutting garnishes and fruit.

Water filter: Tap water's added minerals can distort the taste of a cocktail, so you'll want to get a filter. I have a Pur filtering pitcher, but you can install a filter on your faucet as well.

Hand juicer: Fresh juice is the key to a good cocktail. You can purchase a juice press, but a hand juicer usually comes in three sizes and is portable and affordable (about $15). A medium-size one (typically for lemons) is awesomely all purpose, juicing halves of lemons and limes beautifully, and oranges and grapefruits in quarters.

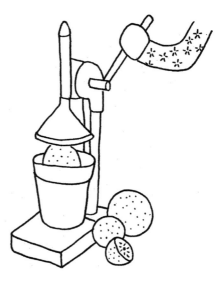

Zester/Grater: I like the handheld
Microplane brand for zesting citrus.
It helps that there are also several
other purposes for it in your kitchen
such as grating cheese, ginger and
garlic, or shaving chocolate.

Bar towels: Pick up a dozen dishcloths from Ikea for 50 cents each
to keep in and around your bar area. You'll want to keep it clean,
and the cloth towels are way more durable and eco-friendly than
paper ones.

UP YOUR GAME: NEXT LEVEL BAR TOOLS

Over time, as you learn what you like to drink, what you like to
mix, and what you like to serve at home, you'll want tools beyond
the basics that make life easier, drink making more efficient, and
cocktailing more fun. Here are a few tools you could do without,
but shouldn't:

Reusable glass straws: An interesting conversation piece when
gathered in a vase or other container, these non-disposable straws
are also eco-friendly. Brands include Glass Dharma and Strawe-
some. Check Etsy.com for bended, handmade straws in rad colors
and designs.

Punch bowl: A punch bowl and ladle are necessities for the savvy, boozy babe with a penchant for hosting, since the easiest way
to serve a large group is via punch cocktails made ahead of time.
Look for a unique and high-quality style at vintage and antique

stores (hint: crystal, or colored glass, are timeless).

Lewis bag and wooden mallet: This is how you make crushed ice when you want to control its size (or if you have an old refrigerator without a crushed ice option, as I do). A Lewis bag is simply a heavy-duty canvas bag you stuff with ice and then whack with a mallet.

Electric juicer: Squeezing citrus by hand isn't such a big deal when making only a few drinks. But it becomes a huge deal when we're talking about a party. Plus, with an electric juicer, you can make several quarts of fresh juice in advance. For a few juicer suggestions, see page 55.

Ice Scoop with Strainer: It makes perfect sense that an ice scoop has holes in it, so that you don't inadvertently dump a spoonful of water into your punch. That's why I love these (I got mine at Crate & Barrel), in addition to the fact that you can use them to strain drinks from shaker to glass.

Blender: Your best friend for frozen drinks, a blender is also handy for making purees. Some electric juicers come with a blender attachment, which will take up less space in your cabinet (always a plus).

SodaStream: Using a soda machine like the SodaStream is cheaper and more convenient and eco-friendly than buying bottles of club soda. Plus, it's extra annoying when a store-bought container of soda loses its fizz before you've had a chance to use it. When you make your own on demand, you reuse the same bottle, and you can make your own syrups to flavor it.

MAKING SIMPLE AND FLAVORED SYRUPS

Basic simple syrup, which hundreds of cocktail recipes call for, can be made by simmering equal parts white, raw or brown sugar and water until the sugar is dissolved. And adding a flavored simple syrup to a cocktail is a great way to up the sweetness and dimension without taking over a spirit's natural flavor. Drop fruits, oils, or herbs in the syrup while it's simmering until they're tender and the sugar is dissolved, and you've got flavored syrup. Try elderflowers, ginger, lavender, blackberry, lemon, rosehips, or peppermint. The proportion of flavoring to sugar is completely up to your tastes, and you can use as much or as little as you see fit when preparing the drink. Experiment with how thick and flavorful you'd like the syrup to be by adjusting your proportion of sugar to water. For example, syrup with two parts sugar to one part water will be thicker and sweeter than a one-to-one ratio. I like my syrups and sodas less sweet, so I normally add one ounce of syrup for every 12 ounces of soda water. You can gauge your preference by starting with that ratio, and gradually adding or reducing syrup until you get the hang of it.

MAKE GRENADINE

Forget bottled Rose's grenadine. Making fresh grenadine is easy. Simmer two cups pomegranate juice with 1 cup raw sugar over medium heat and stir until the sugar is dissolved and the syrup thickens. Let cool. Feel free to add zest of your favorite citrus to the final blend.

FILL 'ER UP: SETTING UP A GLASSWARE COLLECTION

There's no room for plastic cups in a babe's bar. Serving a drink in a well-chosen glass can mean the difference between an elegant cocktail or simply just another boring glass of booze.

Here are a few glassware staples:

Old-fashioned or rocks glasses: Wide, heavy glasses that can be used for any stirred cocktail or neat drink. It usually holds about four to six ounces. You can get double old-fashioned glasses that hold double the amount, too. But the smaller ones are more important to have for reasons I'll get into later.

Highball or Collins glasses: These usually hold 10 ounces or so. They are also the most common glass used for drinks with soda or tonic.

Martini glasses and/or champagne coupes: These are perfect for any drink served straight up (chilled, without ice). I prefer the coupe because I like its elegant shape and rounded edges that prevent liquid from so easily sloshing over them, but either will work. Both hold four to five ounces.

THE COUPE SCOOP
It is often rumored the coupe glass was modeled after the left breast of Marie Antoinette, the 18th century queen whose extravagant endeavors helped provoke the French Revolution. As much fun as this tidbit is to believe, it just isn't true. The origin of the coupe glass can be traced to 17th century England, where it was designed specifically for champagne.

FIZZ WHIZ: START A HOME SODA FOUNTAIN

At the turn of the century, soda fountains were all the rage. Located in pharmacies, soda fountains served carbonated water mixed with botanical-infused syrups, bitters, and fresh fruits that were believed to be the cure to what ailed you. Pharmacists went to great lengths to distinguish their soda from another's, and several unique flavors were available, some of which were mixed in cocktails during the Temperance movement. As Prohibition sent bartenders overseas for work, many others took up working at pharmacies, where they could put their skills to use mixing sodas. By the 1950s, America had sadly ditched the soda fountain for Coca-Cola and the likes.

But in the last few years, soda fountains have made a comeback, partly driven by the mainstream movement away from processed foods and drinks. And for good reason—commercial sodas contain an obscene amount of sugar, chemicals, and preservatives, which give you a hangover and are high in calories. And in terms of cocktails, the natural flavorings of homemade sodas enhance rather than cover up the flavor of spirits.

So, instead of using store-bought sodas in cocktails, expose your friends and family to homemade ones by setting up a soda station. All you need is a selection of flavored syrups, a SodaStream, and a collection of recipes and instructions on display.

Once you've made a flavored soda water, try adding it to cocktail recipes that call for plain soda water and also contain complementary ingredients. For example, a raspberry-and-sage-flavored soda would beautifully jazz up a traditional Tom Collins, which usually contains gin, lemon juice, simple syrup, and plain soda water.

Tulip glasses or brandy snifters: These six-to-eight-ounce glasses are great for tasting and drinking spirits neat. A tulip glass is shaped like the tulip flower, and has a curvacious shape. The snifter is a balloon-shaped glass. Both concentrate aromas in the glass because of the wide bottoms and narrow tops. They can also be  used to serve some iced cocktails instead of a rocks glass. Small, one-ounce snifters are good to have on hand for tastings and samplings (plus they are darn cute).

Cordial glasses: Holding about three ounces, this glass is perfect when you want just a small, taster cocktail or an after-dinner treat. It comes in many decorative styles, to include long, narrow shapes and tulip shapes.

Glassware comes in an endless variety of styles and shapes, which are not only fun to scout for and collect, but also make really beautiful displays on a bar cart, in a china cabinet, or on a shelf. It's all about loving what you're drinking, including the vessel. I like to shop for vintage and unique glasses at thrift stores and on eBay.

Over the last year, I snagged a groovy set of five brown and floral old-fashioned glasses from the '60s for the same price as plain ones from Target, and sets of etched coupe and cordial glasses for a couple of bucks a piece. I also scored a super cool set of four tulip snifters on tall stems for about $10. When choosing glassware, try to resist purchasing large or oversized models. Glasses that hold less allow you to finish a drink before it gets warm. Also, when experimenting with cocktails at home or serving them to others, it makes for a good "test" amount in case you or your guest don't like it.

BOTTLE SERVICE:
BOOZE TO KEEP ON HAND

Building an arsenal of liquor can be expensive and intimidating if you try to do it all at once, so start with a few high-quality, versatile bottles that create tons of drink combinations. Not only will you enjoy your on-hand stash, but so will your guests, who will get a feel for your style and personality based on your liquor choices. My goal is to keep basics on hand that I love and that will inspire my guests to go out and buy the same for themselves (a huge compliment!).

The following are the makings of a perfect, basic starter bar. Don't worry, we'll get into the specifics of these spirits in later chapter.

Fine, small batch bourbon: A 100-proof bourbon will usually also satisfy scotch and cognac drinkers. It can be mixed beautifully, as well as drank neat. There are tons of great options on the market; I like Angel's Envy, Woodford Reserve (both of these are finished in wine barrels), and Michter's.

Midrange, 100 percent agave blanco tequila: Tequila is more versatile than you think. You can use it in margaritas, but also as a substitute for vodka in many cocktails for an earthy, more flavorful spin. Choose a blanco for cleaner, lighter notes in cocktails. Always make sure it is 100 percent agave (it will say so on the label) for the best quality. Brands like Don Julio, El Jimador, and Espolón are good, affordable options.

Midrange London Dry gin: Rarely will folks drink gin straight, so there's no need to go super high-end on this one (unless of course, your G&T loving boss is coming over). Gin can be accented minimally with fresh fruit, citrus, and soda in the summer, or can go well in heavier, winter cocktails. Try Hendrick's, Broker's, or Beefeater.

KEEP YOUR LIQUOR FRESH
Over time, a spirit begins to react to oxygen and lose some of its character. If you have a high-quality, expensive bottle you'd like to keep in tip-top shape, drink it within a month or two. When the bottle is getting low, you can decant it into a smaller bottle with less room for oxygen to hover between the cap and liquid, which will help it taste better longer.

Vermouth, sweet and dry: Vermouth is a crucial component of hundreds of cocktails and goes with just about any spirit. It is a fortified wine, which means that it begins with a base wine and a higher proof alcohol is added to it (sometimes sherry, port, or brandy), along with herbs and spices. Get a red, sweet Italian vermouth like Carpano and a white, dry French one like Dolin or Noilly Prat. But beware, while vermouth doesn't go bad, its flavors do lose their vibrancy over time. Buy or make it (instructions on page 105) in small bottles and use within a couple of months (older vermouths can be used for food recipes that call for wine or to deglaze a pan). You can also use other types of fortified wines in place of vermouth in some instances, such as port, madeira or sherry. Some commonly available fortified wines like Lillet, Cocchi Americano or Dubonnet, have a liqueur–like effect in a drink plus sweetness.

Sweet liqueur: A sweet liqueur can pull triple-duty as a flavor, sweetener, and extra alcoholic kick in a cocktail. I recommend the orange liqueur Cointreau, probably the most versatile fruit liqueur on the market because it is not too sweet, and can be substituted for other fruit liqueurs in a pinch. Other recommendations are Blue Curacao and Grand Marnier (both orange liqueurs), Luxardo Maraschino cherry liqueur, and St. Germain elderflower liqueur. You get what you pay for when it comes to liqueurs, so you'll want to skip cheap triple secs.

Amaro: Amari (plural) are botanical liqueurs that come in a variety of flavors and add the bitter bite you will need to balance many cocktails. Some of the most common are Fernet-Branca, which tastes herbacious and spicy, Campari, which has a bitter orange flavor, and Aperol, which has a profile similar to Campari but tastes less bitter.

Aromatic bitters: Just a few drops of this highly concentrated,

THE FRUGAL BABE

If stocking your bar threatens to break your bank at the moment, and you don't plan on entertaining any time soon, pick one drink you like and purchase the ingredients you need to make that one drink. Master it. When you're ready, find a recipe that calls for a different base spirit with the same or similar modifiers as your first drink, and buy that.

high-proof alcohol infused with fruits, spices, roots, and barks, add that *je ne sais quoi* to a huge number of cocktails. They make great accents for any booze enthusiast's collection and the flavor possibilities are endless: lavender, coriander, mint, peach, grapefruit, lime, chocolate, cardamom, and celery are just a few from companies like Scrappy's and Fee Brothers. But two popular standard bitters everyone should have are Angostura (woodsy and herbal) and Peychaud's (anise-scented). These can be found in any grocery store or liquor store for five to seven dollars. Or, make your own (instructions on page 99).

Whole spices: Sometimes you will be in the mood to make your own vermouth, infuse your own spirits, or *spice* up your garnish game. You can do this with black peppercorn, nutmeg,

cinnamon, allspice, and cloves, for example. You'll want them to be whole so that they are fresher. When you grate them with your microplane, they will smell great! Whole spices are more easily strained and filtered.

CRUCIAL ACCOUTREMENTS: THE WHY, WHAT AND HOW OF GARNISHES

Garnishes are the pretty topping on the cocktail cake. Not only do they add interest to the presentation, but garnishes also add subtle aromas and flavors (from their essential oils) that complete the experience of drinking a cocktail.

I have seen some really interesting garnishes (think mini magolds delicately placed in the drink with tweezers), but a few staples include:

Celery: Whole stalk, without the white part

Cucumber: Sliced with the skin on

Cocktail onions: On a toothpick, on the rim of the glass

Edible flowers: Orchids and hibiscus float well

Herbs: Mint, basil, rosemary, and thyme are placed on the rim of the glass or placed directly in the drink before serving

Lemon, grapefruit, lime, and orange: Served fresh or candied (coated in simple syrup, then dipped in sugar, and baked at 150 degrees for a half hour) in twists, slices, wheels, and wedges

Fresh or liqueur-soaked cherries: Dropped directly in the glass

Black and green olives: Served whole or stuffed, either dropped individually in the glass or on a toothpick

Pineapple: Served as a slice on the rim

Strawberries: Served whole, with a slit, on the rim of the glass

START A COCKTAIL GARDEN

Herbs can be muddled in a drink, infused in a spirit, or used as garnish. Add them to any cocktail for a fresh spin on a classic drink, or put them in clear containers and on platters for sweet smelling décor when guests come over. Herbs are necessary to have around your home bar. To make using herbs über easy, start your own indoor or outdoor cocktail garden.

I have a small plot in my yard where I grow my herbs with a colorful stake and sign that says, "Cocktail Garden." I can't tell you how many people comment on how fun it is.

But even if you don't have a yard, potted herbs in your kitchen, dining, bar, and patio or porch areas make cool accents and are easy to access. All you really need to do is make sure you give them plenty of natural light, water, and adequate drainage. Most herbs are annual, not perennial, so if you live in a place where winter temperatures fluctuate, store the pots inside near plenty of natural sun to keep them alive as long as possible.

You can get the most out of your garden by planting the following herbs most commonly used in cocktail recipes:

Sage: Did you know that sage was once used as a fertility drug by ancient Egyptians? It was also used to treat sore throats and coughs, stop excessive menstrual bleeding, and dry up mother's milk when weening from nursing. Sage adds a peppery, savory flavor to cocktails and pairs well with fruits like blueberries and peaches.

Mint: Calming to our senses, mint grows like a weed. But that's okay, because you'll find plenty of uses for it in drinks. Grow a few different kinds for new twists on the flavor, like apple mint, chocolate mint, spearmint, and peppermint. Look out, it may be a very mojito summer!

Basil: There are hundreds of other uses you can find for this herb in cocktails, but basil goes particularly well with aperitifs and vermouths.

Thyme: Thyme adds a spicy edge to many drinks, and is a hardy plant for growing inside.

Lemon verbena: Lemon verbena smells wonderful and gives a very subtle lemon flavor without the souring effect of lemon juice.

HOW TO CUT 'EM

Fruit garnishes can be cut and displayed several ways, and the method always serves a purpose whether it's the look of a wheel on the glass, or the subtle flavor from the zest. Here's a garnish prep cheat sheet.

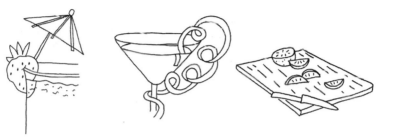

| Slice | Twist | Wedge |

| Wheel | Zest |

LOOKS MATTER:
HOW TO DISPLAY YOUR BAR

Unless you have an actual built-in bar counter at your house, you can use a six-foot or longer table or sideboard to set up drinks when guests come over. This length will provide easy access to all of the ingredients, and if it is set up away from high-traffic areas and doorways, your guests will have plenty of room to mingle.

GARNISHES IN ICE CUBES
For a fun accent to any drink, freeze edible flowers, herbs, and sliced fruits inside ice cubes. The aromatic properties will slowly be unveiled as the ice melts, and it looks pretty too. To do this, fill a large ice cube tray halfway with filtered water, and gently place your desired garnishes inside them. Allow to freeze, and then finish filling each ice mold with water. Freeze again, and voila!

But when it comes to the storage and display of all the unique booze and tools you will acquire, you should give your designated bar area some serious thought, whether you create a fancy full wet bar with a refrigerator and wine cooler, or just convert an old tea cart into a sleek, rolling bar in the corner of your apartment. Whatever it is, the bar can be a pretty focal point in your home, so have fun creating it.

A bar doesn't have to cost a lot, either. I love transforming unconventional pieces of furniture into one-of-a-kind bars. I once

MAKE YOUR OWN BITTERS

Bitters are like the spice rack of cocktails, according to Nick Kosevich, co-owner of Milwaukee-based artisan bitters company Bittercube.

"You can make very simple cocktails, like the gimlet [gin, citrus, and soda], but when you add a dash of bitters it suddenly takes on subtle nuances," he says. "So if you have six different bitters at home, that one drink can suddenly become six different cocktails."

Which is why bitters have become my favorite cocktail ingredient. Highly concentrated, aromatic liquids, bitters are made by infusing high-proof alcohol with all kinds of interesting and obscure, yet specific, bittering roots and barks, fruit peels, seeds, spices, herbs, flowers, and botanicals. They were originally marketed in the 19th century as digestive aids and medicines, but became a key ingredient in classic drinks, adding subtle flavor or balancing sweet notes in the likes of old-fashioneds and Manhattans. Some people still swear by a few dashes of bitters with soda water when you're feeling under the weather or need a hangover cure.

While it's possible to find flavors like lavender, chocolate, mole, celery, orange, Jamaican jerk, and hops bitters made by companies like Fee Brothers, Scrappy's, The Bitter End, and The Bitter Truth online, they can cost upwards of $20 for a small bottle. And in many liquor and grocery stores, the selection stops at Peychaud's and Angostura; while these are classic, hundred-year-old brands you should definitely keep around, I highly recommend experimenting with your own flavored creations.

This basic aromatic bitters recipe comes from Kosevich, who uses it as a jumping off point for new flavors.

Most of the ingredients can be found at a grocery or natural foods store. Note that without the gentian root, this would be a tincture, rather than bitters. A tincture is a high-proof concentration of flavors you use in small doses in cocktails, but they do not have the bittering agents.

2 cups 100-proof bourbon
2 cups neutral grain spirit
   (like vodka or Everclear)
1 1/2 cups water
1/2 cup simple syrup
   (1 part water with
   1 part sugar)
1/4 cup raisins
1 vanilla bean
   (scrape out the inside of
   the bean, and discard
   the pod)
Peel of 1 lemon and 1 orange
1 teaspoon dried spearmint
2 cardamom pods
2 cinnamon sticks
1 teaspoon allspice

1 teaspoon whole clove
1 teaspoon chamomile
1 whole nutmeg, crushed
2 star anise pods
1/2 teaspoon gentian root
   (this can be found at
   natural foods stores and
   online stores like
   Amazon.com)
Gravity filter (optional to get
   bitters with the least
   amount of sediment,
   available at camping and
   outdoor stores) or chinois
   (fine mesh sieve)
Cheesecloth
Patience

1. Combine all ingredients (except the water and syrup) in a glass jar with a sealable lid and shake vigorously, once or twice a day for two weeks.
2. Strain the liquid through cheesecloth and squeeze as much liquid out of the mash as possible.
3. Strain again through fresh cheesecloth, without applying pressure to the cloth so that the sediment doesn't escape.
4. Add the water and simple syrup to this liquid.
5. Let mixture sit for three days.
6. Use either a gravity filter or chinois to remove the sediment that will have settled at the bottom of the jar. Then filter through cheesecloth again. Do this until you have the cleanest liquid you can get.
7. If desired, decant the mixture into smaller bottles (such as two-ounce Boston rounds, which look like pharmacy bottles) with medicine dropper lids for controlled use in drinks. Give them as gifts!

These bitters will work well in any cocktail that calls for bitters. Start your experimentation with an old-fashioned (recipe on page 297). A great book to consult as you experiment with this process is Brad Thomas Parsons' *Bitters: A Spirited History of a Classic Cure-All*. It covers different bittering agents and contains specific recipes for flavors like Meyer lemon, lime, licorice, and coffee.

got a free, 100-year-old upright piano off of Craigslist, only to tear off the front panels, which revealed colorful strings and parts that were way more interesting than the roughed-up exterior. So I installed stemware racks under the top and under the keys, had a piece of tempered glass made to lay over the keys, and stored liquor bottles in the bottom of the piano, where the feet are. Not a single person makes it through my house without commenting on it, and it also makes me very happy that I have a bar no one else has that, in all, cost just over $150. I then mounted the keyboard cover on a nearby wall, where it folds out to hold drinks for folks who are standing. I installed spiral wine racks on the wall above the piano for extra bottle storage. Most anything can be made into an affordable bar that fits the style of your home and the space you have allotted. On my Pinterest page (Pinterest.com/booze-forbabes), I've collected some ideas for small apartment bars, re-purposed bars, vintage bars, outdoor bars, and dream bars to give you some inspiration.

As for how to arrange your stash, here are a few tips for keep-ing your bar looking great and organized:

1. **Keep your most elegant and interesting looking bottles at the front of your bar.** Push the average, less unique – shaped bottles to the back.

2. **Arrange bitters and other aesthetically pleasing accoutre-ments in their own section, at the front of the bar.** Not only do they look professional this way, but they also add splashes of color and diversity to the display.

3. **Show off your self-infused spirits in a collection of funky shaped or colored bottles, Prohibition-style glass jugs, or classy square or swing-top corked bottles** (SpecialtyBottle.com has cool shapes and cheap prices). Jazz them up with la-bels by finding a pretty label template online or cutting black-board contact paper into shapes and writing on them with chalk. If you don't have room on your bar, opt to arrange them on a tray as a table centerpiece instead.

4. **Keep your best glasses on display either on stemware racks or a tray.** Tuck average ones in a cabinet for backup.

5. **Use unique containers to house cocktail stirrers and other**

tools (I keep mine in a vintage toolbox and milk glass vases).

6. *Keep a top shelf.* Your home bar doesn't have to be set up like a commercial one, but you do need a place for your best stuff. Mine is the top of my piano, where my most expensive and collectible bottles sit. Not only does it look nice and regal, but it also keeps people from accidentally opening a commemorative bottle (if your friends are anything like mine, it could happen).

ON THE ROAD:
HOW TO CREATE A PORTABLE BAR

Once you've got some new bartending skills under your belt, you might want to take them on the road—camping, vacationing with friends, or visiting a friend's home. But where to begin without lugging a lot of heavy, breakable stuff? I consulted New York City bartenders Lynnette Marrero and Ivy Mix, who travel often for Speed Rack, a ladies bartending competition, about what they never leave home without. According to them, the key is bringing just a few versatile items that pack well, so that you can mix a lot of different drinks with minimal ingredients. Since you can usually find fruits, sugar, and citrus wherever you may be, here's a portable bar packing list of items that don't take up a lot of space and would be awfully inconvenient to track down while traveling:

Travel set of bitters: A set of flavored bitters which come in 100-milliliter bottles (similar to essential oils or face creams) will allow for several variations of one drink, such as a sour (which includes booze, citrus, and sugar).

Hand juicer: More compact than a pair of shoes, this tool is necessary for making fresh drinks away from home.

Shaker: I have certainly made do without a shaker before at a poorly equipped friend's house and in a vacation cabin, but it wasn't pretty rigging two glasses together and shaking them gently so they wouldn't break. Bring the shaker, and to save space in your bag, tuck your cloth-wrapped bitters bottles and/or a hand juicer in it (if you have an oversized shaker like I do, this will all fit).

IN-FLIGHT PICK-ME-UP
Sick of the airlines' sorry booze selection? To be sure you can enjoy a good drink on the plane, Mix recommends putting a mixed cocktail in a clean travel toiletry container, storing it in a zip-top bag, and whipping it out once you're up in the air. Use the airline's mixers like soda water and orange juice to complete your concoction.

One spirit: Make it the one you and your companions like most. Make this spirit go the distance by planning three to five cocktails around it.

MANDATORY MIXER: MAKE YOUR OWN VERMOUTH

Vermouth is a crucial ingredient in dozens of classic cocktails and can elongate a spirit with its light, yet rich, flavors. Vermouth is a fortified wine, which means that it has a wine base with stronger booze added to up the alcohol content and make its flavor more dynamic.

But it can be difficult to find a great and complex tasting store-bought vermouth that holds its flavor and is tasty enough to drink straight on the rocks. The great thing about making vermouth at home is that you can tweak the flavor to be more spicy, sweet, bitter, light, or heavy as you please.

I always begin with a pinot grigio base wine because it is neither too dry or too sweet but contains some fruity notes. If you want to make sweet vermouth, consider cognac, apple brandy, sherry, or port as a fortifier. If you'd like it dry, consider gin or vodka. Flavor your vermouth with any herbs you fancy—coriander, chamomile, juniper, ginger, elderberries, and cloves are popular.

The following recipe is a base for sweet vermouth, but you can use its proportions and change out ingredients for others based on your desired taste. This may take some trial and error, but don't be afraid! You can then use your vermouth in any recipe that calls for it, and give some away to friends.

Zest of 1 orange
3 1/4 cups white wine, such as pinot grigio
1 cinnamon stick
1 teaspoon juniper berries
8 cardamom pods

1 star anise
1 teaspoon dried lavender
1/4 teaspoon wormwood leaf
1/2 cup grape brandy, like cognac
1/2 cup dry sherry

Combine the wine, zest, and herbs in a pot, stir, and simmer over medium heat until mixture comes to a boil, about five minutes. Reduce heat to low, cover, and cook for an additional 5 minutes. Remove from heat. Strain out solids and return liquid to the pot to cool. Once cooled, stir in the sherry and/or brandy. Let it sit for 24 hours before serving, and decant into an airtight container. Refrigerate for up to a month.

One liqueur or fortified wine: Make your pick based on the booze you choose, and how many recipes you can dig up using both spirits (probably dozens). Some suggestions include Campari, a bitter amaro, sweet or dry vermouth, or Cointreau, an orange liqueur.

Jigger: Great drinks are all about balance. This thing is so small you can fit it in your handbag, so don't leave home without it!

How much of the spirit and modifier you should plan to bring depends on how long you'll be gone, and also whether you'll be flying. If you're carrying on a bag, it may be worth buying your booze when you arrive at your destination, since storing your sauce in the TSA-required three-ounce containers in a one quart zip-top bag would be a total pain in the arse, and would leave little room for your soap! But if you are checking your bag, you can wrap whole bottles tightly in clothing to protect the glass, or transfer the spirits to smaller, reusable plastic or stainless steel water bottles. Or see below for a totally professional way to travel with a bar.

You should know that the Federal Aviation Administration currently does not limit the amount of alcoholic beverages you can send on a plane if they under 48 proof (such as bitters and some liqueurs or fortified wines), but you can only check five liters of sealable alcohol that is between 48 and 140 proof. Anything over that (like . . . a certain type of flammable rum) is not allowed at all, even in your toiletry kit. Overseas, there may be different rules on what's permitted, so be sure to check before you go.

COCKTAILS FOR THE SKIN

Spas around the world are beginning to catch on to wine's benefits and antioxidants for the skin, incorporating it into fancy facials and body treatments. Spirits, because they are not pure alcohols like the kind found in some store-bought cleansers that dry the skin, can help stimulate circulation and fight wrinkles and fine lines when applied topically. Plus, they are extraordinarily aromatic and are all around fun to play with at home. Here, a couple of homemade beauty recipes to get you started on a boozy beauty regimen with your new bar stash.

Between the Sheets Scrub

Based on the Prohibition - era cocktail, this scrub recipe comes from Jasmina Aganovic, founder of the Stages of Beauty skincare line. The brandy and sugar exfoliates the skin, whether used on the body or face, and the citrus brightens it.

1 tablespoon brandy
2 tablespoons packed
   brown sugar
1 tablespoon orange juice
1 tablespoon lemon juice

Mix ingredients for a few minutes until there is a consistent texture. Apply gently to face and/or body in circular motions for 30 seconds and rinse.

Piña Colada Face Mask

The sugar and lactic acid in the coconut milk exfoliates; while the rum and pineapple act as astringents. The yogurt unlocks antibacterial powers to eliminate impurities.

1 tablespoon dried coconut
   milk or dried goat's milk
1 tablespoon sugar
1 tablespoon pineapple
puree
1 tablespoon plain yogurt
1 tablespoon aged rum

Mix all ingredients together in a bowl until there is a consistent texture. Apply to the face and let sit until dry. Rinse thoroughly.

PORTABLE BAR BAGS

Now, how to transport your bar without breaking a bottle (or a sweat!)?

The most important factor is keeping glass intact. You can repurpose a camera bag, which is already equipped with padded compartments, into a bar bag, and turn any knife roll into a carrier for bar spoons, strainers, straws, and a paring knife, for example.

There are also a couple of great bar bags on the market that may be worth the investment if you plan to be the designated bartender extraordinaire away from home:

- *Moore & Giles Bar Rollup by Jim Meehan:* This stylish suede and leather roll designed by the bartender/owner of Please Don't Tell (PDT) in New York City is a splurge at $150, but is ultra stylish. There's even a little insert for a name tag on the outside of it. It holds spoons and tools of various sizes.

- *The Gin & Luck Rucksack:* Designed by bartenders David Kaplan and Alex Day, this backpack comes in blue and black, with side pockets for bottles, a shaker sleeve, a laptop compartment, and a toolkit. At $350 it ain't cheap, but you can sometimes catch it on sale (available at CocktailKingdom. com).

Get creative with how you transport your tools! When I'm driving somewhere and can take it easily, I use a vintage toolbox to hold the things I need like a jigger, strainer, bar spoon, mesh sieves, and swizzle sticks. A small toolbox from Home Depot, or for a more feminine touch, a makeup travel case with compartments, works just as well.

CHAPTER 5

Gin for the Win

Gin—the clear, juniper-forward, and often dry spirit—sometimes has to grow on you. When I was growing up my dad drank gin and tonics and occasionally I'd accidentally pick up his highball and take a big chug, thinking it was ice water. "Yuck! I will *never* drink this nasty stuff!" I'd say, right after I spit it out. My opinion of gin remained this way through my early 20s, until I began drinking better gin, better tonic, and better gin cocktails than my father did (I have since brought him around to the finer stuff). Now, it's my second favorite spirit behind whiskey. The point is that gin isn't always easy on the palate, but it has an interesting, storied history that you'll be able to appreciate. Then we'll get into how you, too, can come around to gin, by knowing the different types available and what to do with them.

Back in the day (I'm talking 11th century), Italian monks flavored crudely distilled spirits with aromatic and tasty juniper berries. Since water was unsafe to drink, people thought this rudimentary gin could protect against the plague when drunk regularly. But it wasn't until the mid-17th century that what we now know as gin was invented by a Dutch physician named Franciscus Sylvius—though numerous small Dutch and Flemish distillers had been making gin-like substances by redistilling alcohol with herbs like juniper, anise, caraway, and coriander to treat kidney and stomach problems, gall stones, and gout (don't try this at home).

"Gin's a spirit unto herself. She's a loner. Gin can gnaw on the back of your neck till she nigh-on draws blood, and she can just as easily kiss you softly behind each ear, stroke the back of your shivering hand, and make you know that everything's going to be okay . . . Gin is for thinkers and doers alike, but she won't be seen dead with the loud, brash braggart down the end of the bar. Gin makes her own statement, too. She doesn't need a sleek black dress and screw-me pumps to make her presence known at the party. She can just sit quietly at the end of the bar, faded jeans and a plain white T-shirt, secure in the knowledge that only the guys and gals who know exactly what they want, how they want it, and how they're gonna go about getting it, will ever approach her. And when they sidle over to her side, they know that they'd better treat her with some respect, too. Don't mess around with gin. She's been known to take off her earrings . . ."

—gaz regan in his 2009 book,
The Bartender's Gin Compendium

Gin became known as an English gentleman's drink in the 17th century when English soldiers discovered that Dutch soldiers had been performing remarkably well in battles after sipping genever from small bottles before the fight. The English wanted a piece of this "Dutch courage" and in the late-17th century passed a law that encouraged their homeland farmers to distill gin. British distillers began to make their own version of gin with a corn base that was lighter and sweeter than the Dutch version.

Once mainstream England caught onto gin—a period known as the "gin craze" between 1720 and 1751—the per capita consumption of cheap distilled spirits tripled. Get this: by 1727, gin consumption hit five million gallons a year for a population of 6.5 million! It was a phenomenon among the working class in London until the Gin Act of 1751 got the black market booze business under control with improved licensing requirements for distillers and retailers.

Fast forward to the early 20th century, particularly during Prohibition, when gin was experiencing a heydey as a speakeasy staple because of how easily it could be crudely put together in makeshift vessels (like bathtubs). Because of the timing of its popularity, gin evokes images of cultural revolutions and heady times like glamorous vaudeville shows and the Harlem Renaissance. In turn, there is something wonderfully classic (and in turn, classy) about gin. After all, there would be no martini without it, and look at what that cocktail has come to represent: sophistication, glamour, and, thanks to James Bond, suave courage in the face of danger.

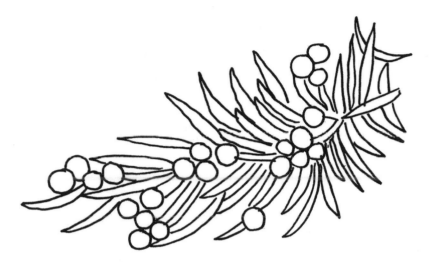

GIN CYCLE: HOW GIN IS MADE

Gin is a neutral grain spirit – like vodka – redistilled with juniper berries. Those berries are what makes gin gin. Gin can contains various other botanicals in addition to the juniper like anise, almonds, angelica, coriander, orange peel, and cinnamon. The amount and combination of botanicals is what distinguishes one gin from another.

WHAT IS RAIL LIQUOR?

Rail liquors are the selection of bottles bartenders keep in the long shelf under the bar counter, called the rail. These bottles are usually the cheapest liquors they carry, and are often used automatically unless you, or the cocktail menu, specify otherwise.

If you haven't tried gin neat, I'm not surprised. Because gin is a popular base for classic staples like the martini and gin and tonic, you probably never even considered it to have its own independently worthy qualities. A web poll by *Imbibe* magazine found that out of more than 1,650 respondents, only four and a half percent picked gin as their favorite spirit to sip neat.

That's because many cheap, rail gins (see below for explanation) contain bitter flavors resembling the taste of a rotten lemon, which is caused by flaws in distillation, or by cheap oil flavorings and the use of poor quality base vodkas.

But there are so many great gin products out there at all price points, particularly by craft distillers across America who are experimenting and adding local botanicals to create products that stray from the spirit's dry and bitter tradition. Now, gin can be floral, herbal, spicy, or earthy with the addition of botanicals like elderberry, sage, orris root, and lemongrass. Though gin is cheaper to make than spirits like brandy and whiskey because it does not need time to age, that doesn't mean it's always a cheap or poor-quality product.

ORIGINAL GIN: ALL OF THE TYPES OF GIN

Unlike scotch or cognac, which must be produced in Scotland or Cognac, France, respectively, to be classified as such, gin can be made anywhere in the world. It is usually about 90 proof.

For gin makers, juniper, like cognac's grapes, is sacred. Juniper shrubs grow in several select places, from the western United States to Umbria and Macedonia. Since this is the single most important ingredient in gin, a distiller may receive several samples during the fall harvest season. Like any crop, finding the perfect product—and matching it year to year—is difficult and precise.

The best gin is always going to be the one you like the most, but there are some general guidelines by which to choose a decent bottle. To distinguish between all of choices out there, you've got to understand what the words on a gin's label means for its taste and style:

Juniper-flavored, genever, jenever, and Dutch gin: This is the earliest class of gin, which is produced by redistilling grain alcohol with botanicals to extract the aromatic compounds. This type is sometimes aged in wooden barrels, retains some grain flavor, and has relatively low alcoholic content. Dutch gins today use barley and age the spirit to give it rich, whiskey-like flavor, but the predominant aroma and taste is always juniper. Genever has to contain juniper, but it doesn't have to taste like it by law, which makes it interesting and almost not like a gin at all. Bols, which started distilling it in the 17th century, is the oldest genever brand, but a few others, such as Boomsma, are available here.

German or Steignhager Gin: This type must be produced from triple-distilled spirit and juniper berries. It is often diluted with purified water before it is bottled because it is so strong. You won't easily find this product in the United States The only one I've been able to find tasted like rubbing alcohol to me, but might taste like heaven to a German. Who knows?

Gin: A product labeled just "gin" or "compound gin" is made by simply flavoring neutral spirit with essences and/or other "natural flavorings" without re-distillation, and is usually not considered a refined spirit. Botanicals are crushed and pressed to extract essential oils and components. The oils are then added to the main tank of neutral grain spirits and mixed for a week. This is how bathtub gin was made during Prohibition.

London Dry Gin or Dry Gin: London gin's flavor is "dry" and redistilled with juniper and other botanicals that could include cucumber, coriander, citrus – you name it. London Gin or Dry Gin may contain very limited sugar in the final product, and cannot have any colorants or additives other than water. I find that London Dry and other dry gins are the most versatile and quintessential type of gin to use in cocktails. Quality and popular brands include Bluecoat, Beefeater, Broker's, and Tanqueray.

Distilled Gin: This classification means the product was produced by redistilling ethyl alcohol with juniper berries and other natural botanicals, though the juniper taste is always predominant. Using this term differentiates it from just "gin" or "compound gin" because the ingredients are fresh or dried, rather than oils or essences. Most American gin brands that are considered Dry Gin fall under this category.

Old Tom Gin: Popular in the 18th century, this type of gin is hard to find now, with the exception of a couple of small brands such as Ransom and Hayman's. This type of gin was named during England's gin ban in the 1700s, after black "tom" cat plaques mounted on the outside walls of pubs and homes. Behind these plaques were tubes leading to bootleg tubs of gin inside, from which patrons could take a  shot for a penny. The spirit is distilled with grain as opposed to juniper, and an infusion of botanicals like juniper, coriander, cardamom, and angelica root. The two distillations are combined and distilled together and aged in oak barrels. Old Tom gin is lighter than genever or Dutch gin, but is fuller-bodied than a London Dry. It's a good style to line up in the middle of a gin tasting.

Navy-strength gins: If you see this on the label of a gin bottle, it means that it is at least 114 proof, which is the same requirement the British Navy had for gins in the 19th century (the sailors were given daily rations of it). It had to  be high proof so that gunpowder could still fire if the gin touched it. These gins are heavier than others, which means they can hold up against vermouth and other liquors well in a cocktail. Brands include Plymouth Navy Strength Gin, Hayman's Royal Dock of Deptford, and Leopold Brothers.

MAKE A GIMLET

The gimlet cocktail was created by British Royal Navy doctor Sir Thomas Desmond Gimlette as a preventive measure against scurvy. Now, it's a popular drink that also serves as a jumping off point for other tasty sour combinations:

2 ounces dry gin
1/2 ounce lime juice
1/2 ounce simple syrup
Lime wedge

Add all ingredients to a cocktail shaker with ice and shake vigorously. Strain into coupe or martini glass and garnish with the lime wedge.

WHAT MAKES A GOOD GIN?

With more innovative gins to choose from than ever before, there is a style to suit everyone's taste. Gin lovers that go way back typically love the heavy juniper taste found in London Dry, Dutch, and Old Tom gins, while others may like lighter, more herbal varieties found in many new American styles.

You can also taste the difference between a gin that has been distilled with botanicals and one that has been infused with botanicals after distilling. You can compare it to the depth of chocolate flavor you'd taste if you were eating a cake made with chocolate batter as opposed to a cake with just a chocolate topping. When you taste a gin that has been distilled with the botanicals, they are woven into the spirit in a fluid and dynamic way. Those that have been blended will retain more of their grain alcohol flavor. If a gin smells highly of ethyl alcohol, it's likely a low quality. If the gin smells perfumey, rather than subtly aromatic, it's probably artificially flavored and you should nix it. In all cases, trust your nose. When I asked Joanne Moore, the master distiller for Bloom London Dry Gin, what makes a good product, she said balance. The juniper notes in a gin should be evident but also complemented by any other botanicals used. That means that you should not take a sip and think, "Wow! That [insert flavor] is really strong!" It helps to get a feel for juniper's aromas by smelling the dried berries by themselves at a natural foods store (I keep them on hand in

INSIDE THE "GIN PALACE"
In Victorian England, the middle class would patronize gin palaces, which were basically just lounges where the spirit was served (the term "gin palace" has since became a nickname for luxury yachts meant for boozing it up). The first gin palaces were built in the1820s—Thompson and Fearon's in Holborn and Weller's on London's Old Street. They were new, fashionable, and scandalous because men often went there to meet prostitutes.

Thomas Miller, a writer for the Illustrated London News, wrote in 1848, "that there are few places in London where so great a variety of characters may be seen popping in and out in a short space of time, as at the bars of our modern gin palaces. Even respectable men who meet each other by chance, after a long absence, must drop in at the nearest tavern, although they have scarcely a minute to spare, to drink a glass together at the bar, and enquire about old friends. Married women, we are sorry to say, many of them the wives of clever mechanics, also congregate when they ought to be providing the dinner for their families."

Now, just like with contemporary speakeasy trend in the United States, London is honoring their drinking traditions of days past by recreating gin palaces with classic cocktails and sultry décor (think velvet curtains and dark color palettes) without the gender discrimination of days past.

my pantry for homemade vermouths and teas).

"Most brands will give you some information on the labels about the flavors and aromas, much like you would expect with a wine," Moore adds. "The important thing to understand is that not all gins are the same. We wouldn't say that all white wine tastes and smells the same! Each recipe is different so if you have had a bad experience with one brand that doesn't mean you don't like gin."

WHEN TO CHOOSE GIN

Most people don't drink gin straight, but that doesn't mean you can't. There is no season for making gin—it can be produced year round. And as a result, gin is one of the most versatile spirits out there, working well in warm weather and cold weather cocktails.

Gin is elevated when mixed with ingredients that highlight,

WHAT DOES DRINKING GIN SAY ABOUT YOU?
"Our mothers and grandmothers drank gin, and so it has had a stereotype as an older person's drink," says Moore. "But that perception is changing. I think the gin we choose to drink as a woman—whether it be spicy, floral, herbal, or dry—can give a little insight to our character or our mood at that time, much like how we choose our perfume due to the occasion."

---

rather than cover up, its distinctive botanical taste. I've found that unique botanical gins should be deconstructed to find the perfect match. If the gin's primary flavor, other than juniper of course, is apple, then work with that. Dry gins can be paired with just about anything, and when you're at a loss for mixes, muddled fruit, liqueurs, and fortified wines, like sherry, port, and madeira, make perfect additions.

I tend to choose gin when...

- *I want a light but dynamic addition to a punch.* Try adding gin instead of brandy to traditional sangria, for example. Because of gin's botanical, yet light character, it's easily mixable without feeling heavy.

- *I want an alternative to vodka.* Next time a bartender asks for your choice of gin or vodka, choose gin and see what happens. In many cocktails, gin provides the punch of vodka but with more dynamic flavors.

- *It's summertime.* You can drink any spirit, any time of year, but gin is a refreshing base for a number of summer cocktails, such as a Tom Collins, French 75, or pretty much anything with fresh fruit muddled with it.

SUPER TONIC:
MAKE YOUR OWN TONIC WATER

When a good tonic isn't available, try making your own.

This recipe from Marcia Simmons, author of *DIY Cocktails: A Simple Guide to Creating Your Own Signature Drinks*, is a great way to get your creative juices flowing, and is a throwback to tonic's old production method of steeping cinchona bark to make tea, which is why this DIY tonic mixture will be brown in color (don't be alarmed!). Mainstream tonic is clear because its quinine content in usually chemically extracted.

If you can get a hold of cinchona bark at a Latin market or online (try the California-based Lhasa Karnak Herb Company) you can

SHAKEN, NOT STIRRED (NOT!): TRY A REAL MARTINI

A gin lesson is not complete without talking about the martini, a classic gin and vermouth cocktail that gained widespread recognition because of Bond, James Bond. While it's become common to make martinis with vodka, they were traditionally made with gin. While some believe the martini as we now know it was born during the California Gold Rush, British journalist John Doxat insists it was first created in New York City at the old Knickerbocker Hotel one evening in 1910. Patrons were hooked, and other bars began the process of recreating the cocktail. And so the evolution began of this popular, yet mysterious and storied drink. The martini—or a version of it—has likely been around even longer than that, however. In 1896, bartender and author Thomas Stewart wrote a recipe for a drink with two-thirds Plymouth gin and one-third sweet French vermouth. And that whole shaken, not stirred thing? Ian Fleming, Bond author, used to have his martinis mixed tableside at London's famed Dorchester Hotel, which provided inspiration for that famous question. But contrary to Bond's shaken preference, a martini should actually be stirred for two reasons: one, shaking the ingredients allows too much air to dissolve in the drink, and two, it becomes too cold when shaken. Both of these alter the taste of the drink by dulling it. That's not to say your martini has to be super high-octane. In fact, those who prefer their martinis extra dry (i.e. a drop of vermouth or none at all) are actually not having a martini, though it is a perfectly fine option nonetheless!

MAKE A MARTINI
2 ounces London Dry gin
1 ounce sweet or dry vermouth

Add both ingredients to a cocktail shaker or glass with ice. Stir and strain into a coupe or martini glass.

make your own tonic water from scratch for a minimal investment.

Once you get the hang of how to create a tonic syrup – which you will mix with soda water to get the fizz – you can experiment with its flavors and nuances. For example, you can swap cane sugar for agave nectar, or add orange or lemon peel. In the end, you'll have an herbal, all-natural concoction that tastes delicious.

"You know what you'll use tonic for. You know if you want it to have a strong floral flavor or a bitter quinine flavor and make it accordingly," Simmons says. "Even though it requires an obscure ingredient [cinchona bark], it's not very expensive, and you don't need very much. If you happen to mess up, there's not much risk in it. Get your friends involved."

Plus, a bottle of homemade tonic syrup paired with a good gin makes a great gift.

Get started! (makes 6 cups tonic water)

2 cups water

1 ½ cups pure cane sugar or ⅔ cups agave nectar

2 teaspoons cut cinchona bark (available in some
    herb stores online)

1 ¼ teaspoons powdered citric acid (found in most well-stocked
    grocery stores or online)

1 lime, juiced

⅔ cup chopped lemongrass stalks

Sparkling water

Medium saucepan

Spoon

Strainer

Cheesecloth

Coffee filters

Funnel

Glass bottle with lid

1. In a medium saucepan, bring the sugar and water to a boil until the sugar dissolves, then turn heat to low.

2. Add the cinchona bark, citric acid, lemongrass, and lime juice. Stir well and simmer for about 25 minutes, until the powder is dissolved and the syrup is thin and runny.

3. Remove from heat and let cool. Strain through cheesecloth and then a coffee filter.

4. Funnel the syrup into sterilized glass bottles, cover tightly, and store in the refrigerator for up to one month.

5. Immediately before consumption, add the syrup to sodium-free sparkling water (about 2 ½ ounces syrup to 10 ounces water), or carbonate filtered water with a CO_2 charger.

PARTY TRICK: SET UP A GIN & TONIC BAR

Now that you know a little about gin's possibilities, set up a gin & tonic bar at your next party to get friends and family exposed to new brands and flavors.

Line up five different types of gin on a table—three diverse botanical gins with different predominant flavors, and two drys.

Then present five different tonics, including one or two homemade versions. Include a tonic made with a botanical and one

HOW TO MAKE THE PERFECT G&T

The gin and tonic has an interesting origin. The drink, which consists of one part gin and three parts tonic, began in the 16th century as a medicine for kidney problems by Dutch scientist Dr. Franciscus Sylvius. Tonic, which contains quinine and was traditionally consumed to prevent malaria, was added to the spirit when the British colonized India as a way to fend off mosquitoes. Gin effectively masked the vile taste of quinine, made from a South American bark called cinchona. Over time, the cinchona tonic was mixed with citric acid and carbonated water and became a staple at every bar.

A properly made gin and tonic with natural, high-quality ingredients is likely to change a gin skeptic's mind about the spirit. Make one right with the following tips based on my conversation with Jorge Figueredo, general manager of Jaleo, a Spanish tapas restaurant by celebrity chef José Andrés in Washington, D.C. Jaleo features six signature G&Ts with six very different gins, small batch tonics, and a house-made tonic syrup made from cinchona bark, coriander, lemon verbena, and citric acid. There's even a G&T sorbet on the menu, which pays homage to Spain's after-dinner G&T *digestivo* of choice.

Taste the gin before mixing it with tonic. The type of gin you choose will define your gin and tonic's characteristics. Do you prefer an herbal drink or a dry one? Do you want to tone down the quinine or enhance it? Botanical gins, which bring out floral flavors, will make a different G&T than a dry gin, which is juniper-forward.

Then choose a tonic. Did you know that there is life beyond Schweppes and Canada Dry tonic water? The quality of tonic water is crucial to creating a dynamic G&T—if you can't use a good tonic, don't bother making one. Try brands like Q Tonic, Fever-Tree, or Fentimans (available at natural foods and specialty stores). These tonics, while more expensive and a little harder to find, are filtered several times and flavored with herbs, fruits, and flowers like lemons, marigolds, and orange oil. They may be sweetened with agave nectar or cane sugar. Q Tonic, for example, uses pure quinine from a cinchona plantation on the border of Congo and Rwanda. Because of the natural ingredients, these tonics usually have less than half the calories of mainstream tonics. These are also packaged in smaller bottles, so that they do not lose their carbonation as quickly. Choose tonic based on the qualities in the gin and counter them for balance, such as pairing a sweet or lighter tonic with dry gin.

Use a proper glass. Nix the traditional Collins glass for a large rimmed rocks glass with a heavy bottom. Doing so makes one feel important while drinking it (screw the martini with three olives!), and allows for more aromas to penetrate the senses. Since freezing gin dulls its flavors, frost the glass instead. Making a bigger deal of the G&T's presentation elevates its status and enhances the experience of drinking it.

Deconstruct the gin for garnish. The beauty of the gin and tonic is in its simplicity, but you can up the ante on presentation and aromatics with a proper garnish. Eschew the typical lime wedge on the rim, and instead choose floating garnishes by deconstructing the gin. For example, if the gin contains elderflower, orange, and coriander, drop a few coriander seeds, an elderflower, and orange zest in the glass before pouring in the liquid. Let it float at the top of the glass.

Ice matters. Some bartenders hand cut blocks of dry ice that won't melt quickly, but home bartenders can get a similar effect by boiling water to close air pockets, letting it cool, and then freezing it into oversize ice cube trays. Use one large cube in your glass to keep the G&T as pure as possible while also keeping it chilled.

Drink G&Ts with food. Gin cuts grease and fats really well so don't be afraid to pair G&Ts with food. The same principles apply to gin pairing as with wine. A light a airy, herbal G&T may go well with shrimp while a drier, juniper-forward or Old Tom gin-based drink pairs well with pork.

Use it as a jumping off point. The gin and tonic is a great base for building a new cocktail. For example, my husband adds a half-ounce of St. Germain, an elderflower liqueur, to his G&T, which subtly tones down the bitter taste of quinine-heavy tonic.

MAKE A GIN AND TONIC: JOSÉ ANDRÉS' GIN & TONIC
This recipe is chef Andrés' personal favorite, which has a fresh cucumber essence thanks to the inclusion of Hendrick's gin.

1 ounce Hendrick's gin
1 bottle Fever-Tree tonic
2 juniper berries
1 lime wheel
1 lemon peel
1 leaf lemon verbena

Add juniper berries, lime wheel, lemon peel, and lemon verbena to wide-rimmed rocks glass or stemless red wine glass with a single oversized ice cube. Pour in gin then slowly add the tonic water. Serve.

sweetened with agave. Encourage your guests to pair their chosen tonic and gin the same way you put together ingredients in a single dish—by contrasting characteristics. For example, don't match a sweet gin with an agave-based tonic.

Using the tasting and nosing tips with which I've armed you in Chapter 12, determine which essences and scents you detect in the gin, and set out bowls of corresponding whole botanicals with spoons, tongs, or tweezers (for delicate flowers and herbs) for garnishing, labeled with chalkboard sticker tags or place cards. Don't tell the guests which ingredients appear in which gins. Give them a little background about the ingredients you've chosen and encourage them to deconstruct the spirits themselves. Voila! Your guests will make their own quality drinks, while learning at the same time.

SLOE-ING IT DOWN: HOW TO MAKE SLOE GIN

You may have heard of sloe gin and thought it was just a different style of gin, but it is actually a gin-based liqueur. And what the heck are sloes, you might ask? Sloes are a type of European blackthorn berry that is sweet, tart, and extra rare in the United States. So rare, that in 2008 when Plymouth released its variety here, bartenders rejoiced. The history of sloe gin goes back to the 19th century, when an army of women would gather the fruit just so this liqueur could be made. The fruit is then steeped in specially distilled gin and matured in old oak casks. The English would pair the liqueur with their London Dry for a warming wintertime drink.

Plymouth Sloe Gin, which uses an original 1883 recipe, and The Bitter Truth's Sloe Berry Blue Gin are quality products on the market, but they are not easy to come by in liquor stores. While on a business trip to London, I was super giddy when I wandered into a local shop and found a sloe gin by Sipsmith's, a small English distillery, to take home with me, serve on special occasions and proudly display on my bar.

If you happen to get your hands on the sloes, sloe gin is incredibly easy to make and results in a beverage with a beautiful, deep red color. This recipe for slow gin is slightly modified from the Women's Institute's 1954 handbook, *Home Made Wines, Syrups, and Cordials:*

1 pound sloes

1 ½ pints London Dry gin

3 ounces raw sugar

1. Stalk and clean sloes, then prick each one with a fork.
2. Pack the fruit in a large, 16-ounce mason jar; add sugar and gin.
3. Store for three months in a dark cupboard, turning over the jar occasionally. Strain through cheesecloth, bottle, and cork.

DRINK TO IMPRESS: SLOE GIN FIZZ

I'll never forget the time I saw a Sloe Gin Fizz, a classic cocktail from the early 20th century, made perfectly. I was in Derek Brown's 10-seat bar, the Columbia Room, in Washington, D.C. The red, foamy drink took 10 minutes to make because of the vigorous shaking required. Some people top the sloe gin fizz with a splash of club soda for extra effervescence, but it's not necessary.

Here's Brown's recipe for the ultimate sloe gin fizz:

1 ounce Plymouth gin
1 1/2 ounces Plymouth sloe gin
3/4 ounce lemon juice
1/2 cane sugar syrup (2 parts sugar to 1 part water)
Orange slice and cherry for garnish

Shake all ingredients with ice until chilled. Once chilled, strain over fresh ice into a 12-ounce highball. Garnish with a flag (an orange slice and cherry on a toothpick).

GATEWAY GIN COCKTAILS

The variety of gin styles available make it accessible and appropriate for any time or place. Here's what to drink when you...

Want to seal the deal: The Hanky Panky

Created in 1925 by Ada Coleman, a renowned female bartender at The Savoy Hotel's American Bar in London, the Hanky Panky is a fresh alternative to the martini. It is a rich, red drink she created for Sir Charles Hawtrey, a celebrated Georgian actor who frequented the establishment. Don't forget to order it with a straight face!

1 1/2 ounces gin
1 1/2 ounces sweet vermouth
2 dashes Fernet-Branca
Orange twist, for garnish

Add all ingredients to a shaker and fill with ice. Stir and strain into a chilled cocktail glass. Garnish with the orange twist.

Want to girl talk: The Orange Blossom

This is the perfect alternative to the popular champagne-based Mimosa brunch beverage, and the addition of peach bitters makes it a well rounded cocktail.

1 1/2 ounces London dry gin
1 1/2 ounces fresh-squeezed orange juice
 (you won't believe how much of a difference this makes)
4 dashes peach bitters

Toss all ingredients in a cocktail shaker with ice and shake vigorously. Pour with the ice into a highball or Collins glass.

Feel Adventurous: The Jackson

Simple but assertive, this drink which is lightened up by the orange bitters, offers a nice vermouth alternative with Dubonnet.

1 1/2 ounces gin
1 1/2 ounces Dubonnet (an herbal fortified wine)
2 dashes orange bitters

Combine all ingredients in a mixing glass with ice and stir well. Strain into a cocktail glass.

Need a standard go-to: Tom Collins

Tom Collins is your man. This drink is refreshing and classic, and allows the flavors of the gin to flourish under the lemon. Fun Fact: The drink was originally named after John Collins, a waiter at Limmer's Old House on London's Hanover Square in the mid-19th century. Later, another bartender made the same drink with Old Tom Gin and changed the name accordingly.

2 ounces Old Tom gin
1 teaspoon superfine sugar
1/2 ounce lemon juice
Club soda
Lemon wheel, for garnish

Pour lemon juice, gin, and sugar in a highball or Collins glass. Fill to top with club soda, garnish with a lemon wheel.

Are feeling fun: Aprés-Hard Day

I created this bevvie after a trip to a local farmers' market found me with gorgeous sweet plums I didn't know what to do with. A simple sour cocktail, it's become a summer after-work staple that represents the start of fun time.

2 small sweet plums
1/2 ounce lemon juice
2 ounces Beefeaters gin
1/2 ounce simple syrup Club soda, optional

Muddle the plums in a rocks glass with crushed ice. Make sure you remove the plum pits from the glass with tongs after muddling. Shake the remaining ingredients in a cocktail shaker with ice and strain into the glass. Top with a splash of club soda if preferred.

Are hosting: Lavender Gin Fizz

Go for this impressive concoction. Best, logistically, for serving to small groups, this drink gets bonus points its use of unique lavender bitters and egg white frothiness.

2 ounces gin
3 dashes Scrappy's Lavender Bitters
1 egg white
Juice of half a lime
Juice of two large strawberries

Shake all ingredients vigorously in a cocktail shaker for about five minutes, until frothy. Strain into a coupe glass.

CHAPTER 6

Whiskey A Go-Go

Whiskey is my absolute favorite spirit. It's versatile, sexy, classic, and worthy of just about any occasion. A refined spirit by nature, whiskey takes a lot of care and attention to produce. And that, lovely babes, is just one of the reasons why you deserve to know about it, and enjoy it.

Just before one of my guy friends popped the question, he was advised never to marry a woman who drank whiskey. And no, this nugget of wisdom didn't come from his 90-year-old grandpa, but one of his 20-something friends. This was only a couple of years ago! Women who drank this traditionally man's drink were unruly, unpredictable, and overly assertive according to this outdated stereotype. I still get surprised reactions from some servers when I order a whiskey straight. I happen to love that my affinity for fine, aged spirits separates me from the rest. But it's time we change the perception that is keeping us from being the gourmet, refined whiskey drinkers we know we can be!

Babes have found an extraordinary amount of enjoyment and interest in wine over the years, and whiskey takes that appreciation for fine booze one step further. Women generally have good palates that allow us to identify complex characteristics and nuances—this advantage ups our appreciation of wine and can give us a similar leg up when it comes to whiskey. Like vino, whiskeys have various flavor profiles (sweet, spicy, smoky, honeyed, even fruity), and are produced in large and small batches from Japan to the United States It can be so fun to experiment with craft variations of a whiskey in any place you visit. Some distillers tweak their versions in really fun ways, like finishing the whiskey in old sherry barrels, making unaged whiskey with malted barley (basically moonshine), or applying beer brewing techniques to achieve flavors like oatmeal stout.

Whiskey is something to savor. It offers more aroma compounds than any other spirit. It engages the senses and deepens the palate the way a delicious meal does, and shows signs of confidence, sexiness, and adventure in a woman who orders it. If you love to enjoy life, whiskey is an affordable luxury. Though this barrel-aged spirit distilled from fermented grain mash is one of the most popular and dynamic types of alcohol, women make up just a quarter of whiskey drinkers. But once you've mastered the world of whiskey, you can master any spirit. There is the perfect whiskey for every woman—you just have to find it and know what to do with it.

Here's a crash course in the main types of whiskey you'll see (and soon savor) in liquor stores and bars: American whiskey, scotch whiskey, Irish whiskey, white whiskey, blended whiskey, and Japanese whiskey.

AMERICAN WHISKEY

America's whiskey tradition is so rich, it's a wonder babes haven't entirely embraced it. Borrowed from the Scots to become one of America's first cottage industries in the 1700s, whiskey was a grain-based, agricultural byproduct endorsed by the country's most influential figures, including George Washington. Frontiersman Davy Crockett even owned a whiskey distillery in Tennessee.

Bourbon: Bourbon, by legal enforcement and classification, can be made *only* in the United States. While it originated in Bourbon County, Kentucky, where the spirit gets its name, bourbon whiskey can be made in any state. Many bourbon distillers choose to base their operations in Kentucky, though, because they can use natural, limestone-filtered water that is ripe for producing a clean-tasting product. The only rules are that the bourbon must be made from at least 51 percent corn, is distilled to no more than 160 proof (or 80 percent alcohol), and is aged in new charred oak barrels, which give it its brown color and smoky character. Before being aged a minimum of two years in the barrels, the whiskey is often filtered through charcoal. No artificial coloring can be added.

Each distiller's mash bill— the recipe of grain proportions used to make the whiskey—is a little different, and that's what distinguishes each bourbon from the next. Most distillers use upwards of around 70 percent corn in bourbon. A bourbon made with a higher corn percentage will likely be sweeter, while one made with mostly corn but a higher percentage of rye may be drier. Those made with some barley may take on more smoke.

Rye: At least 51 percent of rye whiskey must be made with rye, a type of grain that grows well in the United States. Rye is produced using similar methods as bourbon, and is aged in new charred American oak barrels. Rye is never blended; what's in the barrel is what's in your bottle. Whiskeys made with rye are often spicier and drier than those made with wheat or corn. You may know about rye whiskey from watching Mad Men, the classy television drama about advertising moguls on New York City's Madison Avenue in the 1960s. Jon Hamm, who plays ad exec Don Draper, often mixes himself rye old-fashioneds in the comfort of his office. Until the last decade, this grain whiskey was facing extinction, but a new penchant for classics and flirty ad men in sharp suits has upped our interest and inspired several distilleries to start making it again.

BOURBON'S ORIGIN: THE BIG CHAR ACCIDENT
Rumor has it that whiskey maker Reverend Elijah Craig (whose namesake whiskey still exists) experienced a fire that charred all of his whiskey barrels in the early 19th century. But instead of wasting them, he used them and sent his first batch of clear whiskey in charred barrels to New Orleans via the Mississippi River from Bourbon County, Kentucky. By the time it reached New Orleans, the whiskey was a light caramel color with smoky and vanilla notes. The people loved it.

Bourbon historian Mike Veach has a different opinion about this whiskey's origin. He believes it was created by American-based French businessmen John and Louis Tarascon. In an attempt to simulate their homeland's cognac, which was aged in charred barrels and in high demand in New Orleans, the brothers bought whiskey and put it into charred barrels—as opposed to the un-charred barrels whiskey was normally aged in. Voilà, bourbon!

Tennessee Whiskey: People often confuse Tennessee whiskeys like George Dickel and Jack Daniels with bourbon, but they are not. Tennessee whiskeys are similar to bourbons (made with at least 51 percent corn and distilled to no more than 160 proof) but they must – surprise! – be made in the state of Tennessee and are filtered through maple charcoal prior to aging, known as the "Lincoln County Process." The only exception is the Tennessee whiskey from Pritchard's Distillery, whose product is not charcoal-filtered but received an exemption from the state to keep its label.

THE HOT TODDY

A winter classic, this warm bourbon drink is great for a sore throat (hey, we know that alcohol can be medicinal!). I like to make my toddies a little heavier on the bourbon side, with raw honey, which is unprocessed and retains its nutrients. Next time you're feeling a little under the weather, try this recipe:

2 ounces bourbon
1 tablespoon raw honey (available at natural foods stores)
1/4 ounce fresh lemon juice
1/4 cup hot water

Pour all ingredients in a mug and stir.

Tip: Don't use scalding water in a hot cocktail. High heat will cause the alcohol to evaporate and emit a weird odor. I can't tell you how disappointed I was when I made this mistake while making a large batch of hard cider! Instead, simmer or boil the water and let it cool a little so that it is comfortable to the touch before mixing it in your drink.

SCOTCH

Scotch, which is a whiskey made in Scotland, outsells all other aged spirits worldwide—not bad for a spirit that got popular in the late-19th century when a plague devastated all of the cognac vineyards in France. With no French brandy to drink, Scotsman Tommy Dewar used his marketing prowess to create his White Label blended scotch. The rest is history, with countless scotch brands available now and a reputation for refinement.

There are two types of scotch:

Malt: Made from malted barley

Grain: Made from raw corn or wheat

Then, there are two styles from which to choose:

Blended: Accounts for the majority of scotches; neutral grain whiskey is blended with smaller amounts of malt whiskey from up to a dozen distilleries. The malts used are of different ages and are from different regions, so they combine to create a plethora of unique nuances that range from sweet to smoky.

Single malt: Unblended barley whiskey produced by a single distillery. People tend to like single malt scotch because it has really defined flavors and traits. It tends to taste more "pure," like bourbon, because no neutral whiskey is added. Single malts represent about five percent of the scotch that's consumed.

No matter the style of scotch, it is made in one of four main regions, each of which has a unique climate and natural resources that greatly contribute to the flavors the spirit takes on. For example, salty air contributes to the flavoring in Islay, a seaside region known for its heavily peated varieties.

A scotch's region will be noted on the bottle's label, and that can be a great indicator of the flavors you can expect. Here are the main ones:

Lowlands: Known for blends and grain whiskies; brands hailing from the Lowlands include Glenkinchie and Auchentoshan. These are usually softer than other scotches, making them particularly appealing for beginners.

Highlands: Just north of Glasgow, this region features lots of styles—some even resembling bourbon notes—but most are peaty. Brands include Oban, Balblair, Glenmorangie, Highland Park, and Talisker.

Islay: These scotches are often the boldest and peatiest, since the island on which they are produced is one huge peat bog. Brands include Bowmore, Laphroaig, and Ardbeg.

Speyside: This northeastern region produces the majority of single malts, including popular ones like Glenlivet, Glenfiddich, Balvenie, and Macallan. The rivers in the region have clean, purified water that makes for great filtering and there is also a good supply of local barley. These scotches are balanced, sweet, and elegant with a good bit of honey and vanilla notes.

ROB ROY

This classic combines smoky scotch characteristics with sweet, aromatic vermouth.

2 ounces scotch
1 ounce sweet vermouth

Place scotch and vermouth in a glass or shaker with ice and stir. Strain into a coupe glass.

WHAT MAKES A GOOD SCOTCH

One of the most common myths about scotch is that the older it is, the better quality it is. But that is not always the case.

If a spirit ages too long, the original character (in this case, either grain or barley) in the spirit gets overtaken by the wood. The age you like your scotch is all about your preference, which you can only determine by tasting as many as possible. If you'd like to know whether age matters to you, line up three ages of scotches of the same style and made by the same company. Place them in fluted glasses or tulip-shaped glasses. As you nose and taste each, cleansing your palate with filtered water in between, see if you can put your finger on various characteristics. Are you tasting more woody flavors like oak, vanilla, caramel, and do you like that better than those with more prominent grain, barley, and peat character? You be the judge of whether older is better.

YOU KNOW YOU'RE A WHISKEY GIRL WHEN...
Allison Patel, a drinkspreneur I'll talk about later and who advocates women become familiar with the brown spirit she loves, says once you're hooked, there's no turning back. Here, a few indications she gives for how you know you're whiskey girl:

- You've taken tasting notes again when at a busy, packed bar because you MUST remember what you're experiencing! (insert eye roll from spouses and friends everywhere).
- You know from memory what type of oak all of your favorite whiskies have been in and for how long.
- You know what type of flavors specific varietals of oak attribute to whiskey.
- You probably spend the first five to ten minutes just nosing your glass before even taking your first sip.
- You consider being called a "whiskey geek" a very high compliment.
- You can pantomime with ease the different shapes of stills with your hands.
- You can drink a whiskey blindly and correctly guess its age within a year or two.

WORD UP: WIDEN YOUR WHISKEY VOCAB

These terms are not terribly technical, but you may see them on whiskey bottle labels or hear about them during a tasting. Knowing the lingo will also help you when it comes to describing a whiskey you like, or differentiating between products.

Batch number: This number, indicated on the bottle, shows when the whiskey was made. For example, a bottle labeled Batch #1 was bottled from the distiller's first batch made for sale.

Body: The mouthfeel, the fullness of the whiskey.

Branch: Ever heard of the drink bourbon and branch? A Texan phrase, it simply means a bourbon with fresh spring water (the "branch").

Double-oaked: This means that the bourbon has been aged in two separate oak barrels, with one being toasted or charred differently to give it a different taste.

Dram: An old Scottish term for a small pour of whiskey.

Finish: The flavors you taste after you've swallowed a sip of whiskey.

Finished: This means that a whiskey is aged the majority of time in a specific type of barrel before going into a different finishing barrel for just a short time. For example, a whiskey may spend eight years in charred oak before being finished for six months in old Pinot Noir barrels. This imparts some new flavors without overpowering the spirit's main characteristics.

Malt: Germinated barley, or the whiskey product resulting from distilling barley.

Mash bill: The recipe for the blend of fermented grains that goes into making a particular whiskey.

Peaty: Containing a heavy presence of peat, which is partially decomposed vegetable matter with a high-carbon content. This is primarily how scotch is filtered.

Single cask: Each bottle comes from a single aging barrel.

Single malt: An unblended malt whiskey produced by a single distillery.

Small batch: The practice of blending limited exceptional barrels to create a special product.

Sour mash: A sour mash whiskey means that residue from a batch of whiskey is used to start the next, similar to the process of baking sourdough bread.

Straight: Made solely from grain, and not blended or mixed.

Terroir: Simply put, this means the land. It is used to describe soil, climate, and other environmental factors that affect spirits.

Vatted malt: A blend of two or more barley whiskies from different distilleries. There is no grain in them. "Vatted" essentially means blended.

Vintage: Describes whiskey that has been marked with the date of its distillation or bottling.

Viscous: Slightly thicker, stickier mouthfeel.

White dog or white lightning: White (or unaged) whiskey. Back in the day it was called moonshine.

The same goes for color. Whether a scotch is light or dark is not a surefire way to distinguish quality. For example, a common mantra is that darker (and in turn, mostly older) is better. But one of my favorite scotches is Balblair from the Highlands, which is a pale golden color. It can also be deceiving because a lot of brands use a flavorless caramel to maintain color consistency.

Since a scotch can be made several ways (Is it finished in a port barrel? Is it blended or single malt? Is peat used in the process?), its quality depends largely on your personal tastes. Look at what a scotch claims to be and then examine the product by taste in accordance with its marketed characteristics. A good scotch should be balanced, aromatic, and creamy on the palate.

Though scotch has distinctive character that separates it from other spirits, it should not give off a wet hay taste, which tends to happen when a spirit has not been distilled properly.

IT'S A PROCESS

Scotch's arduous production process is one of the things that sets it apart from regular ol' whiskey.

1. First, raw barley is screened for impurities and then soaked in water for two to three days in tanks known as steeps. The damp barley sits on a concrete malting floor to germinate for almost two weeks.

2. The barley is dried in kilns over peat, a type of wood, or coal.

3. The dried barley malt is ground into flour and then mixed with warm water and mashed until fermentable sugars dissolve. The water is important to the process because it affects a spirit's taste; the best is soft water that's passed over indigenous granite. But other scotches, like in the Islay region, are made with water that's passed through peat.

4. Then the mixture, called wort (I realize this doesn't sound the least bit appetizing!), is cooled and transferred to a wooden vessel to ferment. It's basically beer at this point. If a grain whiskey is being made, as opposed to malted barley, it's cooked under pressure to break down the sugars.

5. After fermentation, the mash is distilled with a few possible techniques depending on the desired outcome and type of scotch.

6. The whiskey is then aged for at least three years, typically more, and up to about 25 years. About half of a whiskey's flavor comes from the wood in which it's aged. There is no legal requirement as to the barrel that must be used, but it could be new oak or used sherry, port, or charred bourbon barrels that impart a unique finish on the scotch.

ON BECOMING A WHISKEY GIRL

Allison Patel tells the story like this: she and her husband, Nital, used to share an after-work drink every day. Except she drank wine and he drank whiskey.

Her husband, a brand consultant who frequently traveled to Asia, would call to rave about the new whiskeys he was trying that he'd never be able to find in the United States. But it wasn't until one day, when at a restaurant with Nital that Patel became hooked.

"Yamazaki 18 (a Japanese whiskey) is the one that changed my life," she says. "Because it was so expensive, I remember what bar it was. It was summer, we were outside. He ordered it neat. He took a sip and he told me I should take a sip and I wouldn't give it back."

And so the ballerina became a spirits importer by profession as a way to get the world's finest whiskeys to more places in the United States.

Fast forward a few years and Patel decided to start her own brand by partnering with a French cognac distiller who had been experimenting with whiskey. Named Brenne, Patel's product is a fruit-forward single malt (made from barley) that is finished in cognac barrels. Distilling it like cognac in an alembic still, which is basically two copper vessels connected by a tube (and is a very pretty design), allows more fruity notes like apricot to shine through. It's aged seven years and the bottles are labeled with barrel numbers rather than batch numbers to embrace subtle variances from barrel to barrel that occur based on their place in the rickhouse. She puts out only 30,000 bottles a year.

To put it simply: whiskey is now Patel's baby. The entrepreneur has already broken two pairs of shoes while pounding the pavement, going door to door of New York City bars, where she sells her product. Sometimes, she's surprised at the reactions she gets for being a female whiskey producer.

"When I sell the product, I always say I'm sorry I don't look like a distiller. I don't have a beard," she says jokingly. "The weirdest question I get daily is, 'But do you drink whiskey?' or 'Do you like whiskey?' I think, would you ever ask a winemaker if he likes wine? I don't see myself as a woman first. I see myself as a person first, woman second. But is fun to shatter the glass ceiling."

The stereotypes branch into drinking whiskey, too.

"I think it's really sexy for a woman to walk up to the bar and order a single malt. I went into a bar last night by myself and ordered a whiskey neat and the guy next to me had a Chardonnay. I almost spit out my whiskey, laughing," she says, because "we had ordered the polar opposites of our stereotypes. Bartenders rarely give me any look of surprise, but women, if they are with men, seem to take an interest."

So what's Patel's advice for women looking to branch into the whiskey world?

"The only wrong way to drink whiskey is to not drink it," she says. "I drank a lot of wine before I got into whiskey. I got to travel and got to explore spirits and wineries. I took my cues from that. I would do flights and go to classes and tastings as often as I could."

As for honing good whiskey taste, Patel suggests asking as many questions as you can of educated bartenders and friends in a comfortable environment.

"Put [the whiskey] in the right, beautiful glass. Set the mood. Put the fire on. Savor it and appreciate it. It's easy for people to be intimidated, but you can understand spirits. Wine is definitely more difficult!"

WHISKEY WITH AN "E"?
Sometimes you'll see whiskey spelled two ways: with an "e" or without it. United Kingdom and some Asian products always spell it without an "e." And while a 1968 directive of the Bureau of Alcohol, Tobacco, and Firearms specifies "whisky" as the official United States spelling, using the 'e' is okay and common. Either way is fine, but contemporary poet Stanley Bruce settles the issue humorously in this 2004 rhyme:

A Scotsman who spells whisky with an 'e,'
should be hand cuffed and thrown head first in the Dee,
In the USA and Ireland,
it's spelt with an 'e' but in Scotland it's real 'whisky.'
So if you see whisky and it has an 'e,' only take it,
if you get it for free!
For the name is not the same and it never will be,
a dram is only a real dram, from a bottle of 'scotch whisky.'

Other times you may identify a graininess, soapiness, rotten egg, or sulfur smell that also comes from distilling flaws. The more scotch you drink, the more keen your nose will be to these qualities.

BLENDER BENDER:
MAKE YOUR OWN SCOTCH WHISKEY

If you enjoy several different single malts, or just want to see how different characteristics play together in a blended scotch, experiment at home! It's a fun exercise in flavors and tastes.

To get started, select three single malts you enjoy for different reasons. Perhaps you like the briny character in one, the sherry finish in another, and a peat flavor in a third. Since it is difficult to find a single grain scotch in the United States to use as a base (although you can find some unaged malted barley and rye whiskies made in America), you may have to use a pre-blended

WHISKEY WITH AN AGE STATEMENT

A whiskey is either bottled as a blend that contains multiple ages (such as whiskies that are 7, 10, and 15 years old); or as a spirit that is all the same age (say, 12 years old). With a blend, an age number on the label indicates the youngest of whiskies contained in the bottle.

Whiskey labeled as a vintage indicates all of the whiskey in that bottle is the same age, and was put into a barrel in the year indicated on the bottle. So if a bottle is labeled a vintage 2000 and it was bottled in 2014, all contents in the bottle are 14 years old from the year 2000. Vintage whiskies are special because master distillers believe them to be the finest examples of a batch casked in a particular year. Of the thousands sampled each year, only a limited number are bottled as vintage.

BUT...AGE AIN'T NOTHIN' BUT A NUMBER

The aging process is really important in how all aged whiskeys turn out. A lot of it depends on where the barrels are stored in the dark cellars and barns (called rickhouses), where they are aged. In hot weather, bourbon barrels at the top of a structure age more quickly than those on the bottom, so they may get changed out or rearranged to balance them, or the distillers will blend whiskeys up high with those down low to get their desired taste. The climate of the place where the whiskey is made also plays a factor in the aging, since a certain amount of heat and humidity is required. For example, because it is made in a cooler climate, scotch takes longer to get the same characteristics from aging as a bourbon made in Kentucky, where it gets really hot. And that's why the higher number on the bottle doesn't always mean the product is necessarily better.

scotch. Appreciate each for what it brings to the table, and then write down ratios of formulas to try.

Experiment in small batches so that you avoid wasting good whiskey in the event that you don't like your blend. To mix them, simply stir in a room temperature glass, and roll the mixture between two glasses (this involves pouring the mixture into another glass, then back to the first one, then back again).

A British company called WhiskeyBlender.com allows you to build your own scotch on the web and have it shipped to you, as does a really awesome whiskey retailer called MasterofMalt.com (where you can find even the most obscure whiskies from all over the world). But it's much more fun to be hands-on. If you think your scotch blend is particularly special, consider decanting it with a funnel into smaller, clear bottles with corks (available at SpecialtyBottle.com), adding custom labels, and giving them as gifts. Or you can serve your blend at a party, with a cool little story about how you did it.

HOW TO DRINK SCOTCH WHISKEYS

"A quality spirit is not whether you like it or not. It's that it tastes the same every time and that's an art. The chemistry is informed by human senses. You can't just stick it in a machine."

—Hollis Bulleit, a.k.a. the "Bette Midler of Bourbon" and brand ambassador for Bulleit Distilling Co., which makes rye and bourbon

Just because scotch has a reputation as a fancy-pants drink—the kind we see important businesspeople drink in movies—doesn't mean you have to be all fancy-pants when you drink it. Of course,

A WOMAN'S WORLD OF SCOTCH

For years, scotch has earned a reputation as a business and old man's drink. But thanks in part to leading ladies in the industry like Rachel Barrie, master blender of Morrison Bowmore Distilleries, which makes Auchentoshan, Glen Garioch, and Bowmore scotches, that is starting to change. Here, Barrie explains how we can start to appreciate scotch for more than its reputation has let on:

What makes an awesome scotch?
I want the scotch to take me on a sensory adventure. I want it to tell me a story. Malt whiskey, more than any other spirit, triggers an emotional response because of the aromatics. It can either want to make me get up and dance, or relax in a chair. You can't say one flavor profile is indicative of quality. It's balance and intrigue. The flavors should bump up and down, and they should change every time you sip or smell it. A kiss of peat is wonderful.

When and how did you become a whiskey expert, and what was like it like to be a female coming up in the scotch world?
I had my first taste of whiskey at age seven with honey, lemon, and hot water. But really, when I started in this business, it was very male-dominated. I had a very analytical role at first because of my chemistry degree. Even then, I was the only female in the research institute. When I started in production, it was unusual but I was very, very lucky to have built up credibility. I used to feel like I had to act like a man, but I don't feel like that now.

Why should women drink scotch?
Perhaps some women never had the chance to try it because of social barriers that kept them from drinking it, or maybe they just hadn't thought about it. But drinking it shows they have a sense of adventure, they go out and do what they want and enjoy life. Single malt whiskeys are like the new chateau wines. Scotch is beautiful.

How can you decipher a good scotch from the bottle?
Everything you see on the bottle should be an indication of the liquid inside. Bowmore is in a long bottle with an anchor so that it gives off "ocean" cues. Ladies are quite tuned into their senses and can get a feel for the personality of the whiskey in this way. Also, look at the tasting notes. But you really need to taste it yourself to be sure.

How can you train yourself to be a good taster?
Trust your instincts and use your sense of smell, which is a major indicator of whether you will enjoy it or not. Slow down when you taste. When you rush around, you're less creative. Instead, take it easy, live in the moment and keep an open mind. Beginners should start with a 10- to 12-year-old scotch. It's not too expensive and it's wonderfully balanced.

How do you pair scotch and food?
There is nothing like oysters and salty, peaty whiskeys. It's the synergies with the taste of the ocean. It's also a texture thing because you've got the silkiness of the oysters. With food pairing, look for certain elements in common like that.

there's definitely a time and a place for scotch, and once you know what you like, let your mood decide when and where that is. Some whiskey snobs might be opposed to mixing scotch in a cocktail, but I don't agree with that. You can appreciate a scotch neat, but prefer it mixed with other high quality ingredients.

IRISH WHISKEY

Irish whiskey is often confused with scotch, and it's easy to see why when you look at history. The Celtic monks who preserved and passed on the art of distillation in the Middle Ages were probably the architects of both Irish and scotch spirits. In fact, today's biggest Irish whiskey brands—Jameson and Bushmill's—also have strong Scottish ties: Bushmill's distills malt whiskey in a pot still and Jameson's founder was related by marriage to a powerful whiskey family in the Highlands.

The Irish masses of the early 18th century actually preferred brandy, and Irish booze was drunk by the lower classes. But soon a rudimentary Irish whiskey flavored with roots and herbs was appreciated in Paris and by the end of the 18th century there were 2,000 stills in Ireland to meet newfound demand. Irish whiskey was made traditionally in copper pot stills and as a result was more widely respected because it required more handcrafting. A series of unfortunate circumstances eventually crippled the industry: by 1779, a newly required tax had caused a fourth of all

DREAM CREAM: MAKE YOUR OWN IRISH CREAM

Everybody knows Baileys Irish Cream, a liqueur that is synonymous with coffee after dinner. But did you also know that it's super easy and incredibly delicious to make your own using an Irish whiskey base? Plus, what better way to impress houseguests than with this DIY nightcap, or go ahead and knock the socks off a secret Santa by giving a bottle as a gift. This yummy recipe comes from Yvette van Boven's *Home Made Winter*:

4 ounces heavy cream
1 14-ounce can of sweetened condensed milk
14 ounces Irish whiskey
1 tablespoon instant coffee granules
2 tablespoon chocolate syrup

Add all the ingredients to a blender and pulse until fully mixed. Pour into clean, decorative bottles and seal. It will keep in the refrigerator for up to 2 months.

legal distilleries to close down; after Ireland declared independence in 1919, England enacted a trade embargo against it; and then Prohibition shut down the United States market. By the 1960s only a few Irish whiskeys remained: Jameson, Bushmill's, Powers, and Irish Distillers. Eventually, they all merged, and were then bought by liquor giant Pernod Ricard. In 1988 The Cooley Distillery began making the Tyrconnel, Kilbeggan, and Connemara brands to break up the competition and there's now an exciting renaissance of Irish whiskey. The Distilled Spirits Council of the United States (DISCUS) reported 2012 sales of Irish whiskey in the United States exceeded those of single malt scotch for the first time since tracking began. But there is still a huge disparity in the number of Irish whiskies out there compared to scotch products.

Like scotch, Irish whiskey is made from barley, but typically a mix between malted (barley is soaked in water and allowed to germinate) and unmalted. It is often distilled three times to give it a lighter flavor, while scotch is distilled only two times. Peat is rarely used in the Irish whiskey–making process, so Irish whiskeys are

LEGAL LADY MOONSHINER
Troy Ball started her Western North Carolina distillery, Troy & Sons, when she moved to North Carolina from Texas in 2004 and was first exposed to moonshine. If the people who lived in the mountains liked you, they'd bring you homemade moonshine, but it was awful. She knew that she could do it better, so she did, using a local heritage corn to make a premium product. The former real estate developer has since lobbied to repeal several antiquated liquor bills in North Carolina.

hardly ever smoky like scotch.

Irish whiskey has only two legal requirements:

1. It must be distilled in Ireland.
2. It must be matured in wooden casks in an Irish warehouse for a minimum of three years.

The region Irish whiskey comes from is also not as crucial as it is with scotch. Instead, Irish whiskey nuances vary from brand to brand based on their distillation processes. For example, Bushmill's dries its malt in closed ovens so it never comes into contact with smoke. As a result, they make very smooth single malts. Jameson on the other hand, uses a blend of malted and grain whiskies for its blends, which it makes in pot stills for dynamic character.

MOONSHINE, WHITE LIGHTING AND WHITE DOG (IT'S ALL THE SAME!)

White whiskey, a.k.a. white lightning or white dog, is experiencing a strong resurgence. Let's call it white dog from here on out, since that's more fun.

A white dog is an unaged whiskey and can be made from rye, corn, barley, malted wheat, or any other grain. Moonshine falls into this category, but white dogs are legal when done through the proper channels!

American craft distillers are loving the white dog right now. For one, it's easy and cheap to make since it doesn't require years of barrel aging. And two, these grain mashes can wind up tasting really distinctive, smoky, and interesting because raw whiskey is a purely unadulterated expression of the grain. Unlike vodka, which is typically distilled in a column to near tastelessness, whiskey is distilled only twice, often in a pot still which also adds to the flavor.

White dog can take on many forms, often tasting like scotch or rye but without the vanilla, honey, or other sweet flavors from the wood. This can take some getting used to for novice whiskey drinkers, but white dog also mixes beautifully in cocktails, like a blanco tequila or pisco (more on that to come). Other ingredients in a cocktail are equally highlighted because wood character doesn't take over.

BLENDED WHISKIES:
CANADIAN WHISKEY AND "SPIRIT WHISKEY"

Canadian whiskies are blends that contain at least 20 percent straight whiskey, plus neutral grain spirits, which are similar to vodka. These are not to be confused with blended scotches, which do not contain any neutral grain spirit.

Canadian whiskey became its own category thanks to Canadian Club, a liquor brand started in 1858 by a man named Hiram Walker who was New England-born, lived in Detroit, and started his business just across the border in Windsor, Ontario. His idea was to combine complex, smoky bourbons with soft, neutral-flavored spirits like vodka—easier on the palate and a lot cheaper to produce since the amount of aged whiskey is limited. The brand's mellow character became instantly popular among Americans.

Most Canadian and American blended "spirit whiskies" (this is what they are called when they are not Canadian) are distilled at about 80 proof, the same as bourbon. But as cocktail historian and author David Wondrich has said, American blends amount to basically "whiskey-flavored vodkas" due to their really light flavors. Some of the blended whiskey brands include Canadian Club, Crown Royal, and Seagram's Seven Crown.

WHAT MAKES A GOOD BLENDED WHISKEY

A good blended whiskey should not have a distinctly grain alcohol taste, though you should be able to identify hints of neutral spirit. That is, after all, what distinguishes a blended Canadian whiskey from a single malt, for example. Blends tend to have a lighter or airier taste than single malts, since intense grain and wood flavors are diluted with the neutral spirit. If they are too light, though, and you can't taste sweetness, or if the whiskey is not hitting sensors on your entire mouth, then it's probably not balanced.

JAPANESE WHISKEY

Japanese whiskeys are gaining traction in the United States, particularly Yoichi, Yamazaki, Hibiki, and Hakushu, the latter three of which fall under the Suntory brand, which owns Japan's oldest distillery. And when I say oldest, it's actually pretty new compared to other types of whiskeys, which have been made for centuries—Japanese whiskeys have been sold commercially only since the 1920s. Similar to scotch, there are single malt and blended Japanese whiskeys, the differentiating characteristics of which stem from experimentation with different types of yeasts, peat amounts, and barleys in-house to create really intricate blends from their own distillates (as opposed to buying the liquid from another company and adding it to their blends like the Scots do). They even use different types of stills and barrels. The intricacy of the process means that a Japanese whiskey is usually silkier and less aggressive than a scotch. In fact, most of the time they are bottled at a much lower proof—about 86.

As with scotch or bourbon, the terroir and local resources where the distilleries are located impact each brand's flavors. The Hibiki, for example, is often finished in old plum liqueur barrels, while others may be filtered through charred bamboo. As a result, these whiskeys can get pretty pricey, and must be bought almost exclusively online because they are still scarcely distributed in the United States.

GATEWAY WHISKEY COCKTAILS

A babe who appreciates a refined whiskey enjoys the finer things in life. An aggressive bold Islay scotch may signal you are a ruthless businesswoman; a delicate Hibiki may demonstrate an appreciation for learning and art. A white dog preference may signify you are adventurous and trendy, while an Irish whiskey may signify you are traditional. Whatever it is, there is a whiskey cocktail to suit if you...

Want to seal a deal: Smoky Martini
From author and storied bartender Dale DeGroff, this recipe combines gin and scotch for a really stiff but delicious drink that shows chutzpah.

2 1/2 ounces gin
Splash of blended scotch
Lemon twist

Stir the scotch and gin in a shaker with ice then strain into a cocktail or coupe glass. Garnish with the lemon twist. If you really want to put a spin on it, do as New York bartender Audrey Saunders does and shake a few drops of Pernod absinthe on the ice before adding the gin and scotch to the shaker.

Want to girl talk: The Clara Bow
Named for the Brooklyn-born 1920s silent film star who was defined by her moxie and energetic spirit, this is a light and fun cocktail to try with the girls. It was created by Lynnette Marrero, a New York City bartender.

6 mint leaves
1/2 ounce St. Germain elderflower liqueur
1/2 ounce freshly made grenadine (recipe on page 86)
1 1/2 ounces Bulleit bourbon
3/4 ounce lemon juice

Pour ingredients into a shaker over ice and shake with five mint leaves. Strain into a coupe glass and garnish with a mint leaf.

Feel adventurous: Smoky Mountain Manhattan

A perfect Manhattan replaces 1/2 part of the recipe's sweet vermouth with a dry one. Josh Stevenson at Larkspur, a restaurant in Vail, Colorado, created this version after tasting too many overly sweet ones made only with sweet vermouth. With the balanced vermouths, a quality cherry, and hint of smoke from the scotch rinse, it's the real perfect Manhattan.

2 1/2 ounces bourbon
1/4 ounce Islay single malt scotch
1/2 ounce sweet vermouth
1/2 ounce dry vermouth
3 dashes house made maple bitters* or aromatic bitters
Amarena cherry (it's a small and sour varietal)

Rinse a martini or cocktail glass with the scotch. Stir bourbon, sweet vermouth, and dry vermouth in cocktail shaker until chilled. Add three dashes maple bitters, strain into martini glass. Garnish with the cherry.

*To experiment with maple bitters, start with page 99 in the Home Bar Chapter.

Need a standard go-to: Old-Fashioned

The best thing about this drink is that it works with any kind of whiskey, and no matter where you are, you'll almost always be able to find these ingredients too.

2 ounces whiskey
1/2 ounces simple syrup
3 dashes Angostura bitters
Club soda (optional)

Add syrup and bitters to a rocks glass, followed by a large square ice cube. Top with the rye and club soda if desired.

Are feeling fun: Mauka Grog

This recipe comes from Matty Durgin, a brand development liaison for Cognac Ferrand. I modified it to use ginger beer instead of ginger ale for additional spice, which goes great with the grapefruit.

2 ounces rye whiskey
$1/4$ ounce Velvet Falernum
$1/4$ ounce high quality orgeat syrup, such as Monin, FeeBrothers or St. Vincent's
1 ounce fresh squeezed pink grapefruit juice
2 ounces ginger beer
1 dash Angostura bitters
grapefruit peel

Shake all ingredients except ginger beer vigorously into a shaker and strain into a Collins glass over fresh ice. Top with ginger beer. Garnish with a grapefruit peel.

Are hosting: Tropical Moonshine Punch

This recipe satisfies the clear spirit lovers and brown spirit lovers in one shot, and is also super refreshing. It makes six cocktails but can be easily multiplied.

6 ounces white whiskey (a.k.a. moonshine)
3 ounces fresh pineapple juice
3 ounces fresh mango juice
3 ounces fresh lime juice
3 ounces simple syrup

Mix all ingredients in a shaker with ice. Strain into rocks glasses with fresh ice.

CHAPTER 7

Rum's the Word

There is something about rum that gives it an irresistible appeal.

Perhaps it's the spirit's mysterious history that involves outlaws like pirates, rebels, and rumrunners, or its association with carefree times on the beach. Rum is essentially the spirit of a babe—it represents endless possibilities, the opportunity for reinvention at every turn, and affirmation that a process can be done in different ways but turn out equally awesome.

Speaking of outlaws, unlike with cognac, bourbon, scotch, or tequila, there are no universal legal regulations for the distillation or production of rum. Consequently, there aren't many maxims for drinking it, either. On the one hand, this is actually pretty cool, since it creates a wide variety of products with different tastes and flavors to choose from. It means rum is versatile enough to mix with most everything. On the other hand, it means that you must be ever the more educated to take advantage of all rum's available choices and find what you like best, since, like other spirits, a rum can be refined enough to sip neat or served simply in an old-fashioned.

THE HISTORY OF RUM

Rum is made from sugarcane juice, cane syrup, or molasses before being fermented and distilled to become alcohol.

Compared to other spirits, rum is relatively new, having been first made by colonists in the Caribbean islands during the 17th century. Legend has it that rum was discovered when a Barbadian slave dipped his spoon into a tray of leftover molasses, which had cooked for a few weeks in the hot sun. It was a crude version, but the slaves enjoyed it. Soon after, in the mid-17th century, planta tion owners caught on and a light bulb went off: what if we applied more advanced distillation methods to turn this abundant resource into an export? That's exactly what they did, and rum soon became profitable evidence of colonial progress. Once colonists figured out how to turn rum from a sticky goo into profits, it wasn't long before drinking rum became an American pastime, too.

There are several theories for where the word *rum* comes from. Though Christopher Columbus first introduced sugarcane to the Caribbean, where several rums are made, the Malaysians had a cane drink thousands of years ago called *brum*. English writings from the mid-17th century refer to *rumbullion* in Barbados, which means "tumult." And Dutch settlers who farmed cane in Barbados used to take drinking glasses called rummers with them on trips (they seemed to have their hands in the beginnings of every spirit!).

After its discovery, rum was the spirit of choice for about a hundred years thanks to its versatility, sweet taste and low production costs. When the British captured Jamaica in 1655, it became customary for each member of the naval fleet to receive a half pint of liquor a day. Since rum was cheaper than French brandy, which they had been receiving, it made sense to distribute rum instead. The sailors, who became obnoxious drunks, threatened to revolt if the ration went away. Finally in 1740, an admiral named Edward Vernon proposed a solution: The rum ration would be mixed with water, lime juice, and sugar. In jest, the sailors called that drink grog after Vernon's grogram cloak. This, my ladies, was the first rum cocktail.

Americans quickly caught wind of how yummy rum was, as they took cues from the British fleets, who reigned over the world's shipping industry and frequented United States ports. In 1770, six million gallons of molasses were imported from the Caribbean to distilleries in the American colonies. However, once the American Revolution began in 1763, it became difficult and expensive to get the molasses. Since whiskey could be produced entirely in America, it quickly took top spot over rum among Americans. In fact, in 1790, United States government figures show that the annual per capita alcohol consumption of Americans over the age of 15 included five gallons of distilled spirits, the majority of which were whiskey. But Americans' adoration of rum remained strong, particularly among sailors (this also includes pirates).

Fast forward a couple hundred years, and rum became popular again during Prohibition, when steamships in Florida would take thirsty patrons to Cuba for dancing and drinking. Rumrunners

KILL DEVIL SWILL
Rum was nicknamed "kill devil" by English colonists for its tendency to cause unbearable hangovers. It remains a nickname for the spirit today.

PIRATE'S PICK:
MAKE YOUR OWN GROG
The Royal Navy's original grog recipe included rum, lime juice, spices, and water, and was usually served warm, but we've come a long way since the rustic colonialism of days past. The first time I tried modern grog was at Piratz Tavern outside of Washington, D.C., in Silver Spring, Maryland. Served by staff dressed as pirates, the grog was blended with spices, sweet, easy to drink, and refreshing on a sweltering day since it was served cold. This recipe, a variation of the Colonial grog, can be served any way you like it.

2 ounces dark rum
$1/5$ ounce fresh lime juice
$1/2$ teaspoon of brown simple syrup (2 parts brown sugar to one part water)
4 ounces of distilled or filtered water (can be hot or cold)
Orange wheel
Cinnamon stick

Mix the lime juice and brown simple syrup. Add the water and rum. Garnish with the orange wheel and cinnamon stick.

smuggled the booze from the Caribbean into Florida because rum was not only convenient to obtain, but was tasty, too.

By the time World War II began and thousands of American soldiers were stationed in the tropics where rum was the drink of choice, we had become a tiki-crazed nation. But we'll talk more about that later.

HOW RUM IS MADE

Creating sugar from sugarcane is simple but arduous. First, the stalks are harvested from February through July when their su-

crose levels are sufficiently high. Then they're pressed to get the cane juice. If making cane juice-based rum, you'd stop here.

If making molasses-based rum, the juice is boiled, and then the sugar is transferred to clay pots where it crystallizes and becomes molasses. Sometimes more sugar is added. And exactly how much molasses does it take to make one gallon of 110-proof rum? About 11 $\frac{1}{2}$ tons! (Don't worry. Once this sugary mixture is distilled it comes out with no more calories than any other spirit).

A mash is then created for fermenting by adding yeast, distilled water, and nutrients. Many distillers believe the amount of yeast is the key to their desired outcome, since the yeast is what consumes sugars and converts them to alcohol. This mixture ferments for up to three weeks.

During fermentation, the yeast mixes with molasses and creates compounds called esters. These esters add a fruity taste to the spirit. The longer the fermentation, the higher the number of esters, which increase the rum's acidity and concentration of aromas. The shorter the ferment, the lower the esters and the less fruity a rum will be. The longer the mash sits, the heavier and darker the rum, while the less fermented rums are lighter bodied.

Rums are then usually double distilled and blended with other batches from different stills and of different ages to get the perfect, most delicious proportion. The type of still matters—whether a pot or column still—because of the way the rum condenses and moves through the still as it's being made. Because rum is meant to be rich and complex, you'll likely want a spirit that has been produced in a pot still, which allows more flavor nuances to shine through. Some rums will indicate this on the bottle, while others may take some online digging to find out.

Sometimes caramel or raw molasses is added after distillation to give the rum additional flavor, while giving it a liqueur-like quality, before being filtered, usually through charcoal. While several countries follow the common practice of labeling the bottle's age based on the youngest rum in the blend, some distillers may label it with the average age, or refer to the oldest. This is one of the tricky parts about dealing with rum's vast array of products.

The rum is then either bottled as a clear liquid or aged in barrels. Distillers often use former cognac, bourbon, scotch, or sherry barrels for a twist on the flavor. The longer the rum is aged, the more character from the barrel it will take on.

DANCE TO THE BEAT OF YOUR OWN RUM: TYPES OF RUM

Now that you know how rum is produced, let's talk about the labels on the bottles and how to decipher them.

Rum can be produced anywhere in the world, but some common origins you'll see are in or around the Caribbean, like Puerto Rico (Bacardi), Jamaica (Appleton's), St. Lucia (Chairman's Reserve), Bermuda (Gosling's), Barbados (Mount Gay), Nicaragua (Flor de Caña), Dominican Republic (Brugal), Guatemala (Zacapa), and St. Croix (Cruzan). But there is even rum made in Madagascar (Pink Pigeon) and the United States (Prichard's, RAILEAN, Montanya, The Nobel Experiment). United States rum is experiencing quite a heydey at the moment for its high quality and many styles available and made by craft distillers.

Some, but not all, countries regulate their rum products independently, including:

French rum: Made from fresh cane in Martinique. The aging and blending takes place in Bordeaux.

Jamaican rum: Made from molasses, which is fermented for about three weeks (a lot longer than most rum fermentation times). Must be double distilled.

Cachaça: Brazilian rum made from the juice of unrefined sugarcane. Ferments in wood or copper vats for three weeks before being boiled down. When imported to the United States, it must be at least 80 proof.

No matter where a rum is made, there is a universal vocabulary you're likely to find on the bottles that will help you determine its age and flavors, and these are in no particular order:

Light, clear, white, or silver: Aged for a year or less in stainless steel containers or oak barrels. Lighter bodied with subtle flavors. A great catchall for most rum cocktails.

Amber or gold: Aged at least three years, these rums have a distinctive sweet taste, but with a little more "oomph" in the alcohol department on the tongue.

Dark rum: Aged five years or longer. It may also be referred to as brown, black, or red rum. It takes on a more woody character and is dominated by caramel.

Blackstrap rum: A heavy rum made from the remaining molasses after the extraction of sugar from sugarcane. It's very sweet, but mixes well with hearty drinks like eggnogs and Dark and Stormys.

Spiced: A rum infused with spices like nutmeg, cinnamon, and peppercorn. Tastes like Christmas to me.

Añejo: Age-dated rum blended from different outstanding vintages. These are dynamic and subtly sweet.

151-proof rum: Known as overproof rum; it's often used as a base for bitters or is floated on top of cocktails for an ignited show of flames. Get ready for a burn in your mouth, too.

Demerara: A premium dark rum made in Guyana.

Flavored: Light rums usually artificially flavored with fruit; often contains added sugar. Stay away from them, and instead infuse your own light rum with whole fruits, spices and herbs.

Naval rum, British Royal Navy Imperial, or Pusser's: Based on the old tradition of distributing rum to British sailors, these combine rums from Guyana, Barbados, and Jamaica. They are rich and complex.

Rhum agricole: Rum made in the French West Indies (mostly Martinique) from sugarcane juice rather than molasses; lighter bodied and clean tasting.

Rhum industriel or "industrial rum": The classification for rum made from molasses (which is most).

Solera: To make this particular style, barrels are stacked in rows several levels high. Each row is a different batch or vintage. The rum is bottled from about one-third of each barrel on the bottom row. The space in those barrels is then replaced with rum from barrels above it, and so on. Tastes balanced, with a nice blend of newer and older rums.

American or Colonial: Defines rum that is distilled authentically in a pot still and is aged briefly. It's the way our ancestors did it.

HOW TO BUY RUM

Be careful when purchasing rum. While the universal non-regulation of its production can make for exciting and unusual blends, there are also a lot of imposter products out there, meaning they could be (gasp!) based with plain distilled alcohol. Rum is sold at varying proofs depending on the country it comes from, and the categories vary in their titles as well. I asked Nancy Fraley, a master rum blender and owner of the sensory analysis consulting firm Nosing Services for her shopping guidelines. Here are four tips to keep in mind:

- *Are you mixing it or drinking it neat?* If you are drinking the rum neat or will be giving the rum as a gift, you'll want to spring for a higher quality (and sometimes more expensive) rum; if you're mixing it you can go with a midrange. This is the easiest way to begin to narrow down your options.

- *Enlist the help of trusted reviewers.* Taste is subjective, but when shopping for a rum, consult reputable reviewers like F. Paul Pacult, who writes a quarterly *Spirits Journal* with hon-

CACHAÇA 101:
RUM'S FORGOTTEN COUSIN

For Freddy Diaz, president of mixology consulting firm AlambiQ in Miami, cachaça is not just an obscure spirit reserved only for the caipirinha, a staple Brazilian cocktail consisting of the sugarcane-based spirit, sugar, and lime. Instead, cachaça is a versatile liquor that can be substituted in many classic cocktails and bring earthy notes to innovative creations. Yet many libation lovers know little about it. Here Diaz, who's worked closely with cachaça and rum brands like Cuca Fresca, Rhum Clement, Ron Diplomatico and Ron Dos Maderas, explains how cachaça differs from rum and how it can be used in cocktails to best accentuate its unique characteristics.

What is cachaça?

It's a Brazilian spirit made from fermented sugarcane juice, and most are aged in woods native to Brazil. Silver cachaças such as Cuca Fresca are aged in English Oak. Aged cachaças usually spend two to twelve years in wood. Cachaças are bottled around 80 to 100 proof.

What are the typical characteristics of cachaça, and how do they differ from sugarcane-based spirits of other origins?

Cachaças are similar in style to the rhum agricoles produced in the French West Indies. The sugarcane is fermented within 24 hours of harvesting and that is the difference between cachaça and other rums, which are mostly made from molasses. Cachaças have an earthier scent and taste of fresh vegetation with a hint of spice and are not overly sweet. Cachaça's nuances really lie in the way the product is distilled, filtered, and/or aged, and the subtle flavors that result.

What is the best way to use cachaça in a cocktail?

Cachaça tastes great as a base in most any cocktail as long as you use fresh ingredients. It can even substitute beautifully for gin in some drinks, or in daiquiris, Mai Tais, and Swizzles. You can use it in an old-fashioned or Navy Grog. Its earthy and light notes make for a well-balanced drink.

How do you know a quality cachaça from an average or below-par one?
It really takes research and plenty of tasting. For example, Cuca Fresca does a double distillation in a copper pot still and filters the product three times, which requires more nuance and craft. It can be hard to distinguish between products judging by what's written on the labels, so try a few to find what you like. Weed out products that may taste overly sweet, perfumy, or off-balance. They should hit every sense on your taste buds and they should not be overly pungent.

CAIPIRINHA
Roughly translated from Portuguese, caipirinha means "farmer's drink," but it's actually a quite sophisticated Brazilian drink, in which the natural sweetness of cachaça is countered by lime zest.

1 lime, cut into wedges
2 teaspoons sugar
2 ounces cachaça

Place lime wedges in a rocks glass with ice and sprinkle with sugar. Add cachaça.

est reviews on every new and established product across every category imaginable. Ed Hamilton, who runs the Web site MinistryofRum.com, is also a good resource. Since not many people have the time to spend tasting all the brands reviewers do, they can help steer you away from impure brands before you waste time or money.

- *Ignore marketing jargon on the bottle.* Words like "super premium" were added to the bottle by a marketing pro, and actually have no significance or official weight in the rum category.

- *Ignore the bottle's appearance.* The beautiful bottle may not be the best one out there. In many instances, you are paying for the bottle. Don't immediately ignore the ugly ones, which might contain the best darn rum you ever had. The only way to know for sure is to taste it.

HAVE A RUM TIME WITH IT: HOW TO DRINK IT

There aren't many rules for drinking rum, and that's part of its allure. You could channel your inner Hemingway and sip rum out of a snifter by the fire, or swig it from a coconut with a barbecued rib in the other hand. Both would be acceptable and equally fun.

I like to invoke the spirit of rum's heritage when using it to prepare drinks. Think fresh, natural, and simple. Fraley says she finds the holidays a great time to introduce friends and family to nice rums since the notes in many (e.g. nutmeg, cinnamon, and allspice) pair well with baked goods. But that doesn't mean rum is an exclusively wintertime drink. A white or amber rum can pair just as nicely with good tonic and a lime as gin does, making it a refreshing go-to for summer.

MIXING RUM

While some rums have more complex characteristics best enjoyed neat, the spirit generally likes to play with others. Here, we'll discuss several rum classics and how to make them the right way— simple and fresh. You'll see that an unfortunate consequence of rum's anything-goes reputation is that many rum drinks devolved for a while somewhere in the 20th century, taking them from their historic, interesting, and fresh concoctions into bottled and poorly mixed crap. I'm talking about you, daiquiris and rum and Cokes!

OUT WITH THE RUM AND COKE, IN WITH THE CUBA LIBRE!

I've said before that you shouldn't mix a good spirit with Coke, and I still stand by that. But if you love the flavor of cola with rum, opt for a naturally sweetened cola by Q Tonic, Fentimans, or Fever-Tree. Even Mexican Coca-Cola—which you can get your hands on it at some international and Latin markets—is better because it is sweetened with agave nectar rather than processed sugar.

And if you want to take the flavors one step further, you can get authentic with it and mix a Cuba Libre, which can also be found in some Cuban and Latin restaurants.

It came about in 1900, when a United States soldier in the Spanish-American war for Cuban independence combined Coca-Cola (which at that time was not the brand we know today but a mix of cola nut syrup and cocaine) with rum, gin, lime, and bitters. Folks in the American South loved this drink after Prohibition ended, mostly because rum was so much cheaper than whiskey.

Try this recipe (sans the cocaine, of course):

1 1/4 ounces light rum

1/2 ounce London Dry gin

Juice of 1 lime

1 dash Angostura bitters

3 ounces cola

Fill a rocks glass with ice. Pour rum and gin over it. Squeeze the lime over the mixture and leave lime in the glass. Pour cola into the glass. Top with a few dashes of bitters and stir.

THE DARK AND STORMY

Another great mixed rum drink combines two of the best inventions ever to come out of the Caribbean: rum and ginger beer. Ginger beer can be found at some supermarkets and in some liquor stores, and packs a lot of natural flavor.

2 ounces blackstrap or dark rum

1/4 ounce lime juice

6 ounces ginger beer

Combine the rum and lime juice in a highball glass. Top with ginger beer and stir.

ISLAND FLAIR: THE WONDERFUL WORLD OF TIKI

Tiki bars are back. They are popping up in the middle of big cities and reinventing themselves in beachside towns. Technically, tiki

MAKE YOUR OWN GINGER BEER

Ginger beer is delectable and fermented, non-alcoholic drink made from ginger and other spices. Plenty of ginger beer options out there (such as Fentimans, Barrit's, Reed's, and Ginger People) are of good quality and make excellent mixers with many spirits (namely the Dark and Stormy, see opposite page). I find it to stand it well most of the time for mainstream ginger ales, which are packed with fructose. But it is just as easy to make your own. It will keep for several weeks, plus you'll feel like a badass who made her own ginger beer!

Here's how to do it:

1 gallon filtered water
1 1/4 pounds peeled ginger root
Juice of 2 limes and their peels, pith removed
1/2 cup brown sugar
1/4 teaspoon black peppercorn
3 cinnamon sticks

This recipe makes about two large pitchers.

1. Bring the water to a boil in a large pot then remove from heat.
2. Pulse the ginger root with a few drops of boiling water in a food processor until minced.
3. Add ginger, sugar, lime juice and lime peels to hot water.
4. Stir and cover for an hour.
5. Strain through cheesecloth and pour into glass containers to cool. When ready to drink, make it fizzy by shaking in a shaker with ice.

refers to those really cool wooden and stone warrior carvings found in Polynesia, but the term has come to represent general Polynesian pop culture—thatched huts, rattan furniture and tattoos. In a nutshell, tiki represents *fun,* and tiki drinks are an extension of a culture that promotes relaxation and living the good life.

MAINTAIN AN AUTHENTIC TIKI BAR AT HOME

Everybody loves tiki drinks, and if you make them well and naturally, they are a big hit any time of year. In the summer, tiki cocktails are a perfectly refreshing complement to gorgeous weather. In the winter, they are a nostalgic reminder of days spent with friends and family among beaches and barbecues. But you've got to do them right.

"There's nothing worse than a really bad tropical drink," says Julie Reiner, a renowned bartender and owner of the Clover Club in New York City, who also happened to grow up in Hawaii. "That's why they got such a bad rap is because there are so many places doing them poorly. Don't just go get a bottle of Trader Vic's Mai Tai mix. Get a couple good recipes and test them out."

Tiki drinks don't always have to be made with rum, either. "You can tiki-fy any spirit," Reiner adds, but what defines a tiki drink is more about its other flavors. What are they, you might ask? So that you can make the best tiki cocktails anytime at home, there are a few main ingredients you need to keep around:

Orgeat: Originally made with barley, this is an almond milk–based syrup with a little clove and fresh lime essence. You can make your own orgeat, which is time intensive, but Monin and Fee Brothers make a nice bottled one.

Coconut water and coconut milk: What better way to celebrate the islands than with coconuts? Plus, coconut water packs a ton of electrolytes like sodium and potassium, helping prevent and relieve hangovers. Coconut milk serves as a great way to thicken cocktails or neutralize overpowering flavors.

Guarapo: Because you can't make a tiki drink without the sweet stuff. Guarapo is simple syrup made from freshly pressed sugarcane stalks. You can purchase these stalks at natural foods stores.

Cinnamon bark syrup: Popular in tiki drinks, but versatile enough to use in other drinks, all you have to do is simmer one part raw sugar with one part water and three cinnamon sticks for five minutes until the sugar dissolves. Strain out the sticks and let cool.

Garnishes: The big, fancy things sticking out of your drink is part of what makes tiki tiki. So stock up on umbrellas, and chunks of fruit like guava, pineapple, and mango.

Tiki Mugs: These wooden mugs with funny faces carved into them are fun to serve drinks in for guests, especially. Find vintage sets on sites like Etsy.com and Ebay.com, or in thrift stores.

MIXING UP AUTHENTIC TIKI TIPPLES
Oh, Mai Tai!
Vic Bergeron, a restaurateur who opened Hinky Dinks, and later the famous Trader Vic's, in the San Francisco Bay Area in 1934, originally created the Mai Tai cocktail to enhance the flavors of an aged rum without overpowering it. He and a rival, who became known

as "Don the Beachcomber," battled for the better mid-20th century over secret, tropical recipes (Don the Beachcomber even hired professional set designers to create his bars' exotic settings). In his book, *Trader Vic's Book of Food and Drink*, Bergeron called rum "the nectar of the gods, the drink of the ancients."

I'll never forget my first experience with a Mai Tai at The Tiki Bar near my hometown along Maryland's Chesapeake Bay. Mai Tais are what this Solomon's Island bar is known for, and they have a dangerous reputation as the kind of drink that'll knock you on your butt for the next three days. I don't know what was in them, but they just tasted fake and my body knew it. They were too sugary, and used so-so rum, and my head paid for it the next day.

Don't make the same mistake I did the next time you go to a tiki bar. If there isn't a real Mai Tai, then don't order one at all. Begin by asking the bartender whether they make the drink from scratch or if they use a store-bought mix. If they use a mix, the conversation should end there and you should order a beer. When I visited Hawaii, just about every restaurant and bar had a Mai Tai available and each took pride in the way they made it. At the Halekulani Hotel, a high end resort in Waikiki, a waiter told me that their Mai Tai didn't contain pineapple juice like "all of the touristy places." At La Mariana Sailing Club, an authentic and wonderfully kitschy tiki bar

MAKE A LEI

Want to throw a tiki party now that you know how to make a few authentic tiki drinks? You've got to have leis for your guests! Thread the heads of 50 colorful marigolds, carnations, or other sturdy flower on a 24-inch long piece of dental floss. Spritz with water and store in the refrigerator for up to a few hours.

MAKE TAHITIAN COFFEE

Tiki isn't only about partying in the tropics. It's also about relaxing. For those evenings when you just want to unwind with a blanket on the couch, we have this recipe from Trader Vic:

5 ounces warm, but not steaming, black coffee
2 ounces gold rum
1 teaspoon coconut syrup (recipe below)
1 ounce lightly beaten whipping cream

Preheat the mug by filling it with boiling water. Dump it after one minute and combine coffee, rum. and coconut syrup. Float the whipped cream on top.

COCONUT SYRUP

Bring 1 part sugar, 1 part water, and 1/4 part coconut flakes to boil until the flakes dissolve. Remove from heat, cool, and strain.

from the 1950s near Pearl Harbor, the Mai Tai is made with a secret blend of white and dark rums with a house made mix that tasted great to me. Play your Mai Tai indulgences by ear.

The Mai Tai's name comes from the Tahitian words for "out of this world" and in a well-made one you should be able to taste the rum. Your drink should taste naturally sweet and it should whet your appetite.

The Original Mai Tai

2 ounces aged Jamaican rum

1/2 ounce orgeat syrup

1/2 ounce curacao

1/4 ounce rock candy simple syrup (to make this, saturate water with sugar until it won't dissolve anymore)

Juice from one lime

Sprig of fresh mint

Add all ingredients to a metal shaker with ice. Stir well and pour into a rocks glass or tulip-shaped glass. To add to the fun, serve in pineapples that have been carved out. Add a straw.

The Original Daiquiri

Believe it or not, a daiquiri is not a red slushie from a plastic bottle at the grocery store. Writer Ernest Hemingway, who loved daiquiris, would have never drunk that.

The daiquiri was made famous in the late 19th century in Havana, Cuba, by a man named Constantino Ribalaigua Vert. He owned a bar called El Floridita and took a recipe from an American engineer, Jennings S. Cox, who was working in an iron mine called Daiquiri in eastern Cuba. After work one night, Cox created the drink with what he had: lemons, sugar, and rum. He rattled it in a shaker with ice. Vert put his spin on the drink by adding maraschino cherry liqueur and crushed ice, and blended it to be served in a frosted glass. I prefer this rocks version, though.

2 ounces gold rum

1 ounce fresh lime juice

1 teaspoon superfine sugar or simple syrup

1 ounce maraschino liqueur (such as Luxardo, optional)

Cherry

Combine all ingredients in a shaker with ice. Pour into a tall glass and garnish with the cherry. If you'd like your daiquiri frozen, simply use a cup of ice made from filtered water and add all ingredients to the blender except the cherry.

To create a flavored daiquiri, simply muddle your fruit of choice (mango, melon, peaches) over crushed ice before adding the other ingredients. You can use frozen fruits (but *not* sugared frozen fruits) if you prefer a blended version, and nix the addition of ice.

SPICE YOUR OWN RUM

With the medley of fresh and delightful ingredients found in tropical places where rum is produced, it's no surprise that spiced rum evolved as a way for local shops to distinguish themselves. They made it with overproof gold rum so that it already had some wood character, and infused it with vanilla, fruit, nutmeg, allspice, and barks over several weeks or months.

You can do the same, since Captain Morgan and Sailor Jerry sometimes overly sweet spiced bottlings don't always cut it. The best part is that you can adjust the level of spice in your own batch, and bottle it in mason jars or corked bottles to give as gifts. The amount of each spice can be tweaked to your taste, but the following is a recipe from which to base your experiment. Check the concoction's taste and smell each day. If one ingredient is taking over, take it out. The infusion could take one day to a week (any longer and you get close to bitters territory). Once you're happy with it, strain the rum through cheesecloth and get rid of the solids. Be sure to use all whole spices because the ground ones are impossible to fully strain out.

1 750-ml bottle of gold rum

1 vanilla bean, with ends cut off and split lengthwise

4 whole cloves

2 cardamom pods

5 black peppercorns

1 whole nutmeg (or $1/_2$ teaspoon ground nutmeg, though it will
    require more filtering)

3 whole allspice berries

1 star anise

1 orange peel without the pith

1 cinnamon stick

Piece of peeled fresh ginger (takes up half a teaspoon)

Toast the ingredients in a dry pan before placing in a mason jar with rum. When the mixture is to your liking, strain through cheesecloth and then, if necessary, through a coffee filter. Funnel into a decorative bottle.

MAKE THE PERFECT MOJITO

There's nothing like a mojito. It's crisp, light, sometimes fruity, and not too boozy. It conjures images of poolside lounging, beach bummin', and club-going. But this beloved Latin classic that's come to symbolize summer fun is often made wrong.

Mojito comes from *mojo,* the Spanish word meaning to assemble or blend. Like many classic cocktails, the origins of the mojito are fuzzy, but legend claims its roots come from Cuban plantation masters adding highly alcoholic sugarcane distillate to slaves' energy-boosting sugar water. Over time mint and lime were added. Fast forward a couple hundred years to the 20th century, and the easy-to-drink combination was a go-to cocktail at Havana bars and clubs, eventually making its way to the United States.

The difference between a perfect mojito and an average one is the quality of ingredients.

"The mojito must be all natural. It must have a rustic flavor, no metallics [that ruin the simple taste]," says Vance Henderson, bar manager at Washington, D.C.'s Cuba Libre Restaurant & Rum Bar, which features a dozen signature mojitos and 98 rums to accompany its Cuban fare. "Fresh is always best. And it's not meant to be strong and knock you on your butt."

Fresh mojitos are lower-cal, healthier, and tastier. Here are Henderson's best tips for making a classic mojito the right way:

Always start with white rum. Since aged rums change a classic mojito's flavor with their woody character, start with white rum for the purest expression of sugarcane. Once you experiment with various fruit mojitos and learn your rum preference, change out the white with a higher proof or aged rum for spins on the classic.

Use guarapo rather than simple syrup. Squeezing the green-colored juice from sugarcane stalks is the most authentic way to sweeten a mojito. Stalks can be purchased at some natural food stores, such as Whole Foods, peeled, and extracted with a high-powered electric juicer. When making fresh *guarapo* is not possible, combine one part raw or unprocessed sugar with one part water on a stovetop until sugar is dissolved. Remove from heat and let cool before mixing into the mojito.

Tear, rather than muddle, fresh mint leaves. When shaken with ice, torn mint releases its essential oils easier and becomes more aromatic. Muddled leaves, on the other hand, retain much of the fresh flavor characteristic of the drink. The quality of mint also counts. Henderson recommends Israeli mint when possible, which contains more oils. Make sure mint leaves are not dry or browning.

Avoid bottled lime juice and sour mix. Bottled lime juices contain unnecessary preservatives and since limes are widely available most of the year, you have no excuse for using it. Choose limes that are somewhat firm and roll each one to loosen juices before squeezing.

Ready to get your real mojito on? Here's how to make one:

Six mint leaves
1 1/4 ounces fresh lime juice
2 1/2 ounces guarapo
1 1/2 ounces white rum
1 ounce club soda or sparkling water
Lime wedge for garnish

Combine mint leaves, lime juice, and guarapo in a shaker. Add rum and fill with ice. Shake vigorously and pour in a Collins glass. Splash with club soda and garnish with lime wedge.

I can hear you sipping from here. And it sounds *good*.

GATEWAY RUM COCKTAILS

Rum can be anything you want it to be, and thanks to the many expressions out there, there is a perfect rum drink for every mood. Here's what to drink when you...

Want to seal a deal: Rum Old-Fashioned

This drink shows you can kick back while keepin' classy.

2 ounces of aged rum
4 dashes of aromatic bitters
$1/2$ to 1 teaspoon simple syrup depending on your tastes
1 orange slice
1 cherry

Muddle syrup, bitters, orange slice, and cherry in the bottom of a rocks glass. Add the rum, one large ice cube, and stir.

Want to girl talk: Bee's Kiss

Not to be confused with the dreaded Bee Sting, this sweet drink, adapted from *Trader Vic's Book of Food and Drink* in 1946, goes down easy.

1 teaspoon fresh heavy cream
1 teaspoon fresh honey
2 ounces gold rum

Shake all ingredients in a metal shaker with ice. Strain out the ice and pour into a chilled coupe glass.

Feel adventurous: Sparkly Summer Lovin'

This recipe from Carlos Splendorini, a bartender at MICHAEL MINA in San Francisco, uses champagne to bring effervescence to an unlikely combination of balsamic vinegar and rum.

1 sugar cube soaked in quality balsamic vinegar
1 ounce light rum

3 ounces champagne
twist of an orange peel

Soak the sugar cube in the vinegar and place at the bottom
of a champagne flute. Add the rum and slowly top with
champagne. Garnish with the orange peel.

Need a standard go-to: Spiced Citrus Punch

This recipe is refreshing and has just the right amount of sweet.
It is also complex, thanks to the spiced simple syrup.

2 ounces white or gold rum
$1/2$ ounce fresh lemon juice
$1/2$ ounce fresh orange juice
4 dashes of peach or
    Angostura bitters
1 ounce spiced simple syrup (recipe below)
Orange slice for garnish

Add all ingredients except the orange slice to a metal shaker
and vigorously shake with ice. Pour into a water goblet or rocks
glass. Garnish with the orange slice.

MAKE SPICED SIMPLE SYRUP

To make the spiced simple syrup, combine $1/2$ cup of sugar and
$1/2$ cup filtered water with $1/4$ teaspoon each of fresh ground
cinnamon, allspice, cloves, and nutmeg in a saucepan. Bring to
a simmer and stir until dissolved. If you are out and about and
request this drink or a variation of it be made, a plain simple
syrup is just as tasty.

Are feeling fun: Banana Cow
Adapted from Trader Vic's Rum Cookery and Drinkery, 1974

Trader Vic called this drink the greatest hangover cure, which is
perfect for the party girl.

1 ounce light rum
1 dash Angostura aromatic bitters
1 whole banana
1 teaspoon raw sugar
1 dash vanilla extract
3 ounces skim milk

Blend all ingredients with ice and serve in a Collins glass or tumbler.

Are hosting: Fresca Frambuesa
Adapted from Freddy Diaz, president at Miami mixology consulting firm AlambiQ, this recipe can be easily multiplied for a group of guests.

1 ounce cachaça
1 ounce raspberry puree
$1/2$ ounce lemon Juice
$1/2$ ounce simple syrup
3 ounce Champagne

In a mixing glass, combine all ingredients and gently stir together with ice. Strain into champagne flutes.

CHAPTER 8

You Say Tequila, I Say Mezcal

I love mezcal and tequila. No, I *adore* them. Let me tell you why.

First of all, Mexico, where both mezcal and tequila originate from native agave plants, is a mecca of the world's best ingredients. For example, did you know that's where chocolate, peanuts, and maize came from? And had Spanish conquistadors not brought Mexico's native tomatoes to the Old World in the 15th century, Italian cuisine as we know it would have taken a completely different course.

Mexico may be rich in (yummy) culinary tradition, but many people have never even heard of mezcal, one of its *mas importante* contributions to the gastronomical world. Though mezcal lists in Latin restaurants and bars around the country are growing in size and popularity, the spirit is mostly drunk locally in and around Oaxaca, Mexico, where it is made in small batches by mezcaleros, almost the way moonshiners make whiskey in the United States. A few brands export to the States, but in many cases, if an American establishment has a large collection of mezcal, it is because their staff physically brought the bottles back from Mexico. And this game of hard-to-get is part of the reason I can't get enough of it. The other reason is mezcal's unique, smoky taste is oh-so-interesting in cocktails, particularly with spicy or savory ingredients.

Myth has it that the first agave-based spirit was first created in 1000 A.D., when a lightning bolt struck the spiky, leafy plant species, causing a sweet and smoky aroma to emanate as the heat cooked it. Once the Aztecs tried the juice—which they named *pulque*—it was over. The Aztecs loved the crude liquid so much they offered up human sacrifices to ensure its abundance forever. Mezcal was born as natives learned to refine the rudimentary liquid through distillation, and tequila – a less smoky version from a different type of agave plant – followed shortly after, when the Spanish began producing it after they ran out of their own brandy in the mid-16th century. The rest is history—sort of.

THE DIFFERENCE BETWEEN MEZCAL AND TEQUILA

All tequilas are mezcals, but not all mezcals are tequila. Both are made from different types of *maguey*, which are spiky, leafy agave plants. Agave is often mistaken for cactus and looks kind of like an aloe plant. Here are the primary differences between the two classifications of spirits:

Tequila	Mezcal
Distilled from the blue agave plant	Distilled from about two dozen species of the green agave plant
Is produced by steaming the leaves in an above-ground oven	Is produced by cooking the leaves in an earthen oven (which gives it a smoky taste)
Made in the state of Jalisco, Mexico (most is produced in the city of Tequila)	Made in five Mexican states: Oaxaca, Durango, Guerrero, Zacatecas, and San Luis Potasi

HOW MEZCAL WINDS UP IN THE BOTTLE

Mezcal goes through a rustic process to get its distinctively smoky taste. The agave leaves and *piñas* (their pineapple-like cores), are placed in wood-fired holes in the ground and cooked with hot stones and compost from previous distillations. The hole is covered with leaves that trap the smoke, so the plant takes on an earthy flavor, almost the way a pig does when it is cooked traditionally in a sub-ground pit. The leaves and *piñas* are left to rest for a day or two before being ground into a pulp. Water is then added to the pulp and natural yeast ferments for up to three weeks before the mixture is distilled, usually twice. Sometimes the mezcal is bottled immediately, other times it's aged in oak barrels first.

HOW TO PICK A DECENT MEZCAL

There are not enough mezcals available in the United States to make your head spin, but navigating quality standards and finding one you like can be tricky because of their unique and varying characteristics. There are two types of mezcal as established by the Mexican government: 100 percent agave and *mixto*, which is a mix of agave (80 percent) and other sugars.

When shopping for or buying mezcal, you always want to choose the 100 percent agave option—it will always be the most natural and pure. There's no telling what makes up the non-agave portion of a *mixto* because producers aren't required by law to tell you.

In addition to going for the 100 percent agave, keep your eyes peeled for mezcal from a certain *type* of agave. The finest green agave are called *espadín,* and they are grown for a minimum of eight years before being plucked from the earth and separated from their *piñas*. Because of *espadín's* prestige, a brand that uses it in their blend will proudly note it on the bottle.

There are also four age types to consider when choosing mezcal. The age doesn't indicate quality, per se, but youngest offers the purest expression of the agave, meaning it tastes the most authentic:

Joven or silver: Unaged, clear

Abocado: Unaged, but can contain additives like caramel, flavorings, and colorings

Reposado: Aged a minimum of two months in oak barrels

Añejo: Aged in oak barrels at least one year

SPOTTING THE GOOD FROM THE BAD MEZCALS

Some aficionados say the best mezcals in Mexico are usually sold under a mezcalero's private label and reserved for family and friends. Go to clandestine Oaxaca bars, and many small production bottles are hand-blown, which is a very impressive sight, and a collector's and gift giver's dream. In the United States we have fewer choices, but there are still good options available here.

One thing is for sure, though: you'll want to stay away from *bronco* and *granel* mezcals. Unfortunately you have to taste a mezcal to know if you got one of these imperfect blends, 'cause the maker sure won't announce it on the label. Luckily, they're not common in the United States, because our mezcal laws adhere to the quality standards set by the Mexican government. But occasionally, bad eggs do work their way into obscure and not-so-obscure places at home and abroad.

Bronco mezcals use more heads and tails, which means that the distiller didn't take much care eliminating the off-tasting, flawed liquid that comes out of a still at the beginning and end of the process. *Broncos* are therefore cheaper and of lesser quality, and are usually bottled by different companies than the ones that make them. *Granels* are bulk-made mezcals that don't follow legal classification standards. You'll know you've got a *granel* if you smell or taste hints of nail polish remover or aldehydes (like apples that are too ripe).

If mezcal has a harsh grain alcohol taste, ditch that sucker

THE WORM, DEMYSTIFIED

First, let's dispel the myth that some tequila bottles come with worms. If a bottle has a worm in it, it's mezcal, not tequila. At one point the worm's preservation in the alcohol was proof to the purchaser that the liquor contained sufficient alcohol content, but now a worm in a mezcal bottle is nothing more than a marketing gimmick. While the worms, which are the larvae of a giant butterfly, are thought to be a powerful aphrodisiac and witch curse deterrent, they actually attack the agave plant and ruin its quality. In the bottle, they do the same thing—tainting the liquid's flavors and aromas. Repeat after me: worms in bottles are *no bueno.*

'cause it's not good, and probably contains a high percentage of methanol and saturated alcohols, which cause hangovers. You'll also want to stay away from *abocado* mezcals that contain additional flavorings and colorings. Remember: a quality spirit doesn't need coverup help.

Good mezcal is often defined by its finish—the way your mouth feels after you've swallowed a taste. The mezcal should radiate and warm your palate, not burn it. It should maintain a smoky character, almost like a peaty scotch does, and it should taste complex, hitting every taste sensor in your mouth.

DRINKING MEZCAL FOR NEWBIES

If you're not so down with the smokiness of mezcal, try a *reposado* or *añejo.* Their woody flavors tame the spice and smoke of the agave, which can be easier on the untrained or unaccustomed palate. The purest expression of mezcal comes through in *joven*.

Mezcals that extract the juices of the agave before steaming the leaves, such as Zignum, eliminate the smoky taste altogether, making the mezcal taste more like tequila. This can be a great introduction for new tasters, but the eventual goal should be to drink the real mezcal, since its intense, smoky flavor makes it what it is.

TEQUILA'S REAL DEAL

Now that you've got a handle on mezcal, tequila is a piece of cake. It may bring back notions of all-night ragers or getting wasted at Señor Frog's with Jose Cuervo, but there's more to this complex spirit than college ever led you to believe.

It's not surprising that most of us wouldn't know a good tequila if it hit us over the head. The United States is tequila's largest market, and in the last several decades tequila companies have

---

ORDER A BETTER TEQUILA

If you find yourself at a Mexican restaurant or bar hankerin' for tequila, you'll need to be specific about what you want. If you aren't you'll probably receive a rail mixto. Instead, specify that you want 100 percent agave and the style you are looking for. If you know the brand you like, ask for it and if it is not available, ask for the bartender's recommendations of brands that might display similar characteristics. Drink a quality, top shelf tequila neat, but ask for a side of lime juice and pure, filtered water to open it up. This also helps separate and pinpoint various aromas you might otherwise miss. In any situation, get adventurous!

marketed it as the party spirit (and consequently, the country's biggest culprit of stomachaches and hangovers). It has hardly received the credibility it deserves as a refined sipping spirit.

Tequila's production process is somewhat similar to mezcal, but there are a few key differences. Jimadores—the machete-wielding guys who harvest the agave plants—manually harvest blue agave for tequila by skillfully removing *hijuelos* (agave offspring) without ruining the mother plant, and cutting away the heavy *piñas*.

Unlike mezcal, which is made by cooking green agave plants over wood in the ground, the hearts of the blue agave are steamed in ovens. Then they are shredded and juiced. The juice ferments and after a few days is distilled twice to remove the cloudiness. Tequila is named after the region where it is made in the state of Jalisco, Mexico, which is teeming with fertile, volcanic soil. Only blue agave spirits made in Jalisco can be labeled as tequila.

HOW TO PICK A GOOD TEQUILA

Authentic tequilas will have a *Norma Oficial Mexicana* (NOM) number on the bottle, which identifies the distillery and tells you the tequila has gone through all of the proper legal channels. If you come across a bottle that doesn't have one—though unlikely in the United States—don't drink it.

Similar to mezcal, there are two main ways of producing tequila:

100 percent agave: Made totally from the agave plant.

Mixto: Only 51 percent agave required, the rest consists of unknown sugars and additives.

Like when choosing mezcal, you always want 100 percent agave. Mixtos are a mixed bag, often diluted with water and other nasty sugars like glucose and fructose, while you're none the wiser. All bottled flavored tequilas are mixto, so you're better off flavoring your own pure tequila (more details on that later). If 100 percent agave is not on the bottle, then it is a mixto by default. There are many affordable 100 percent agave products out there, so there's no need to settle for less.

Beyond that, your choice of tequila is mostly a matter of taste and the biggest decision you'll make is about its age. There are five different categories:

Blanco ("white") or plata ("silver"): Unaged or aged less than two months in stainless steel or neutral oak barrels.

Joven ("young") or oro ("gold"): A mixture of blanco tequila and reposado tequila of various proportions.

Reposado ("rested"): Aged at least two months but less than a year in oak barrels of any size. Some distilleries use former whiskey, scotch, or wine barrels to impart a twist on the flavors.

Añejo ("aged"): Aged at least one year but less than three years in small oak barrels.

Extra Añejo ("extra aged"): Aged at least three years in oak barrels.

Like mezcal, the purest expression of the blue agave will come out in the blanco. In fact, aging tequilas is a relatively new concept that goes against the spirit's tradition. Don't get me wrong; I love me a well-balanced reposado or añejo. But when mixing cocktails, a blanco will give you the best agave flavor. I also like how malleable and versatile it can be in cocktails, particularly because it accentuates many fruit flavors.

All brands use the same type of agave for all of their products, no matter what age the product is intended to be. However, different brands use different species of the blue agave plant, which help determine a tequila's flavors. For example, tequila made with blue agave grown in the highlands (like Don Julio, El Tesoro) are larger, floral, and sweeter, while those harvested in the lowlands (like Partida, Casa Noble) taste earthier and spicier.

TASTY TEQUILA FOOD PAIRINGS
Tequila doesn't just go with Mexican food. Notes in the spirit that range from earthy to vanilla to citrus pair well with unlikely dishes like sushi rolls, créme brûlée, and caviar. For specific pairing ideas by top chefs, check out the Casa Dragones website at www.casadragones.com/pairings.

Some distillers market their tequila to be served chilled, which is a fancy way of saying "this tastes bad!" Since freezing booze dulls the aromas and flavors in most spirits products, this usually means that it is low quality and the chilling advice is meant to hide imperfections. Avoid these.

HOW TO DRINK TEQUILA
Forget the whole gringo ritual of taking a shot of tequila with salt

INFUSE TEQUILA: FOUR TIPS FOR CREATING TASTY, NATURALLY FLAVORED TEQUILA

Joe Cleveland doesn't believe in rules when it comes to matching flavors with tequila. That's why the head bartender infuses various blanco, reposado, and añejo tequilas with everything from cassis to dandelion burdock for cocktails at José Andrés' Washington, D.C., restaurant, Oyamel. Infusing tequila involves choosing a style and allowing an ingredient to steep in the spirit from 12 hours to 10 days in an airtight container. Fruit, herb, spice, and even meat infusions offer clean, yet subtle punches of flavor that mix beautifully, but not overbearingly, in cocktails, Cleveland says. Producing a great infusion requires some trial and error, but more importantly, a fearless attitude and willingness to experiment beyond habanero peppers and limes.

Here are Cleveland's four tips for infusing tequila at home:

Start with one ingredient. While you may eventually blend several ingredients into one infusion (Cleveland's team once made a "gin-quila" with over 30 spices), the easiest way to get started is with just one ingredient so you can get a feel for how long—and to what extent—certain flavors will infuse. The pithy part and membranes of vegetables and fruits can give the infusion a bitter taste, so leave those out. Keep your infusion in a sealed container in a cool place. Sweeter ingredients like oranges and pineapples are good starters because they infuse easily and taste natural on the palate. You can use reposado or añejo tequilas, but blanco tequilas will maintain the most agave character, taste crisper, and take on color more obviously. Citrus elevates flavors in most drinks, so try your infusion in a sour to start, or simply add a lemon or lime peel to your infusion.

Taste test the infusion regularly. Since the length of time required to infuse tequila varies based on your desired intensity, check on the infusion daily to see if it's where you want it to be. Shake vigorously once a day. Begin with a small amount of material (like one pepper) and work your way up based on your desired flavor. Taste the liquid, adding more of an ingredient or taking some out if desired. When it tastes good (the flavors should not overpower the tequila but should definitely be present), strain the fluid through cheesecloth and remove the solid parts. Then bottle it, serve neat or on the rocks, or experiment with cocktails.

Think like a cook. When determining which ingredients will infuse well together, draw inspiration from the flavors in a favorite dish, smoothie, or dessert. For example, Cleveland has been inspired to create infusions based on a chocolate and pig's blood dessert and a roast turkey (see their Sacrifice cocktail recipe on page 203). Once you've got the hang of it, don't be afraid to layer ingredients and experiment with proportions in each infusion. If you're afraid of ruining good tequila, start with a batch in a small mason jar.

No tequila is sacred. Even Don Julio 70, a refined white añejo, was not off-limits when it came time to select tequilas for infusing, Cleveland says. "Sometimes you find that magical combination where only that one will work," he adds. While blanco tequilas often pick up the most flavors while retaining their agave character, reposado and añejo tequilas add a woody, and sometimes spicy or sweet flavor to an infusion.

and a lime. The tradition originated in Palm Springs, California, just after World War II, when businessmen visiting on golf trips were introduced to tequila at the city's bars. The spirit was pretty new to the United States at the time, and there were few brands to choose from—many of which were awful. The bite of lime was meant to enhance the tequila's flavor while a lick of salt from your hand eased its burn.

Today, we don't have that problem. Salt can be a great complement to a tequila cocktail on a rim, but you shouldn't rely on it to be anything but that. If you have chosen a great, 100 percent agave tequila and know how to drink it, it won't burn. And you shouldn't be wasting the nuances of a good tequila worth savoring by shooting it! Not to mention that doing so gets you really drunk, really fast.

It's important to taste every tequila on its own before attempting to build a drink with it. This will enable you to identify notes by which you can choose other ingredients, and figure out the most enjoyable way for you to drink it. Is the tequila citric, peppery, crisp, clean, balanced, fruity, or herbal? Or are you getting a hint of seaweed or peanuts? Is it wimpy, strong, mellow, or robust? Does the tequila seemed balanced, rather than overwhelmingly expressing one or two notes? How does your mouth feel in the finish? Is it oily, heavy, thin?

Since tequila has such a distinct taste, I sometimes find it difficult to pinpoint the aromas in a single pour, but when placed next to several others, you notice *grandé* differences. Express them verbally. The more you do, the better your nose will get and the more refined and defined your tequila preference will become.

THE SACRIFICE
Courtesy of Oyamel in Washington, D.C.

This cocktail pays homage to a biannual Aztec religious festival, in which people offered a sacrifice to the gods and feasted on turkey and maize cakes.

2 ounces turkey-infused reposado tequila (recipe below)
1/2 ounce agave syrup
1/2 ounce curaçao liqueur
3/2 ounce lime juice
1 dash of molé bitters

Pour everything in a shaker and shake vigorously. Strain into an ice-filled rocks glass rimmed with salt.

~~~~~~

TURKEY-INFUSED TEQUILA
1 bottle reposado tequila
2 grilled turkey thighs with the skin on
1 orange (whole, skewered 20 times)
3/4 cup almonds
1 chipotle
1 apple
1 pear
3 whole cloves
Pinch of salt

Grill the turkey thighs. While the turkey is cooking, wrap the remaining ingredients (except tequila and salt) in foil and broil for five minutes. Let both the turkey and wrapped ingredients cool to room temperature. Pull turkey into bits and place in a bowl or container (bones, skin, everything included). Unwrap foil and cut the apple and pear into quarters. Place everything in the container and pour in the tequila with a pinch of salt. Allow to steep for four days. Strain.

SISTER SIP:
A Q&A WITH THE WORLD'S FIRST FEMALE TEQUILA MASTER

Bertha González Nieves, the world's first female master of tequila, knows a thing or two about good agave-based spirits.

It was by chance that she met Bob Pittman, the founder of MTV, at a Brooklyn, NY, party. González Nieves, who had worked for many years in the tequila industry, and Pittman, a tequila aficionado with a home in San Miguel de Allende, Mexico, got to talking about their common love and vision for tequila. In 2008, they started their own brand, called Casa Dragones, a 100 percent blue agave joven tequila made in Tequila, Mexico.

In a short time, their $275 bottle has made a big splash in the industry. I spoke with González Nieves about what true sipping tequila is, the future of the spirit, and what it's like to be a woman in a male-dominated industry.

How did Casa Dragones get started and why did Bob Pittman choose tequila?

Bob is passionate about Mexico and the culture. He's an entrepreneur and visionary marketer. Once Bob and I met, we realized we had a very consistent idea and vision of where to go with our tequila. We functioned well as partners and we set out on a quest to deliver a true sipping tequila, one that's meant to be savored. We only produce one type of tequila—*a joven*—which is rare in the industry. The consumer is looking to drink less and to drink better, and that also applies to tequila.

How did you get to know tequila?

I was a young ambassador of Mexico to Japan in my early 20s and needed to be able to speak eloquently about Mexico's economy, culture, and industries. I made a lot of visits to our tequila distilleries and I fell in love with the industry. I went on to finish a master's degree and work in management consulting for Booz Allen Hamilton. Then I held key positions for 10 years with Grupo Cuervo. As time went by, my passion and interest in tequila kept growing.

Why did you choose to produce a joven tequila, which adds a hint of añejo to a silver product?
We didn't start thinking we were going to develop a *joven* tequila, but we had an idea of how we wanted the tequila to taste—we wanted to create a tequila with a complex, smooth taste that was perfect for sipping. I convinced one of the industry's master tequila makers, Benjamin Garcia, to come out of retirement and help us push the boundaries of what had been done before.

What is it like to be a female leader in a male-dominated tequila and spirits industry?
I was so passionate and determined to go into the tequila business that I didn't think about that at all until I got into it. When I became the world's first female Maestra Tequilera by the Consejo Regulador del Tequila, which regulates the industry, I said to my mentors, "I almost had to grow a mustache for you guys to accept me." We still joke about that. Yes, it's a male driven category but it's also a professional category. Everyone welcomes professional people.

What does drinking a fine tequila say about you, in business and leisure?
I think it sends the same message as drinking a fine wine or single malt scotch. It says that you are willing to make an effort to research what you drink. We know our consumer appreciates the details of our process and enjoys talking about them with others. It's important to ask questions to get to know a category better. The more curiosity you have, the more you will learn. There are a lot of producers trying to take the industry forward. Buyers should see it as something fun to explore.

Once you've honed what you like, it's time to experiment with whatever ingredients tickle your fancy. Tequila is perfect for sour and fruity drinks but also works beautifully in savory ones because of its earthy character, so try mixing it with vegetable bases. For example, I prefer tequila as a delicious substitute for vodka in a Bloody Mary because it goes so well with tomato juice, celery, and bacon. In Mexico, the most traditional way to drink tequila is neat or with a side of sangrita (orange juice, grenadine or tomato juice, and hot chilies). You can also try ingredients like fresh apple, vermouth, anything!

MAKE SANGRITA
Served traditionally in Mexico on the side of a fine, neat tequila, this nutrient-stacked mixture packs a punch.

5 ounces fresh tomato juice
4 1/2 ounces fresh-squeezed orange juice
1 ounce fresh-squeezed lime juice
1/2 ounce freshly ground chili peppers
Pinch of salt

Shake all ingredients in a cocktail shaker with ice, and strain into a highball glass over fresh ice.

HOW TO MAKE A MEAN MARGARITA

Like many popular, classic cocktails, no one actually knows exactly how the margarita came about, but there are several theories. One concerns a bartender named Danny Herrera, who loosely created the margarita (tequila over shaved ice with lemon and triple sec) for actress Majorie King in Rosarita Beach, Mexico, in 1938. Another claims that a Dallas socialite, Margarita Sames, hosted a pool party in 1948 at her Acapulco vacation home, where she made an eponymous cocktail of tequila, Cointreau, and lime juice. But could that really be true? Jose Cuervo began advertising with the tagline, "Margarita: it's more than a girl's name" in 1945, according to Anthony Dias Blue's book, *The Complete Book of Spirits.*

To get the most likely story, I spoke with Al Lucero, author of *The Great Margarita Book* and owner of Maria's New Mexican Kitchen in Santa Fe, which carries over 170 tequilas and serves over 200 types of margaritas. Remember that mid-century, salt and lime concoction created for businessmen and Hollywood stars on Palm Springs getaways? Lucero believes that the margarita was created when those men began bringing their wives and girlfriends to the area, who did not appreciate the rudimentary shooters. So a bartender decided to mix the ingredients together instead. "You had all the elements of what the guys were doing except adding the Cointreau," Lucero says.

So there you have it: the margarita was created for babes, but is now equally and emphatically enjoyed by men and women around the world! There's more to this drink than meets the glass, however. Here are a few tips from Lucero on how to make a perfect margarita:

Use good tequila. Tequila must be 100 percent agave for the best taste and quality. If a reposado, the tequila should be a golden color, and the añejo just slightly darker. If either is too dark, it may be an indication that coloring has been added, even among the 100 percent agave varieties. Lucero recommends Don Julio, El Tesoro, and Herradura for the best bang for your buck.

Always make it fresh. Never, I repeat never, use a bottled margarita mix, which contains nasty sugars, salts, and preservatives. Instead, use fresh citrus, which enhances the taste of the drink 100 fold and is naturally healthier. It's also just as easy.

Ice matters. Lucero swears by using small, clear ice cubes from a store bought bag as opposed to ice from the refrigerator, which tend to have lots of air pockets that throw off the dilution necessary for making a proper drink. Rather than stirring the ingredients in a pitcher, you always want to shake the ingredients with ice, which allows it to chip into tiny pieces that melt quickly.

Experiment with different liqueur and tequila combos. The characteristics of the tequila determine which orange liqueur complements it best, Lucero says. For example, because Grand Marnier has a cognac base, it tends to mix better with finer, flavor-packed tequilas, while Cointreau mixes well with tequilas that would be overpowered by Grand Marnier. When Lucero gets a new tequila, he uses it to build three margaritas using Bols Triple Sec, Grand Marnier, and Cointreau to see which one allows the tequila to shine best.

Try lemon instead of lime. Every margarita served at Maria's includes lemon juice instead of lime juice. Why? Because the lemon maintains a more consistent flavor all year round, and in blind tastings it beat out the limes every time. Sure, it's not traditional, but you be the judge.

Put your own spin on it. Do you a have a penchant for sour tastes? Maybe you like things a little spicier? Don't be afraid to experiment with the proportions or flavors in a margarita. The traditional way is two parts tequila with one part liqueur and one part citrus. But try adding muddled seasonal fruit (plums, anyone?), more or less lime, or a different age of tequila.

EL BAILE DEL SOL MARGARITA
Meaning "Sundance" in Spanish, this margarita, created for Robert Redford at Maria's New Mexican Kitchen, uses two kinds of tequila and lemon juice for a unique spin on the classic.

1 ounce El Tesora añejo tequila
1 ounce Chinaco tequila
1 1/4 ounces Cointreau
1 ounce lemon juice

Combine all ingredients in a cocktail shaker with small and transparent ice cubes. Shake and pour into a rocks glass.

GATEWAY AGAVE COCKTAILS

Tequila and mezcal are more versatile than you think. Go ahead, find out for yourself! Here's what to drink when you...

Want to seal a deal: Don Julio 70, neat
A quality blanco tequila, it shows you can handle yourself, that you are an experienced drinker, and that you know what you like.

Want to girl talk: The Mexican 75
This is basically a margarita, but with a champagne topping that makes your tongue tingle.

1 1/2 ounces blanco tequila
1/2 ounce agave nectar
1/2 ounce fresh lime juice
2 1/2 ounces champagne

Combine everything except the champagne in a cocktail shaker. Shake for five seconds and strain into champagne flute. Top with champagne.

Feel adventurous: Deadman's Boots
This recipe that mixes tequila with rye whiskey was created by the folks at High West Distillery. The owner, David Perkins, is kind of like a mad scientist. Okay, he doesn't wear a lab coat and play with beakers all day, but the spirits he makes are really unique and original. Take a look in the basement of his distillery-slash-restaurant on your next ski trip to Park City, Utah, and you will see tons of formulas scribbled on a chalkboard in what seems like a foreign language. Whatever he does, it's yummy. This stiff drink shows gall.

1 1/2 ounces High West Rendezvous Rye
1 ounce blanco tequila
3 lime wedges
1/4 ounce simple syrup

1 bottle of ginger beer

Muddle two lime wedges and simple syrup together in a shaker. Add rye and tequila. Shake and strain into a highball glass and fill with ginger beer. Garnish with a lime wedge.

Need a standard go-to: The Paloma

Branch out from the margarita with this Mexican mainstay, in which I sub the traditional tequila for mezcal.

2 ounces mezcal
2 ounces fresh grapefruit juice
½ ounce lime juice
1 teaspoon sugar
2 ounces soda water

Combine all ingredients except the soda water in a highball glass with ice. Stir and top with the soda water.

You're feeling fun: Tea-Quila Highball

Jim Meehan, the owner of speakeasy PDT (Please Don't Tell) in New York City, created this cocktail that subtly complements tequila's naturally robust nature with tea.

4 ounces lemon verbena tea
¼ ounce agave nectar
2 ounces blanco tequila
½ ounce St. Germain elderflower liqueur
1 lemon peel

Make tea and combine with agave nectar while warm; set aside to cool. Then combine everything in a cocktail shaker, fill with ice, stir, and strain into a Collins glass garnished with lemon verbena leaves and a lemon peel.

You are hosting: The Christopher Oaxacan
This recipe from Julian Cox, beverage director for restaurants
Short Order, Playa, Rivera, and Picca, in Los Angeles, is perfect
for novice mezcal drinkers because its smokiness is balanced by
the other fruit ingredients. It has a tiki-ish vibe with the orgeat.

2 ounces mezcal
3/4 ounces fresh-squeezed lemon juice
1/2 ounces high quality orgeat syrup, such as Monin, Fee
   Brothers or St. Vincent's (available online)
1/4 ounces agave syrup
1/2 passionfruit pulp
2 dashes Scrappy's Lavender Bitters
lemon twist

Shake all ingredients in a shaker with ice and strain into a
cocktail glass. Garnish with a lemon twist.

CHAPTER 9

Brandy's Dandy

For me, brandy has two distinct associations, neither of which make it appealing: my grandpa sipping it after dinner, and crunk juice (Hennessy and Red Bull), a truly terrible concoction I learned about when hip hop artists Lil' Jon and the East Side Boyz named one of their albums after it in 2004 ("crunk" is short for crazy drunk, by the way). Perhaps you have similarly unsexy (and misguided!) impressions. Well, I'm speaking from experience—it's time to give this sweet and complex spirit a chance.

Brandy is a type of spirit made from fruits like apples, plums, raspberries, and grapes. It comes from Dutch and German words meaning "burnt wine." Brandy can be made anywhere wine is produced, or where fruit is grown, which makes it a monster category to conquer. In fact, some types of brandy have become their own, regulated categories, like Calvados, apple brandy from Normandy, France; Pisco from Peru; Jerez de Brandy from Spain; Grappa from Italy; and cognac and Armagnac, which are French grape brandies. For the sake of clarity, these are the ones we're going to stick to in this chapter (and believe me, it's enough!).

Brandies in general are like extra fine wines and some carry unbelievable cachet. I was touring the Rémy Martin chateau in Cognac, France, when I was led to a small attic of barrels teeming with cobwebs. It was where Louis XIII, Rémy's collection of 1,200 eaux de vies dating back almost 200 years, were resting. I couldn't believe that this small, dark, and dungeon – like space in an elegant French mansion was where delectable, $3,000 bottles of cognac brandy came from. But that's precisely why I became intrigued. A spirit isn't always what it seems, and sometimes its refinement comes from wonderfully unexpected places.

For this reason, I love brandy. But there's no need to be alarmed. There are plenty of affordable and approachable brandy brands and varieties. Know your brandies, and how to pick 'em, and you'll be guaranteed a lifetime of blissful boozin' because brandy is a universal spirit that is found and appreciated around the world. It's also highly versatile, able to sub in for whiskey in many a cocktail as well as stand on its own when you're too lazy to mix. If you're a wino, you'll probably love it even more, because it's a richer extension of the grape and fruit notes you're already bonkers for. Now, let's tackle this brandy beast.

COGNAC

Cognac is like the Cadillac of brandies, mostly because of its romantic history as the drink of the rich and royal going back hundreds of years. All cognacs are brandies, but not all brandies are cognacs. Cognac identifies the origin of the brandy—the tiny idyllic town southwest of Paris defined by its namesake industry. The streets are narrow, the houses are made of ancient stone, there are a few shops

and restaurants, and it's divided by the Charentes River.

Cognac is made exclusively from grapes. After the grapes have fermented for a few weeks, it is distilled twice in copper stills and the result is colorless. At this stage, the liquid is called eau de vie. Cognac is then aged in Limousin oak barrels for at least two years where it takes on its brown color. The master blender or maître de chais (cellar master) is responsible for ensuring that a cognac produced by a company today will taste almost exactly the same as a cognac produced by that same company 100 years ago. He or she will taste the eau de vie periodically and decide when it has reached its prime. When it does, it is removed for blending.

Like scotch, various cognacs of different ages and from different local areas and vintners are blended and bottled into different categories. This blending, or *mariage*, of different eaux de vies is crucial to the complexity of flavors absent from an eau de vie from a single distillery or vineyard. The age of cognac is calculated as the *youngest* liquid used in the blend. So if the blender used a 17, 10, and two year-old cognac, it would be labeled as a two year-old cognac on the bottle.

Cognac is a slightly easier product to buy than, say, bourbon because of the monopoly there is in most liquor stores and restaurants. Four companies dominate 90 percent of the American cognac market: Martell, Rémy Martin, Courvoisier, and Hennessy. But each

CHAMPAGNE, BUT NOT THE BUBBLY STUFF

In the case of cognac, the meaning of the term champagne has nothing to do with sparkling wine. Champagne actually means "field" in French, and is a measure of the soil's effect on the spirit. If Cognac has "champagne" on the label, it is among the best because its grapes came from the richest soil.

Let me explain: like with wine, the quality of grapes used for cognac is largely determined by an area's climate and soil. The cognac region is comprised of six zones over about 220,000 acres, called crus. The best soil is found at the dead center of the region, almost like a bullseye, and the quality deteriorates from there. So cognacs made with grapes from Grande Champagne—the bull's eye—are considered the best, while those from the outside regions become gradually inferior. Here's what you can expect from cognacs made from each cru, starting with the best:

1. *Grande Champagne:* Characterized by floral notes and a long finish.
2. *Petite Champagne:* Similar to Grande Champagne cognacs but are usually shorter on the palate. When mixed with at least 50 percent Grande Champagne grapes, cognac may be marketed as Fine Champagne.
3. *Borderies:* The smallest cru, Borderies contains nutty, sometimes floral, aromas and flavors. Martell's Cordon Bleu is Borderies heavy.
4. *Fins Bois:* Since it ages quickly, Fins Bois is often a good, fruity base.
5. *Bons Bois and Bois Ordinaires:* The furthest out, these crus are more influenced by the Atlantic Ocean climate nearby. They age quickly but are not as interesting or complex in taste.

of these big guys treats the production process differently. For example, Courvoisier relies solely on small farmers while Hennessy manages most of its own vineyards. As a result, Hennessy claims to have the largest reserve of cognac in the world—enough to fill 45 million bottles. Occasionally you may see a small cognac brand in the liquor store, and if you do, pick it up because they are few and far between, even in Paris.

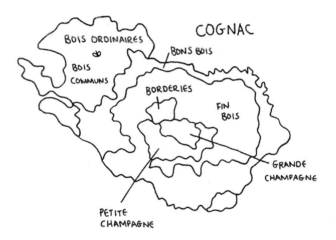

WHAT MAKES A GOOD COGNAC

Aging time and grape quality are the two biggest factors in determining a cognac's quality. The *Bureau National Interprofessionnel du Cognac* keeps the industry in check with the following label designations.:

V.S. or "Very Special": A blend in which the youngest brandy has been aged for at least two years in cask. These will have light, floral, and fruity notes like pear and apple.

V.S.O.P. or "Very Superior Old Pale": A blend in which the youngest brandy is aged for at least four years in a cask. These tend to have more vanilla and dried fruit notes.

Napoleon or XO, or "Extra Old": A blend in which the youngest brandy is aged for at least six but an average of 20 years in cask. You'll get more cinnamon, cocoa, and coffee notes in these.

THE SIDECAR

The origins of this classic sour brandy cocktail are hard to pin down, but my favorite story is that of David Embury's, the author of *The Fine Art of Mixing Drinks*. He claims the drink was created during the first World War by a friend of his who traveled to his favorite little bistro in Paris called Harry's New York Bar in the sidecar of a motorbike. When he arrived he requested this drink, which was then named after his mode of transportation. Others say Frank Meier at the Ritz Paris' Hemingway Bar created it. The bar, which is still open today, stocks what were Ernest Hemingway's favorite single malt whiskeys and is now run by Colin P. Field, Ritz's barkeep since 1994, who invented several famous original cocktails. It's even possible to purchase a Ritz Reserve cognac from 1830 that costs several hundred bucks.

The original drink may have contained six or seven ingredients but was eventually streamlined to include orange liqueur, French brandy, and lemon. A handy tip: you may confuse some bartenders, no matter how knowledgeable they seem, when you ask for this drink, because a beer-and-a-shot combo is also called a Sidecar. Avoid this confusion by making the drink for yourself at home. You can use any grape brandy in a Sidecar but cognac is the traditional way to go, and, since brandies can vary so much in taste and style—

from dry to sweet, for example—you should experiment with the kind you like best, and see how each affects the proportions.

2 ounces cognac

1 ounce orange liqueur (such as Grand Marnier or Cointreau)

$1/_2$ ounce fresh lemon juice

Pour the ingredients into a shaker with ice and shake vigorously. Strain into a chilled coupe or cocktail glass.

ARMAGNAC

Armagnac is cognac's forgotten little grape brandy sister, at least in the United States market. Like cognac, Armagnac is the French region between Bordeaux and Toulouse where the spirit is produced. It's the birthplace of Henri IV's mother, and legend has it that the French king was given his first taste of Armagnac when he was barely out of the womb. Since the region doesn't have a large river like Cognac does, or easy access to the sea, Armagnac remained a local drink because there was no easy way to ship it. In fact, most Armagnac distillers remain small farmers with limited distribution. In France, only 10 percent of brandies consumed are Armagnac.

Those who love Armagnac *love* Armagnac, and there are plenty of reasons to adore it. For starters, most are older than cognacs. There is also less emphasis on strict age categories. Once the master blender tastes eau de vie in a cask and determines it to be complete, he or she will begin blending whether it's two years old or forty. As a result, Armagnacs are close to the XO style of cognacs; they are often woodier, earthier and sometimes higher in alcohol content than cognacs, but have amazing aromatics. What's best is that Armagnacs are not monopolized like cognac, and are often cheaper, too. Bonus!

Armagnacs follow a labeling structure, which gives you an idea of the product's age:

Blanche d'Armagnac: Distilled eau de vie without aging. Blanche means white. This is unique because you will never see a blanche cognac.

Three stars or VS: A minimum of two years in cask.

VSOP or Reserve: A minimum of five years in cask.

XO or Napoleon: A minimum of six years in cask.

Vieil Armagnac: Aged six years.

Hors d'age: A minimum of 10 years in cask.

Vieille Reserve: Aged 15 to 25 years.

CHOOSE A GOOD ARMAGNAC PRODUCER

While the bottles' labelings are important in showing the bottle's complexity, it is important to choose a great Armagnac producer. At quality wine and liquor stores with good selections, you can find balanced brands like Tariquet and Larressingle that have perfected how to carry the brandy with subtle sweetness.

Cognac and Armagnac are made pretty much the same way, but there are a few differences in the process:

	Cognac	Armagnac
Still	Uses a copper pot still	Uses a special, Armagnacais copper still, which is more squarish in shape
Production	The least amount of heads and tails, the better	The heads and tails of the batch—the first and last cuts of what distillers often label substandard material—are actually kept in for complexity
Distillation	Distilled twice	Distilled once
Aging	Aged in Limousin oak barrels, usually four to six years	Aged in local black oak, usually more than 10 years

CALVADOS

As if France didn't have enough claims to fame in the brandy department, just north of Cognac and Armagnac in Normandy is Calvados, where an eponymous apple brandy is made.

Calvados is one of those brandies you either love or hate because trying one that doesn't suit your taste can be like taking a swig of sour apple cider. Pas bon. The finest apples come from the Pays d'Auge region, which includes the town of Calvados. In the

French way, all Calvados brandies must submit to a tasting committee before a certificate of quality is granted. This is why French products rock!

DID YOU KNOW?
It takes 7,000 pounds of apples to produce one barrel of apple brandy. Savor it!

It takes an impressive 30-plus varieties of apples to make Calvados. Some Calvados brandies are also made with pears, but apples are always dominant. This gives the brandy a precise blend of sweet, bitter and acidic tastes. The apples ripen in stages from September through December before being crushed into a pulp called pomace. The pomace sits for a few hours before juice is extracted from it. Once the natural cycle of fermentation is complete, the distillation process for eau de vie begins. Calvados must adhere to these rules:

- Only cider apples from the Pays d'Auge region, which includes Calvados and Orne, are used.
- It's double distilled traditionally in a pot still.
- Approval of the Institut National des Appellations d'Origine is obtained after tasting.
- The juice ferments for at least one month.

Like cognac, most of the barrels used for aging are Limousin oak, but sometimes old sherry and port casks are used, which gives the brandy fruiter and spicier notes. The optimum age for an old Calvados is 25 to 30 years.

The classifications noted on a Calvados bottle are similar to those of cognac and Armagnac. Like the others, the younger the brandy, the more fruity notes you'll get, while the older the brandy, the more wood, chocolate, cinnamon, and other richer and complex notes you'll get:

Three stars: Aged a minimum of two years.

Vieux or Reserve: Aged a minimum of three years.

VO or Veille Reserve: Aged a minimum of four years.

VSOP or Grand Reserve: Aged a minimum of five years.

Napoleon/Hors d'age/Age Inconnu or Extra: Aged more than five years. You'll get more orange, mahogany and other wood notes, maybe even chocolate or nuts, like other aged brandies.

ON AGING IN YOUR LIQUOR CABINET
Brandies stop aging once they leave the wooden casks, so no matter how long you want to save a bottle, it will not get any better, unlike some wines. So don't feel guilty about opening them! Once the bottle is open, you have about six months before oxygen begins to noticeably change the spirit's characteristics. It may not taste bad, per se, but it will taste different. Never store a corked bottle on its side, since contact with a cork could spoil the brandy.

GRAPPA

Grappa is an Italian pomace grape brandy, which means that after juice has been extracted from grapes for wine, the skins, seeds, and stems are smashed gently and distilled into brandy. These remnants contain the acidic, less hearty parts of the fruit, so grappas are usually stronger and more tart in flavor than other brandies. Because of the intricate way one must handle and store the pomace, it is difficult to get grappa right and the spirit got a bad rap because back in the day it was harsh, like moonshine. But practice makes perfect, after all, and by and large it is a much tastier product than it used to be. Grappa is matured in oak barrels, leaving it a light brown color. Grappa can be made from red or white grapes but distillation takes the color out of it, so it can be clear, too. It is common to find grappa packaged as vintages, which means that the product in the bottle has been made with grapes harvested in just one year. Old bottles are called *vecchia* and the even older ones are called *stravecchia*. The name of the single grape used, such as moscato, is usually on the bottle.

Collecting grappas is fun partly because their packaging is so pretty. Some are even bottled in hand-blown Murano glass. But that doesn't mean it's a quality product. Brands like Nardini, Nonino, Marolo, and Jacopo Poli have been around for a long time, are sold in the United States, and are reliable, but don't be afraid to ask helpful staff at Italian restaurants and liquor stores for recommendations.

HOW TO DRINK IT

Grappa should be served at cellar temperature of 65 degrees or lightly chilled. To do it like the Italians do...

- Bask in the Italian tradition of a grappa on top of coffee or espresso called the *Correto*, or just rinse the coffee cup with

CATCHING UP WITH THE COUNTESS OF COGNAC

Béatrice Cointreau is practically liquor royalty. She is great-granddaughter of the Cointreau empire and granddaughter of the founder of Rémy Martin cognac. She's also a refined drinker and masterful businesswoman with degrees in law and marketing, and an education at the Bordeaux Institute of Oenology. I asked her about the nuances of cognac and how to get the most of it.

What makes a good cognac?

A good cognac is defined by its expression of the soil, climate, and grape varietal. These factors reflect the sensitivity, sensibility, and style of the cellar masters, like a work of art. It's a pleasant journey through emotions. Some are very expensive, with prices reaching dizzying sums, but the most important thing is not the rating or price on the label but what you like best and how you feel when you drink it.

So how do you keep in touch with how you feel as you drink it?

The important point is to express impressions and sensations in your own words and keep it simple and true as you taste. Some of the most incredible professional tasters even with encyclopedic knowledge will express with simple references. Most importantly, trust your instincts.

What's your favorite cognac pastime?

Exchanging bottles. Sharing a bottle you've discovered is part of the pleasure of drinking it. In every case it reflects generosity and dares others to try the unknown cognacs and learn.

a tablespoon of grappa before filling with coffee ('rasentin' in Italian).

- Mix a little grappa with lemon sorbet or gelato for aprés-dinner sweets called sgroppino.

- Experiment with purchasing a nice, unaged grappa and infusing it with fruit and herbs in a jar for a year or two.

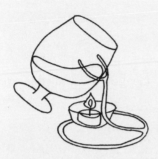

WARM BRANDY, DEMYSTIFIED

It's a common image in popular culture to heat brandy in a warmer, a funky contraption that tilts the snifter on its side under a candle. While warm brandy may feel good when you drink, it's not good for getting the true essences of the brandy since heat causes its volatile compounds to rapidly release, leaving behind only the alcohol taste.

Pour the glass to about a quarter full and swirl the drink in your glass, observing its legs. The legs on any spirit are the drips inside the glass. If the legs drip slowly, it indicates a high alcohol content, while runny drips indicate a low alcohol content. To add to your fancy vocabulary, the first fragrance released from a brandy is known as the *montant*, or 'that which rises' in French.

DOMESTIC BRANDIES

Brandies are being made by distilleries all over the United States, but since California dominates the America's wine production, it consequently dominates its brandy production also. California brandy must be made from grapes grown and distilled in California but there is no restriction on the type of grape. Ugni Blanc, Folle Blanche, Flame Tokay, and Colombard are most common. The brandy must be aged for two years in white oak, otherwise the label must read "immature brandy." Some distillers age their brandy about four to eight years, and most of the brandies in the United States are mass-produced and good for mixing and cooking. But the demand is growing for artisan, more refined domestic brandies and so they are coming! The most popular United States made brandies are from fruits other than grapes, like raspberries and plums.

BRANDY DE JEREZ

As if we haven't covered enough grape brandies to make your head spin, we've got to make room for one more: Brandy de Jerez, named after the Spanish region where it's made.

To be Jerez brandy, it must be aged in American oak barrels with wines from the Jerez region. Maturation of Jerez is similar to that of sherry, in that when barrels on the *solera* (bottom row of a warehouse) are taken out, brandy from a row above it is moved down a tier, and the new brandy is placed at the top. Because of temperature changes, this smooths out disparities across all casks in the blend. Some of the Jerez brandies are aged in former sherry barrels, since sherry and Jerez are produced in the same Andalusian region. The type of sherry has a big effect on the way the Jerez tastes and looks.

There are three types of brandy de Jerez:

Solera: Youngest, aged at least six months.

Reserva: Aged over two years.

Gran Reserva: Oldest and finest, aged over three years.

HOW TO FIND A GOOD JEREZ

Jerez brandies are bold, and while they can be paired with bold,

AMERICAN AS APPLE BRANDY
There are other apple brandies besides Calvados, too – like applejack, which has a United States history as old as the country itself. When the first settlers arrived here, they brought apple seeds with them, and in the 18th century, a man named Robert Laird supplied George Washington's troops with applejack—aged apple brandy blended with neutral grain spirit (like vodka), that is now its own category. Laird later established America's first commercial distillery for producing Laird's Applejack brandy, and it still exists as a family-owned company. One of the head honchos is a babe named Lisa Laird Dunn, who gave me the lowdown on brandy and how to drink it:

What are the biggest misconceptions about brandy?
Women think of brandy and they think of old men smoking a pipe, or Santa Claus drinking it right after a long night of delivering gifts. Some look at the product and say, "Oh, it's strong." But a good brandy should be soothing.

What else makes a good brandy?
There should be a mingling of all of the flavors, and it should not taste harsh. In fact, in most brandies, the wood has mellowed the product through the aging process. I'm looking for a fullness and roundness to the product. The finish is important. It should not be too sharp and should instead be smooth.

What does brandy represent to you?
Brandy represents refinement, intelligence, and adventure because you don't find many people ordering it.

How do you advise women learn about booze and brandy in a non-pandering way?
The least intimidating way would be through cocktails, and any cocktail you prepare with whiskey can be prepared with brandy for totally different nuances. Start with the lighter cocktails then progress to more stirred and strong cocktails. At first, it may be hard to ween off sweeter drinks. After all, we're the Pepsi generation. We grew up on sugar and we're used to sweet. A good bartender can really help you develop your affinity. Tell them flavors you do not like and don't go on a busy night so you can ask questions. It's the most inexpensive way to learn because you don't want to buy a 750 milliliter bottle and get home and realize you don't like it.

spicy meals, they also make great digestives. Keep this in mind upon tasting one for the first time, since its distinctive taste can put some people off initially. While younger Jerez brandies will most truly exhibit characteristics of the grape, like with tequila, new Jerez drinkers may appreciate older ones that have been mellowed by the wooden barrels.

Though Jerez never caught on in the United States the way cognac did, it is still possible to find great bottlings of it here at well-stocked liquor stores, such as Cardenal Mendoza, Lepanto, and Gran Duque d'Alba, which have bright, concentrated notes of raisin and caramel, for example.

PISCO'S NEW DAY IN THE USA

Pisco is an unaged grape brandy from South America. It is my favorite unaged brandy, not only for its vibrant, Latin flair that pairs well with strong ingredients like habanero and citrus, but also because of its dynamic variances and history. For example, in its home countries of Peru and Chile (the two battle over origin), pisco comes from an Incan word that means clay vessel, which was used to distill corn mash (like a rudimentary beer). Distillation of pisco can be traced to the 1500s.

Peruvian pisco is usually of better quality than Chilean pisco because the government regulates its production and distribution. There are other differences, too: Peruvian pisco is distilled in copper pots and stored in casks lined with paraffin, which keeps the liquor clear and flavor pure, while Chilean pisco may contain added flavoring, neutral spirits, plus is aged in oak casks.

There's no doubt pisco is having *un momento*. Bartenders are having more fun with this spirit, since more pisco brands are entering the market. And they're getting bigger and better. But its still finding its legs in the United States. Pisco remains one of the oldest spirits in the Americas that Americans know little about. Pisco can be made from several grape varieties, and the two most popular brands in the United States are Porton and BarSol.

I asked Diego Loret de Mola, founder of the Peruvian BarSol Pisco, why consumers are taking to pisco, and why now.

Why did you start BarSol, even when pisco was not yet well-known in the United States?
A good friend of mine, Dale DeGroff, once told me that America has developed an incredible love affair for all things Latin: food, music, fashion, and certainly drinking. And indeed, I have experienced that since living in the United States since 1985. In 2000, Peru was undergoing a positive economic turnaround after 30 dark years with a military government and terrorism. I wanted to contribute to that change by exporting

our forgotten Peruvian pisco to the world. I wanted to share our amazing history and legacy through a glass of our great spirit, but the product had to be good and a lot of education would be required. I began tasting good, small batch piscos in Peru, and believed the quality would be good enough for the United States market. I partnered with my friend Carlos Ferreyros and acquired the 100-year-old Bodega San Isidro distillery. From 2001 to 2004 we made pisco without selling it. I wanted it to be perfect. I started traveling around the United States [with it] and bartenders loved it.

How was pisco affected during the "dark years"?
Pisco was initially affected by the agricultural reforms applied by the military coup d'état of 1968. Most of the agricultural land owned by the aristocracy in Peru was expropriated by the government and handed to the working class. But they didn't know how to run the businesses. Vineyards were destroyed and subsistence produce was planted instead. No grapes meant no pisco, and any that became available was low quality. We didn't really drink pisco through the 1990s. We grew up drinking scotch like many neighboring countries.

Why is pisco suddenly showing up in the mainstream, beyond traditional Peruvian and Chilean restaurants?
It's a little category that's starting to blossom. By far it is not an ethnic product at all, but a fantastic cocktail base for the American imbiber. You can substitute pisco for any other spirit such as vodka and wind up with a fuller, more complex cocktail. The price is also accessible at $20 to $40 a bottle. Imbibers are also learning that the quality of Peruvian pisco is extraordinary because it's made 100 percent of grapes.

Can you drink pisco neat?
Certainly. But the most popular way to drink pisco in the United States is in cocktails. As imbibers understand how pisco tastes in the cocktail, then they will request it straight.

Like a bourbon or tequila, it's fun to taste the difference among different varietals and expressions, whether it is made of Quebranta, Italia, or Torontel grapes—or a blend of any of them called Acholado.

How do you know you're drinking a good pisco?
The show is in the bottle. Taste it! It should taste complex, full, and without a funky grain or sugarcane alcohol taste. It should reflect clean and crisp floral and spice characteristics of the grape. The fastest growing piscos on the market are Peruvian products, which must adhere to the country's regulations (100 percent from grapes, distilled to bottle proof, with no added water, yeast, enzymes, or sulfites). Peruvian pisco can also never rest in wood, so that the final product is a pure expression of the grape that makes it. Look for cleanliness, clarity, and purity.

Who are the American pisco customers?
They're young—21 to 49—with disposable income and adventurous spirit. Women are typically more adventurous and are consuming more pisco cocktails. That's because its storied history and Latin heritage is romantic and traditional. The spirit itself is clean, pure, sensual, and exotic.

Why should someone pick up a pisco instead of another white spirit or pomace brandy like grappa?
Once you try it, you will love it. There are so many expressions due to the variety of aromatic and non-aromatic grapes that will certainly satisfy all preferences amongst imbibers. When comparing to a pomace brandy, pisco is cleaner and less aggressive since the skins are removed at fermentation. That means there is less bite from tannic acid. Compared to other white spirits, pisco is extremely expressive when consumed straight.

How can a gal choose a pisco she will like?

If you love white tequila, you most likely will like a non-aromatic pisco such as one made from Quebranta grapes, since it presents similar taste characteristics but with fruiter, rather than earthy tones. If you like gin, you'll probably enjoy aromatic piscos made from Italia, Torontel, or Moscatel grapes, which show subtle floral and spice characteristics.

MAKE A PISCO SOUR

The Pisco Sour, which was invented by an American bartender in Lima in the 1920s, is very similar to the Sidecar, though slightly more sour because of pisco's tart nature. The other big difference is the use of egg whites, which adds to the frothiness of the drink. The following recipe comes from gaz regan, a well-known spirits expert, author, and former bartender:

2 ounces pisco brandy
1 ounce fresh lemon juice
$\frac{1}{2}$ ounce simple syrup
1 small raw egg white
Few dashes Angostura bitters

Pour all ingredients but bitters into a cocktail shaker with ice and shake vigorously. Strain into a coupe glass and garnish with the bitters.

GATEWAY BRANDY COCKTAILS

Brandy is so underrated among the young masses in the United States that choosing it—whether to serve to guests or at a bar—shows you think outside the box, especially when you drink it in a way other than its typical state as an aprés-dinner digestive. No matter what you're feelin', there's a perfect brandy drink for you. Here's what to drink when you...

Want to seal a deal: Armagnac, neat
Sip on this to show you appreciate the finer, and rarer, things.

Want to girl talk: French Quarter
This concoction's name is not meant to be reminiscent of rowdy bachelorette parties. On the contrary, it speaks to the simplicity and refinement of a quality aperitif paired with an elegant brandy.

2 1/2 ounces cognac
1/4 ounce Lillet Blanc
Lemon wheel for garnish

Stir both ingredients with ice and strain into a chilled cocktail glass. Garnish with the lemon.

Feel adventurous: Vieux Carré
I call this adventurous because it mixes sweet cognac with rye whiskey, and because it is a boozy and stirred short drink. Created in New Orleans in the 1930s, it's one of my favorites.

1 ounce cognac
3/4 ounce rye whiskey
1/2 ounce sweet vermouth
1/4 ounce Bénédictine
4 dashes equal parts Peychaud's and Angostura bitters

Combine all ingredients in a glass with ice and stir vigorously.

Strain into a rocks glass with fresh ice. You can also serve this straight up if you prefer, by straining into a chilled coupe.

Need a standard go-to: Jack Maples
This cocktail is warming and refreshing at the same time—perfect for babes who want to unwind in style.

2 ounces Laird's Applejack
1 teaspoon pure maple syrup
1 dash aromatic bitters
Cinnamon stick

Stir all ingredients with ice in a metal cocktail shaker and strain into a chilled martini glass. Garnish with the cinnamon stick.

Are feeling fun: Sevilla 75
This drink is refreshing, simple, and incorporates the bubbly effervescence we associate with celebrations—sparkling wine.

1 1/2 ounces Jerez brandy
1/2 ounce fresh lemon juice
1 teaspoon simple syrup
2 ounces cava sparkling wine

Shake the brandy, lemon juice, and simple syrup in a cocktail shaker. Pour into a rocks or Collins glass with one large ice cube in it. Top with the cava.

Are hosting: Baltimore eggnog
Sweet, strong, and dynamic, this spin on traditional eggnog is a big hit at wintertime fiestas (plus, it gives a shout-out to my home state of Maryland).

1 egg
1 1/2 teaspoon sugar
1/2 ounce brandy

½ ounce blackstrap rum
½ ounce Madeira (a Portuguese fortified wine)
7 ounces skim milk
Grated nutmeg for garnish

Put all ingredients into a cocktail shaker and shake vigorously.
Strain into a chilled Collins glass and sprinkle with nutmeg.

CHAPTER 10

The Clear Choice in Vodka

I remember when vodka was my jam. In fact, I'm pretty sure vodka was the first alcoholic drink I ever tried. At that time, I was just getting used to the taste of alcohol, and I had seen vodka ads everywhere. Wasn't this what I was *supposed* to drink?

Plus, I was under the influence of Carrie Bradshaw, the babe-about-town protagonist of the hit series Sex and the City, and her Cosmopolitan-loving friends.

That vodka based, rose-colored cocktail, made popular through television and creative marketing helped make vodka the best-selling spirit in the United States in the last decade and a half, particularly among women. But hey, it's not 1998 anymore, and there's so much more to vodka and the world of cocktails (as you've been learning throughout this book), than that. And to many people, including me until a few years ago, vodka is just a way to add alcohol to a drink. "Savor" and "vodka" are rarely used in the same sentence. Plus, most of us have probably been drinking bad vodka.

Which, of course, is our first mistake. Turns out there is a gang of good stuff to learn about vodka, including how to drink it, how to appreciate it, and how to spot marketing ploys that lure you into buying subpar products. Plus, this clear spirit's got an interesting history with a few fun traditions and classics to discover (like a lady-who-brunch's BFF, the Bloody Mary!).

In order to fully appreciate vodka, it helps to know this booze's roots. Vodka has been distilled in Russia, Poland, and Czechoslovakia since the 1100s, but is now produced all over the world. While it can be made from any fermentable matter, vodka is distilled mostly from potatoes and grains and is often filtered (usually up to eight times) through charcoal, sand, peat, lava rock, limestone, or cloth to remove most traces of aroma and flavor.

In the United States, the only additive vodka can legally contain is water; distillers pride themselves on what type they use, whether it be iceberg, spring, filtered, or distilled. Adding water brings vodka, which is almost 200 proof when it comes out of the still, down to an acceptable 80 to 100 proof.

WITH LOVE, FROM RUSSIA:
VODKA'S HUMBLE BEGINNINGS

Whether vodka originated within the borders of Poland or Russia is up for grabs—both claim it. Since Russia has a more documented history with the spirit, we'll stick to telling that story.

Vodka started as a medicinal drink infused with herbs, berries, and barks for healing properties. The alcohol later became recreational but the flavors were still added to mask the crude distillation. It eventually evolved into a more refined spirit.

Like other anti-alcohol measures throughout time around the

ALL ABOUT AQUAVIT

Vodka infused with spices and herbs, namely dill, caraway, fennel, and anise is called aquavit, or akvavit, in Scandinavia where the style originated. Aquavit gets its name from the Latin phrase "water of life." But unlike in Denmark or Sweden, where it may be clear, made from grain, and served chilled, Norwegians prefer "akevitt" (pronounced ah-keh-veet) aged, room temperature, and served with a beer. It is especially popular during the holiday and winter season. One of Norway's most notable native aquavits, Linie (pronounced lin-yuh), is matured in sherry oak casks during a roundtrip to Australia with United States stops in Savannah, Georgia, and Long Beach, California. The concept happened by accident in the 1800s when liquor tycoon Jørgen Lysholm's family sent a batch of aquavit to Indonesia. What didn't sell got shipped back to Trondheim, where the family noticed it had a richer flavor. It began loading barrels of aquavit onto freighters that carried dried cod, a Norwegian specialty export, and retrieved them after their trip around the world. This method is still practiced today and the boat each bottle traveled on is typed on the bottle's label. Its journey can even be tracked online. Though aquavit can be hard to find in the United States, other popular Danish, Norwegian, and Swedish brands include Glide, O.P. Anderson, and Allborg.

world, an effort in 1400s Russia by Tsar Ivan III to restrict vodka consumption failed, so he instead instituted a monopoly on vodka and by the mid-16th century, kabaks, official Russian taverns, were the only places vodkas could be purchased and consumed. No food was sold there so patrons just got wasted. Then in the 18th century, the laws loosened to allow nobility to own distilleries. Since vodka taxes were 40 percent of the nation's revenue, the Russian government encouraged people to drink more Russian vodka and it became the national drink. Vodka was sold in government-licensed shops, where men went for daily benders.

Smirnoff opened a distillery in Moscow and by 1886 was a purveyor of vodka to the czars before Russia nationalized the industry again at the turn of the century. Once the monopoly ended years later, so many vodka distillers sprang up and produced so much product that even the poorest citizens could afford it. But thanks to a vodka distillation ban in the early 20th century (because being drunk was being a bad communist), Russians didn't produce vodka legally until after World War I, when Russian soldiers got daily rations of vodka. Meanwhile, during this time Poland's vodka production and consumption was growing at a fast and steady pace as well.

IN HIS ELEMENT
Dmitri Mendeleev, who created the periodic table of elements, determined through experimentation that the ideal vodka was 76.4 proof, when the concentration of alcohol would not overpower natural flavors. Most Russian vodkas, and some others, are made by this measure today.

HOW TO DISTINGUISH BETWEEN VODKAS

You may think that vodkas all taste the same, but there are actually some subtle differences between them. For example, traditional vodkas produced in Poland and Russia differ starkly in character from those made in the West.

To get a handle on this, vodkas can be loosely lumped into four styles with varying characteristics:

Russian: Usually made from wheat or rye; thicker, and slightly fruity. Stolichnaya, Russia's crown jewel, is a good example. Bad ones taste oily in the mouth.

Polish: Usually on the sweeter side, and mostly made from rye; some are made from potatoes and sugar beet molasses. Chopin, Potocki, and Żubrówka (a vodka flavored with grass that grows only in eastern Poland), are reputable brands.

DID YOU KNOW?
The majority of vodka produced in the United States is distilled by a handful of companies. Then a manufacturer puts its spin on it through filtration and bottles it. Tito's and Square One distill their own, however, along with several other craft distillers experimenting with the category.

Western: Neutral flavor and smell; made from corn, potatoes, molasses, wheat, barley (mostly in the U.K.), rye, and grapes. Tito's Handmade, Finlandia, and Absolut are good choices. There are also grape-based domestic vodkas like Hangar 1, and those made from organic fruits with a rye base like Square One.

Flavored: Many flavored vodkas are created artificially—often with essential oils—because fresh produce contains oils and acids that cloud the spirit or discolor it. Depending on the flavor, some taste nasty (think whipped cream) and some taste okay (think citrus). You be the judge. If you do want to buy a flavored vodka, look for Skyy Infusions, which use actual fruit to create a quality flavored product, or something from California distilleries Square One and Charbay, where flavored vodka is produced with organically grown fruit like lemons, oranges, basil, and pomegranates. Look for ingredient lists on bottle labels to be sure. You can also infuse your own vodkas to get unique and natural flavors.

WHAT MAKES VODKA VODKA

If vodka can be made from any fermentable matter, what then, distinguishes a vodka made from grapes from an unaged brandy? Essentially nothing—and that is the source of much debate.

For example, once Cîroc, a vodka made from wine grapes in

AMERICA'S LOVE AFFAIR WITH VODKA

Vodka sales in the United States were so small in the 1930s and 1940s that it was not yet recognized as an official spirit category. Legend has it that vodka caught fire when a Los Angeles tavern called the Cock n' Bull began mixing it with ginger beer to create the Moscow Mule at the advice of Jack Martin, who owned a ginger beer brewery and a vodka distributor (clever marketing, eh?).

Its neutral taste is another reason vodka gained popularity. In 1956, House Beautiful magazine's food editor, Poppy Cannon, said women were one of the main reasons why vodka consumption was skyrocketing, even at a time when Americans weren't too fond of the Russians. Why? Because she said that women preferred not to taste their booze. Vodka was also compatible with a wide range of mixers. Young adults at this time, who had been influenced by their Prohibition-era parents to think that gin and whiskey were the devil, felt vodka was a lesser evil. By the 1960s vodka production had reached 19 million gallons per year—20 times greater than a decade before.

There are now over 100 American vodka brands. Smirnoff has the most established history in the United States—it was launched in 1934 in Connecticut by Rudolph Kunett who licensed the name from the original Russian company.

France, came out in 2006, Poland got pissed. They wanted the EU to mandate that only spirits made in their traditional fashion from cereals, potatoes, and sugar beet molasses be labeled vodka. The compromise was that vodkas made from anything other than those items say, "Vodka produced from. . ." on the label. Nowadays, many brands will specify that their product has been distilled from 100 percent grain spirit to differentiate themselves.

A GENDER-NEUTRAL SPIRIT

Vodka has long enjoyed a gender-blind status like no other spirit, but only when served a certain way. In his 1958 paper, "Factors Motivating Social Drinkers in Accepting Vodka," (presented to the American Association for the Advancement of Science), I.M. Altaraz calls attention to this phenomenon. "Vodka enjoys a rather strange advantage in that it is considered a manly drink even while it appeals to women," he wrote. "Men tend to shy away from such 'sissy' concoctions as 'orange blossoms,' yet will readily drink the vodka version called 'screwdrivers.'" It's just another example of how we've associated gender roles with the libations we drink throughout history.

THE GOOD AND THE BAD: MARKETING PLOYS TO AVOID

Vodka's rapid popularity in the latter half of the 20th century led to companies making serious cash, and therefore paying for really elaborate marketing campaigns aimed to sell customers on a fun and sophisticated lifestyle.

"In most cases, those big consumer vodka brands churn and burn the spirit and reduce the cost as much as they can. They assure that it is tasteless and that is not the point of vodka," says vodka expert Dushan Zaric, co-owner of popular Manhattan bars Macau Trading Company and Employees Only. "It's one of the only spirits out there meant to be paired with food. The world of vodka is huge, with all of the styles of production and possible infusions."

The best way to make sure you are buying a flavorful vodka, no matter where it is from is to research your choices beforehand. Ask:

- *How many times was it distilled?* The more times it is distilled, the less flavor and character it will have.

- *What is it made from?* This may change your mind entirely about which spirit you ultimately opt to buy.

- *Where was it made?* Use my guide to types of vodkas to deduce the type of taste you can expect. This also helps determine the type of strength you desire. The more starch the original fer-

A NUMBERS GAME

Many vodka distillers are quite proud of the high number of distillations their product has gone through, as if it means that it is a better product, but that is not true. First, vodka is often distilled several times to remove impurities and imperfections. Second, what counts as a single distillation is a little fuzzy. For example, a copper still has several plates in the condenser through which the distillate travels, and the producer may say a product has been distilled as many times as the number of plates the still has. It means nothing and is technically incorrect. Other marketing techniques in the vodka category have cleverly grabbed our attention as well. By creating and marketing Grey Goose as a "super premium" French vodka in a pretty bottle, owner Sidney Frank was able to charge double the price of the priciest vodka on the market at the time, even though it was no better a product.

menting matter contained, the more alcohol content there will be in the resulting vodka, which is why potato vodkas are usually a higher proof than rye, for example.

- *How was it filtered?* Filtering is the single most important part of the vodka distillation process, according to Zaric. Some vodka brands claim to be filtered through diamonds or platinum, which is just a gimmick. But charcoal filtration, on the other hand, often gives vodka a crisp and clean, but flavorful, taste.

DIRTY LITTLE SECRET...ER, HANDS
Many big brand vodkas add glycerin, a type of sugar alcohol, to their blends as a flavor-masking agent. It covers up the impurities and ethyl alcohol smell you get, and puts a coating on your palate the way a well-made spirit would. Next time you try one, try this test: put a few drops of vodka in your palms and rub your hands together until dry. If it contains glycerin, your hands will be sticky. If it doesn't, your hands will be clean, as if you'd just used hand sanitizer.

When tasting or buying a vodka, you'll want to look closely also at the clarity of the product. Vodkas distilled with water that has a high mineral content becomes cloudy or yellowed, which is no good.

HOW TO DRINK VODKA
What many babes don't know is that vodka is actually intended to be drunk with food, even as an aperitif. Russians believed that vodka helped with digestion and paired well with heavy, meaty meals. James Beard, the revered food critic, even said that vodka was "one

of the few spirits that does not ruffle your taste buds so that you miss the true flavor of the wines served at the dinner to follow."

And unlike other spirits, it is not a faux-pas to serve vodka cold with foods like smoked fish, bacon, charcuterie, and seafood. Doing so helps cut their grease and enhance their flavors in traditional fashion.

As for mixing vodka in cocktails, what type goes best depends on the other ingredients you use. Appropriately mixing vodka is truly the best way to put the spirit to its highest use, and promotes balance in the glass. Here are a few general guidelines:

Type of Drink	Type of Vodka	Examples
Fruity or Sweet	Wheat or Potato	Absolut, Ketel One, Luksusowa, Russian Standard
Savory	Corn or rye	Tito's, Potocki, Belvedere
Boozy or stirred	Winter wheat	Stolichnaya Gold, U'luvka

THE BLOODY MARY: BASICS OF THE BRUNCH STAPLE

This classic hangover cure and brunch favorite was named after Mary I, who ruled England from 1553 to 1558 and was determined to revoke the Protestant Reformation with her father, Henry VIII. She ordered the execution of 300 Protestants. Fernand Petiot, a bartender at Paris' famed Harry's New York Bar, later named this tomato-based concoction to acknowledge her "bloody" reign.

Here's how to make the original, fresh, and delicious recipe from Harry's New York Bar (don't ever let someone mix canned tomato

MAKE BLOODY MARY MIX FROM SCRATCH

If you want to serve Bloody Marys to friends, don't slave over each individual cocktail: make a homemade Bloody mix ahead of time. It is particularly amazing in the summer, when tomatoes are in season. You'll need an electric juicer to do this efficiently, but a hand juicer will work with some elbow grease.

Makes 6 drinks
3 pounds yellow and/or red vine-ripened and cored tomatoes
6 stalks celery
1 teaspoon Worcestershire
Tabasco to taste
Grated horseradish root to taste
1/2 sweet onion, soaked in cold water for 30 minutes*
and then pureed

Crush tomatoes in a large bowl or pitcher. Strain the tomatoes through fine mesh, pushing gently on the pulp to ease it through quicker. You can also use a juicer to do this. Juice celery and set aside. Combine the tomato juice with the celery juice, horseradish, Worcestershire, onion, and Tabasco. The mix will only stay fresh in the fridge for about a day, so try to prepare it the day you plan to serve it.

When you're ready, add a grain-based vodka or spice up the mix with pepper- , dill- , or bacon-infused vodka to your taste. I typically add one-third parts vodka to three parts mix.

*Soaking the onion will take the "bite" out of the onion taste which is palatable in food, but not so great in a drink.

juice and vodka and call it a Bloody Mary again):

2 ounces vodka

5 ounces fresh tomato juice

1 teaspoon lemon juice

1/4 teaspoon Worcestershire sauce

Few dashes Tabasco sauce

Pinch of white pepper

Pinch or two of celery salt

1/2 teaspoon fresh dill

Celery stalk for garnish

Combine all ingredients in a shaker and very gently shake with ice. Pour into a Collins glass. Garnish with celery stalk and a few ice cubes.

INFUSE YOUR OWN VODKA

In the early days of Russia and Poland's recreational enjoyment of vodka, every tavern, monastery, or home had its own still for vodka making. When important guests came over, the house would offer a custom infused vodka using the best available ingredients like fruit, berries, spices, and herbs. These secret, VIP recipes were passed down from generation to generation. Make your own vodka legacy!

It's easy peasy 'cause thanks to vodka's neutral character, it happens to be the simplest spirit to infuse. It will take on any flavor you want beautifully, and rather fast.

Just keep in mind that every ingredient will behave differently and successful concoctions will take some trial and error. Infuse

SET UP A BLOODY MARY BAR

I've seen every kind of Bloody Mary, from one with a burger on top at the Hotel Madeline in Telluride to one that was nothing more than a large hunk of beef jerky and a splash of bourbon tucked into a glass in a New York dive. Everybody loves Bloody Marys, and setting up a station for guests to make their own is a fun way to introduce them to new ingredients and combinations. To create the ultimate Bloody Mary bar, set up a station for the base spirit (suggestions below!), fresh juices, and garnishes. Serve the juices and sauces in decorative containers, rather than in the bottles you purchased them in. For display, write directions on a chalkboard behind the station, with labels or notes on the dishes so that guests know what they are. Provide small rocks glasses, rather than highballs, in case guests don't like what they've put together. No need to waste perfectly good booze! Here are some ideas to get you started:

Base	Juices/Sauces	Garnish
Pepper-infused vodka	Yellow tomato juice	Cocktail onions
Bacon-infused vodka	Red tomato juice	Bacon strips
Plain grain-based vodka	Equal parts tomato/mango juice	Black and white pepper
Blanco tequila	Hot sauce	Celery stalks
Joven mezcal	Fresh lemon juice	Fresh green beans
Reposado tequila	Worcestershire	Pepperoncinis
Gin	Horseradish	Shrimp

vodka with horseradish for more than a day and it will become a tincture palatable only in small amounts; infuse ginger for a day and you'll barely be able to taste it.

One of my favorite infusions is a combination of orange, lime, grapefruit, and lemon. It's crisp and refreshing, and goes well with soda or freshly juiced or muddled cranberries. The jar itself is a stunning and colorful display for the kitchen. You can make your infusion an aquavit by using dill, caraway, or pepper, or a combination of all three. Think about all of the other combos you could make with vodka—blueberry, basil, pepper, mint, juniper berries, elderberry, sage, mango, ginger, bacon, you name it!

READY, SET, INFUSE!

Start your experimentation with small batches so you don't get stuck wasting booze you don't like. If any of the ingredients you want to use have pith, stems, or leaves, remove them before infusing, because they'll impart a bitter taste. Citrus peels, however, are wonderful jolts of flavor, so remove the pith, eat the fruit and just use the peels. Get creative! For more control, tie each ingredient of your infusion into a separate piece of cheesecloth (a quarter cup is a good amount to start with).

Place the sachets in a 16-ounce mason jar and cover completely (air could discolor or rot them) with a midrange vodka. Remember that infusing a crappy vodka doesn't make it taste any better. You want something decent.

Each day, nose the jar and taste. If one of the ingredients is taking over in a way you don't like, just pull its cheesecloth-wrapped ball out for the remainder of the infusion, or simply take out some of its bulk and put it back. Infusions can take up to two weeks,

CHEERS!
A tradition in Russia and Poland is to toast each and every time a new round is served. When hosting a tasting party with vodka, play up the tradition for a fun spin on the rarely celebrated spirit.

depending on what it is and the intensity you are going for. You'll have to play around to see, and check your creation regularly. Here are a few delicious combinations to get you started:

Strawberry, blueberry, or raspberry and basil vodka: Leave berries whole; put basil leaves in whole; infuse for about a week. The basil flavor can get very intense, so you may decide to take the basil out after a day.

Ginger or lemongrass vodka: Slice fresh ginger or lemongrass thinly; infuse for up to two weeks. This is delicious with club soda.

Rosemary vodka: Bruise rosemary leaves with a muddler or pestle and place stems in whole; infuse up to two weeks.

Blueberry and mint vodka: Leave blueberries and mint whole; infuse about three days to a week.

Lemon, blood orange, and/or lime vodka: Peel and remove the pith from the peels. Infuse with the peels for up to a week.

Green Tea Vodka: Use bruised, whole green tea leaves; infuse up to one week.

Cucumber vodka: Peel and slice cucumber; infuse for about a week.

INFUSE, DRINK, AND CELEBRATE!
If you've created several varieties of infusions, that's reason enough to throw a party! If infusing liquor inspires you and you want to try a lot of combos, encourage everyone to get together by creating a standing happy hour every week at your house. After all, it does no good to hoard them. Have friends over for a tasting and send them home with an infusion recipe. Display the raw ingredients in vases for décor.

VODKA: NOT JUST FOR DRINKING

Vodka's neutral character makes it a wonderful household product all around. And if your stash is low and you don't have enough vodka for more drinks, these options are a great way to finish off the bottle and make room for new ones.

GETTING BACK TO SQUARE ONE

Forget Jolly Rancher and whipped cream–flavored crap.

When Allison Evanow started her vodka brand Square One Organics in 2006, she saw a gap in the market—there were no organic vodkas and few viable flavored ones.

"The time had come. I am a foodie and I realized that a drier, more sophisticated palate was coming into play in the cocktail world. You either had straight vodka, and super froufrou vodkas or gins on the market, and nothing in between," she says. "For me, it was about bringing sophistication to the category."

She then enlisted Dill Scott as her distiller, a former perfumer who had developed a line of organic aromatherapies, and went to work creating four organic, rye-based products: a straight vodka, cucumber vodka, basil vodka, and botanical vodka, all of which are made from whole fruits. I asked her how customers can pick a decent vodka:

How can we know whether a product contains artificial flavorings?

It's so hard for a consumer to find this out. The word 'natural' does not mean real ingredients were used. People would be shocked to know that some brands charging $35 a bottle use synthetic flavors in a lemon product. You want flavored vodkas where they've used the whole real fruit in the process. The brands that do will make it clear in their marketing, but that takes some research. For example, Hangar 1 posted videos of real mandarin blossoms steeping in the alcohol they make on their website. It's more of the big international brands and mass marketed ones that are importing tanker trucks full of neutral spirits from Archer Daniels Midland—a food and biofuel processing company—and making it their own. This type of sourcing isn't just in vodka, it's in lots of other types of spirit categories as well.

What can a vodka label tell us about what's inside the bottle?

The more specific it is, the better. We always mention that we're using 100-percent organic rye so customers know that's the base grain that we produce in house. We also list out our ingredients. We demonstrate that we don't use citric acid or glycerin as additives. Under organic label laws we couldn't use glycerin or anything fake in our product anyway. But don't be scared of the words "flavoring" and "essences" on the label. In our case, it refers to a technical process of distilling the whole fruit into individual essences that are blended at the end.

Can we even tell the difference between artificially flavored and organic vodkas?
Absolutely. Because of the neutral nature of vodka, there are far fewer flavor variations than in other categories so it's harder to differentiate between the nuances. But you can tell between a product that burns and a product that tastes fresh and smooth.

Should consumers always buy small indie vodkas?
It used to be that drinking the big, well-known brand showed you were "in the know." Now it's the other way around. The art of discovery and authenticity is more important than name recognition. I could have done something easy and froufrou and laughed all the way to the bank. But it's not who I am.

How can you train your palate away from sweeter products?
Begin by mixing a bone-dry spirit with other ingredients in the cocktail that play the sweet role. A lot of the brands take their vodkas down to 70 proof and add sugars, and we've been trained to expect that. Once your palate starts adjusting to natural sugar, then you start drinking drier over time. Throw an herb into it instead of a sweetener and see how your world will change.

Homemade vanilla extract: One Christmas, in lieu of cards, I made our family and friends homemade vanilla extract. I bought four-ounce, clear Boston round pharmacy bottles from SpecialtyBottle.com, filled them with vodka, and added a Madagascar bourbon vanilla bean, split in half, to each. I let them steep for two months. To enhance the bottle's appearance, I had labels made by MyOwnLabels.com, and voilà! I had a gift I knew everyone would use at some point. You can do the same, and when the jar gets low, simply add more vodka and the flavors from the bean will continue to develop. You won't need to replace the bean for another year or so.

Medicinal: In the Soviet era, vodka was a cure-all, and Russians would drink it with teaspoons of black pepper or turmeric to cure colds and ailments (there's not proof that this works, but pepper-infused vodka is fabulous in savory drinks). Many people in Ukraine drank vodka in the aftermath of the Chernobyl nuclear power plant explosion of 1986 with hopes it would fend off radiation poisoning. But the most interesting medicinal use is one claimed by herbalists that lavender-infused vodka soothed aches and pains when baked in the sun and drank. Vodka also tightens the pores and helps reduce foot odor when applied topically.

Sterilization: Since vodka is about 80-proof alcohol, it can be used to disinfect wounds or sterilize surfaces in a pinch. Infuse vodka with some peppermint essential oil and water, and you have a mouthwash. Housekeepers can dilute vodka with water and wipe glass and other surfaces with it for streak-free shine. In 2011, Moscow's Bolshoi Theatre's gilt was restored using an ancient recipe of egg whites, gold leaf, and vodka. Vodka can also remove minor mold, mildew, and stains from surfaces.

Perfume and air fresheners: To make a fabric spray, simply mix two-thirds parts vodka with one-third part of your favorite essential oil, letting it sit for a couple of days and shaking before use. Make your own perfume by mixing one part vodka with about 20 drops of essential oil, in any combo you please (lavender and orange blossom is divine).

GATEWAY VODKA COCKTAILS

Thanks to vodka's chameleon-like traits, you can mix it with anything, and there is always a way you can use vodka in a drink so that it works for your mood at the time. Here's what to drink when you...

Want to seal a deal: The Soviet Cocktail

The sherry adds a fruity twist to this martini-like mixed drink, but it's boozy and stirred, which shows you mean business.

2 ounces vodka
½ ounce dry vermouth
½ ounce dry sherry
Lemon peel for garnish

Add all ingredients to a shaker with ice. Stir vigorously with a bar spoon. Strain into a coupe glass. Drop a twist of a lemon peel into the glass.

Want to girl talk: The Moscow Mule

The dynamic flavors of this tall cocktail are perfect for sipping over conversation.

2 ounces vodka
1 teaspoon simple syrup
½ ounce fresh lime juice
1 cup ginger beer
Fresh mint for garnish
Slice of lime for garnish

Stir vodka, simple syrup, and lime juice in a shaker with ice. Pour into a highball glass, or if you want to get authentic with it, a copper mug. Top with ginger beer before garnishing with the lime slice and mint sprig.

Feel adventurous: Garden in a Glass

I came across this recipe on Liquor.com and love how balanced and refreshing it is with the addition of cucumber. The dill is an unlikely ingredient that reminds me of summer.

3 cucumber slices
2 dill sprigs
1 ounce lime juice
2 ounces vodka
$1/2$ ounce agave nectar

Add all ingredients except one cucumber slice and one dill sprig to a shaker with ice and shake vigorously. Strain into a rocks glass with fresh ice and garnish with a cucumber slice and dill sprig.

Need a standard go-to: Basil Vodka Gimlet

Take it back to the days of *Mad Men*, but with a modern twist, with this elegant and refreshing cocktail.

2 ounces vodka
1 ounce fresh lemon juice
1 ounce simple syrup
1 sprig basil, torn

Shake all ingredients, including the basil, vigorously in a shaker so that the basil leaves bruise and release their flavor. Strain into a chilled coupe glass.

Are feeling fun: Orange Crush

Refreshing and crisp, this drink is a sweet but classic alternative to the screwdriver.

2 ounces fresh squeezed orange juice
2 ounces vodka
1 ounce Cointreau

1 lime wheel for garnish

Pour all ingredients into a shaker with ice. Shake vigorously. Pour into a rocks glass and garnish with a lime wheel.

Are hosting: Spiced Vodka Delight

Sometimes you gotta entertain picky drinkers. This punch will satisfy their desire for the familiar with vodka and fruit while also bringing a new perspective to it with the spices.

Makes about 25 drinks
1 750 ml bottle of plain vodka
1 750 ml bottle of dry sherry
3 cloves
2 cinnamon sticks
1 teaspoon brown sugar
1 whole nutmeg, cracked
1 ounce fresh lemon juice
3 ounces honey
3 pineapple slices
3 orange slices

Combine all ingredients in a large saucepan and simmer over low heat for 20 minutes. Let cool; strain herbs and fruit, and serve in a punch bowl or carafe with ice.

CHAPTER 11

The Sweet and Lowdown on Liqueurs

Liquor lovers typically turn their nose up at liqueurs—distilled spirits flavored with herbs, spices, and fruit, and sweetened with added sugar. It's not because they aren't tasty, but because they seem like the sugary antecedent to the good stuff. To a certain extent, that is true, but they also play a crucial role in cocktails—elevating them with new flavors and punching up the proof.

The word liqueur comes from the Latin word, *liquefacere*, which means to dissolve. Hippocrates was believed to be the first person to flavor alcohol with herbs, and as early as the fifth century, herbalists and monks made liqueurs with herbs and botanicals in apothecaries they hoped would achieve immortality and overcome sickness. Once Columbus brought sugarcane from the New World, monks began using it to sweeten their crude elixirs.

These ancient recipes evolved over time, and a few brands honor this romantic tradition today. Chartreuse liqueur, for example, is made from a 17th century recipe with over 100 herbs, and Bénédictine, which begin in 1510 at Fécamp Abbey in France, is still made from the same secret recipe of 20-plus herbs including angelica, balm, cinnamon, clove, juniper, nutmeg, tea, and vanilla. You can find both in most liquor stores today.

Liqueurs sold in the United States must contain at least 20 percent sugar and those labeled "cremes" must contain at least 40 percent sugar. Purity is crucial in liqueurs, and they should not contain any chemical extracts or fake essences. However, artificial coloring is allowed and must be indicated on a bottle's label. The sugar's purpose is not only to make the spirit sweet, of course, but to also moderate the acidity of certain ingredients like rhubarb and orange.

Like rum or gin, liqueurs can be made anywhere in the world, and are known by different names, depending on where you are. For example, cordial is another word for liqueur. Though it used to refer to a fruit-based liqueur rather than an herbal liqueur, the two are now interchangeable throughout the United States. In France, liqueurs and cordials are almost exclusively called apéritifs, and in Italy, aperitivos. Several countries make liqueurs from their native herbs, plants, and vegetation, like France's St. Germain, a liqueur made from local elderflowers. But no matter what they're called or where in the world they're made, good liqueurs have always been considered to be curative and particularly good at aiding digestion. Today a good liqueur is defined by how well it stands on its own as a pre- or post-dinner treat, and also what it adds to cocktails.

HOW LIQUEURS ARE MADE

Liqueurs have distilled spirit bases of rum, cognac, Armagnac, vodka, absinthe, grape brandy, neutral grain spirits, or whiskey. If a bottle doesn't signify what type of spirit makes up the base, you can

LIQUEUR LINGO
Elixir: A liqueur with a lighter texture.
Crème: A sweet, heavy, dense liqueur, with usually double the sugar than a regular liqueur; the flavor is often attributed to one ingredient. Crème liqueurs are flavored with fruits, flowers, herbs, and nuts but do not actually include dairy products.
Fruit brandy: Brandy-based liqueurs with added sugar.
Amari: Plural for amaro, this covers a category of Italian liqueurs that are often distinctively bitter, and usually with a grappa or vodka base and botanical flavorings. Some vermouths are considered amari, such as Punt e Mes.

safely assume it's a neutral or grain spirit like vodka. With so many great ingredients and extraction methods available, you can find liqueur flavors made from everything under the sun. New types of liqueurs are popping up every day, and they are an interesting item to collect while traveling since every country has its own artisan style based on its native vegetation (I picked up a damiana liqueur while traveling in Baja, Mexico, for example, where the damiana herb grows rampantly).

Some liqueur companies like Marie Brizard have 30-something flavors, while others make one product extremely well, like Cointreau, the famous orange-flavored liqueur. Some of these recipes are super hush-hush, passed down through generations. Bénédictine and Chartreuse, for example, will never publish their 500 – year – old recipes, and only a few people at a time in the world know them.

Liqueur production boils down to this:

→ All ingredients are fully matured, inspected, cleaned, cut, pitted, crushed, stemmed, peeled, or sorted.

→ The ingredients are then macerated (steeped in tanks of alcohol), percolated (a process also used to brew coffee), or distilled (flavors are extracted by heating and condensing) with the alcohol.

→ Batches are combined to create a house blend.

→ The booze is redistilled and other herbs and spices may be added.

→ The finished product may be aged in wooden casks in temperature-controlled warehouses.

→ It sits for as long as it takes to get it perfect (that's one step technology hasn't managed to speed up), which could be several months.

→ The liqueur is refined through filtering.

→ Simple syrup or honey, water, or alcohol may be added. If cloudy, the liqueur may be filtered again, and then bottled.

TYPES OF LIQUEURS

The many different styles of liqueurs can be loosely lumped together by their flavors, and each flavored liqueur can be made by several different brands with subtle nuances. It would take an entire book to break down the various liqueurs you could find around the world, and their histories and origins, so I'll spare you. The important thing to know for your own experimentation is what various flavors are available, and who makes them so you can look for them in the store and at the bar. There are essentially four types:

- Seed, nut and plant liqueurs
- Fruit liqueurs
- Herbal and spiced liqueurs
- Amaro, singular of amari

Here are a few you may commonly find:

Flavor	Notes	Brands	Type
Absinthe	Made from wormwood and herbs, this distilled spirit has no added sugar so it's not technically a liqueur. But for practicality purposes—it has a very strong licorice taste and you'll probably only use a tiny bit in drinks—it is listed here.	Pernot, Pastis	Distilled spirit
Amaretto	Almond-flavored	Disaronno, Luxardo, Hiram Walker	Nut liqueur

Flavor	Notes	Brands	Type
Anisette, arak or ouzo	Licorice-flavored liqueurs and one of the first liqueurs produced commercially— by Bols in Denmark in the 16th century	Sambuca, Marie Brizard	Herbal and spiced liqueurs
Artichoke	Very bitter because it is *made* with artichokes, but does not overtly *taste* like artichokes	Cynar	Amaro
Caraway	A seed that is an excellent digestive aid	Kummel	Seed liqueur
Cherry	Tastes very sweet, and mixes well with just about anything	Cherry Heering, Luxardo, Kirsch	Fruit liqueur
Crème de banana	Banana-flavored	Hiram Walker, Leroux, DeKuyper	Fruit liqueur
Crème de cacao, chocolate	Chocolate-flavored	Godiva, Cadbury Cream, Mozart	Plant liqueur

Flavor	Notes	Brands	Type
Crème de cafe, coffee	Imparts a strong coffee taste, typically with a rum base	Tia Maria, Kahlua, Frangelico	Plant liqueur
Crème de Cassis	Made from black currants	Bols, Hiram Walker	Fruit liqueur
Crème de Menthe	Mint	Bols	Plant liqueur
Floral	The main ingredient is a flower; tastes light and airy	Crème Yvette (violet), St. Germain (elderflower), hum (hibiscus)	Plant liqueur
Ginger	Prominently made from ginger root	Domaine de Canton	Plant liqueur
Orange	Made with various types of oranges, which could be sweet or bitter	Grand Marnier, Cointreau, Triple Sec, Blue Curacao, Mandarine Napoleon, Solerno, Aperol, Amaro Nonino	Fruit liqueur and Amaro (Aperol, Amaro Nonino)
Herbal	Uses combinations of herbs and botanicals for a sweet, but dynamic taste	Bénédictine, Chartreuse	Herbal and spiced liqueurs

Flavor	Notes	Brands	Type
Honey	Honey is the predominant flavor	Drambuie (scotch base)	Plant liqueur
Peach	Flavored with peaches	Southern Comfort (bourbon base)	Fruit liqueur
Raspberry	Fruity and sweet, these mix well with just about any spirit.	Chambord	Fruit liqueur
Spiced	Flavored with a smorgasbord of items you'd find in your spice cabinet, like cloves, cinnamon and vanilla	Velvet Falernum, Fireball, Jägermeister	Herbal and spiced liqueurs
Sloe gin	Gin-based liqueur made from sloe berries	Plymouth, Sipsmith's	Fruit liqueur

"Cordials and liqueurs are the province of the lady of the house and she should study them not only as cocktail ingredients, but as to their individual service."
—*Crosby Gaige's Cocktail Guide and Ladies' Companion,* 1941

THE APERITIF TRADITION

Liqueurs can be poured over ice or drunk neat. In many European countries the ritual of the aperitif is a big deal. An aperitif is a pre-dinner drink aimed at relaxing the imbiber after a long day's work and preparing her for a meal by stimulating the digestive system, liqueurs' original intent. Popular aperitifs include Cynar, Campari, Aperol, and fortified wines and vermouths like Lillet or Carpano Antica. And while they can be enjoyed in any glass, it is fun to make a production out of them by serving them in small decorative, high-quality glasses like cordial glasses or mini snifters. Because of liqueurs' sweetness, a small pour is ideal anyway. Then take your seat on a porch rocking chair or patio at sunset and enjoy.

WHAT IS A DIGESTIF?

Certain ingredients in liqueurs such as aniseed, caraway seed, and peppermint have indisputable digestive benefits. While you could drink many different types of spirits as digestives, such as scotch or Armagnac, it is also traditional to help your dinner along with Sambuca, Kahlua, or other liqueurs. A digestif is often sweeter, so it doubles as dessert.

OTHER USES FOR LIQUEURS IN THE KITCHEN

Thanks to liqueurs' sweet and widely flavored nature, you can find other ways to put them to good use in the kitchen. Which comes in handy when, say, you can't get rid of that 750-milliliter bottle of absinthe (most cocktails only require a drop or two). Here are a few things you can do with any extra liqueur you've got lying around:

- Add two tablespoons to the batter of any sponge cake.
- Pour a shot over vanilla ice cream.
- Add two tablespoons to the mixture of cake or brownies before beating in the egg whites.
- Pour a small amount into a fruit salad.

THE PROPER PROPORTION

To add just the right amount of liqueur to a homemade drink without overpowering or over-sweetening the cocktail takes some tinkering. In general, Marcia Simmons, who wrote *DIY Cocktails: A Simple Guide to Creating Your Own Signature Drinks*, says she does it by starting with a 3-2-1 ratio—three parts spirit, two parts liqueur, and one part citrus, juice, fruit, or bitters. Since liqueurs can vary so drastically in their consistency and level of sweetness, taste the ones you may use separately before adding them to a drink. Mix a smaller proportion in a shot glass so as not to waste the ingredients, and tinker from there.

COMPOSING CORDIALS: MAKE YOUR OWN LIQUEURS

Making homemade liqueurs is fun, and they make amazing gifts (trust me, everyone will be impressed). They will keep for several months. The following are traditional recipes from 1954's *Home Made Wines, Syrups, and Cordials: Recipes of Women's Institute Members*, which date back to the mid-19th century, including a limoncello, which Italians traditionally made at home. You can loosely use the same instructions to create liqueurs from different

TO THE MAX:
EVERYTHING YOU NEED TO KNOW ABOUT LIQUEURS

With so many liqueurs available on the market and so many flavor profiles to choose from, I turned to Adam Seger, a Chicago-
based cocktail consultant and creator of hum, a rum-based
botanical liqueur, to help us decipher what's out there and how
to get the most out of them.

What are the most common misconceptions about liqueurs?
That they should be low-alcohol. A Grand Marnier, for example,
is 80 proof and brings a good amount of base spirit to the drink,
and that's what you want. There are a lot of liqueurs that are
only 15 percent alcohol and that makes them more of a syrup. In
those cases, you may be better off adding a fruit puree to your
drink. I think an area of liqueurs that gets forgotten about are
amari, which are usually 70 to 90 proof.

What is the best way to use a liqueur?
Anytime you're making a drink, do everything you can to avoid
putting simple syrup into it. It brings nothing to the drink but
sugar. With a liqueur, you've got the sweetness for balance but
you've got all of those flavors and nuances. It makes for a much
more dynamic cocktail. Liqueurs, at their best, are an amazing
way to freeze time and enjoy something out of season, because
they are made from botanicals and ingredients when they are at
their prime freshness and ripeness.

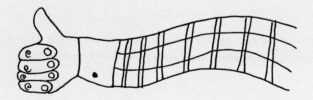

How can we tell if a liqueur is good or bad?
It's all about the quality of the sweetener and the quality of the

actual fruit or flavoring that they add. Think about it like food: a black raspberry ice cream made with fresh cream from no-hormone cows, real vanilla, and real raspberries is going to taste a lot better than one made with mass-produced milk, black raspberry flavoring, and corn syrup. If there's artificial flavor or coloring, they have to put that on the label, so look for it.

You get what you pay for, and you can never make a good cocktail with poor quality liqueurs. If you get a strawberry liqueur that is $10, it has cheap sweetener and will be far re-moved from actual strawberries. Find out what the base spirit is, which will give you an indication of the product quality. Grand Marnier uses beautiful cognac as a base. It goes without saying that they are not going to start adding flavorings. Hum uses a rum base, which goes well with its hibiscus, ginger, and carda-mom flavorings. If you're ready to drop $40 on a liqueur, test it first in one serving at a bar, even up against its competitors. It should taste natural. Also watch the hangover factor. Because of the sugar in liqueurs, if you are using a low quality distillate you can hide a lot of flaws with sugar initially, but you will notice headaches from it the next day.

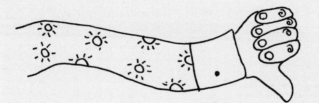

What are the five most versatile liqueurs you know of and why?
Everyone should keep five types of liqueurs on hand to make just about anything:

1.   Grand Marnier—an orange liqueur, it can stand on its own after dinner and also come through in a cocktail, dessert, and savory food like shrimp.

2. One amaro—a choice of Fernet-Branca, Campari, Aperol, or Gran Classico can bring instant complexity to anything you add it to.

3. One floral—St. Germain, an elderflower liqueur, offers quality with a base spirit from Burgundy, is light and floral, and offers good consistency in drinks; hum offers a unique profile that lightens heavy spirits in a drink.

4. One herbal—choose something like Chartreuse or Bénédictine, which bring a savory element to a drink that makes it a little more food-friendly and will get your appetite going.

5. One other fruit—whether plum, cherry, whatever—that is based on your personal taste and what types of things you like to mix. With those, definitely splurge because it is a real treat.

What's a liqueur's shelf life?
Definitely use them within a year of opening for the best and fullest flavors.

What advice would you give for experimenting with liqueurs at home?
For Christmas gifts, it's the coolest thing ever to give homemade liqueurs, but making them in the summertime is great too.

Whether you have a garden or a farmers' market, or even a fruit-of-the-month club, making liqueurs is a great way to use produce before it rots. When the fruits are so ripe and soft and aromatic you know the next day they will be inedible, throw some booze on top of them in a jar. In general, three days is a good infusion. The firmer the fruit, the longer it can go. The softer the fruit, the faster the alcohol will start breaking down the fibers and it will get cloudy. At that point filter it, then sweeten it with your choice of maple syrup, cane syrup, or maybe honey syrup. Personalize them for your home bar. The process is pretty bulletproof. Booze and sugar are two of the oldest natural preservatives out there.

fruits, herbs, and spices. In time, you'll find your best flavors and concoctions just the way the monks and Martha Washington (see her recipe on page 275) did before us—through trial and error! For a fun test, put your homemade liqueur up against its commercial counterpart for a blind tasting with friends and family. Identify the differences in taste, as well as the aromas.

Whiskey Currant Cordial

1 pound white currants

1 lemon rind without the white pith

$1/2$ ounce grated ginger

1 quart whiskey

1 pound sugar cubes or regular sugar

Strip white currants from their stalks, wash and drain the fruit, then place in a large jug. Add lemon rind, grated ginger, and whiskey. Cover the jug and let stand for 24 hours. Strain through cheesecloth. Add sugar to the liquid and let stand another 12 hours. Then bottle and cork.

Raspberry Liqueur

1 quart gin

1 pound raspberries

1 pound raw sugar

$1/2$ pints water

Put gin and raspberries in a mason jar, cover, and keep at room temperature for a few days. Separately, make a simple syrup and let it cool. Strain gin and fruit through cheesecloth and add cooled syrup to the liquid in the jar. Filter the mixture, bottle, and cork.

Cranberry Cordial

2 cups sugar

1 cup water

1 cup cranberry juice

24 ounces fresh cranberries

2 1-liter bottles of vodka

Combine sugar, water, and cranberry juice in a large saucepan over medium high heat. Bring to a boil, stirring constantly. Once the sugar has dissolved, stir in cranberries and bring to a boil. Then reduce the heat and continue to stir the cranberries, thoroughly mashing them. Turn off the heat and let the mixture cool. Transfer cooled cranberries to a large pitcher with lid, pour in vodka and stir well. Refrigerate 2 days then pour through a colander. Strain mixture again through cheesecloth and pour into decorative bottles.

Limoncello

12 lemons

1 $1/_2$ cups sugar

1 1-liter bottle of vodka or grappa

Juice the lemons and reserve juice for another purpose. Cut the rinds into quarters. Place the lemon rinds and sugar in a large pitcher with a tight-fitting lid and stir well, using a spoon to break up the lemons to extract remaining juice. Add the vodka or grappa and stir well. Cover and refrigerate for 24 hours, then stir well and taste, adding more sugar if necessary. Refrigerate for six more days, stirring every day. Strain the mixture through a fine mesh strainer, pour into bottles, and store in the fridge.

MISS AMERICAN PIE . . . LIQUEUR

George Washington loved his wife Martha's Cherry Bounce— a homemade cherry liqueur the first president took on his journeys and also served to guests at his home. We know this because Martha recorded her recipe in a memo on her hus- band's stationary.

But in this modernized recipe, we forgo using the fruit's juice, as Martha did, and instead simmer and bottle whole cher- ries. We also amp it up with a little 18th century American flair with the addition of cloves, cinnamon, and nutmeg. Feel free to substitute the brandy for other spirits like an aged rum or whiskey, but you may find that the one made from brandy is smoothest and sweetest. You can make it in late summer, when cherries are at their ripest, and store the bottles in a cool, dark place until Christmas, when you can give them as gifts.

6 cups whole cherries
1 quart cognac
2 cups cane sugar if using sour cherries; 1 cup sugar and 2 ounces fresh lemon juice if any other cherries
3 whole cloves
1 whole nutmeg, cracked in half
1 cinnamon stick

Combine the cherries, sugar, and spices (and lemon juice if nec- essary), in a saucepan and simmer over medium heat. Reduce heat to medium-low and continue to simmer for 20 minutes, stirring occasionally. Remove and let cool. Pull out the whole spices and pour the mixture into a large glass jar and add the brandy. Attach the lid, shake, and store in a cool, dark place for three months. Strain into a new, clean glass jar (or several smaller jars). It will keep for about two months.

GATEWAY LIQUEUR-LADEN COCKTAILS

No matter what base spirit you prefer—rum, gin, tequila, whiskey, you name it—there's a liqueur-loving cocktail that's just perfect for you. Here's what to drink when you...

Want to seal a deal: The Negroni

This boozy Italian aperitif is a classic first created in 1919, and basically consists of sweet vermouth, gin and bitters. Campari, an orange amaro, is most often used as the bitters part, but not always. Order this drink to your specifications, which could be straight up or with one large ice cube; with an orange peel or a lemon peel, and you show you know exactly what you want and how to get it.

2 ounces gin
1 ounce sweet vermouth
1 ounce Campari (or other preferred orange liqueur)
Orange peel or lemon peel

Mix all ingredients in a rocks glass with ice and stir. Drop in the peel for garnish.

Want to girl talk: The Anacaona Apéritif

This recipe comes from the Ladies United for the Preservation of Endangered Cocktails (LUPEC) in Boston. The bubbly, interesting, and herbal concoction is named after Queen Anacaona, one of the earliest Taino leaders to resist the Spanish conquistadors in Haiti in the late 15th century. Its unique ingredients make for lively cocktail conversation.

1 ounce Dubonnet Rouge (a fortified wine)
3/4 ounce Grand Marnier (orange liqueur)
1 teaspoon St. Elizabeth Allspice Liqueur (rum-based spiced liqueur)
3 dashes Angostura bitters
2 ounces chilled brut champagne
Wide orange peel

Fill a shaker with cracked ice. Add all ingredients except the champagne and orange peel, and stir well. Strain into a flute or coupe glass, and top with the champagne. Squeeze the orange peel over the drink to release those fragrant and essential oils, and then gently rub the peel around the rim of the glass. Discard it and drink up!

Feel adventurous: Ladies' Cocktail
While I don't usually go for drinks with names geared specifically for babes (since many fall short of my liking), this one has interesting flavors and uses whiskey as a base, giving it a badass-ness alongside the anise and sweet pineapple.

Cracked ice
2 ounces bourbon
1/2 ounce Pernod (absinthe)
1/2 ounce any anise liqueur (for a licorice taste)
2 dashes Angostura bitters
Pineapple chunk for garnish

Fill a shaker with ice and add all of the ingredients. Stir very well. Then add the pineapple chunk to the glass, and strain the mixture over it.

Need a standard go-to: The Aviation
This classic cocktail combines cherry with citrus and gin in a balanced way. Lovely and sophisticated!

2 ounces gin
1/2 ounce lemon juice
1 ounce maraschino liqueur (such as Luxardo, which is
    cherry flavored)
Teaspoon of créme de violette (a floral liqueur)
1 maraschino cherry for garnish

Rinse a chilled cocktail glass with créme de violette. Shake the rest of the ingredients in a shaker with ice and strain into a chilled cocktail glass. Drop in the cherry for garnish.

Are feeling fun: D.O.M. Iced Tea

You can't get much closer to Mother Nature than green tea and the über-herbal Bénédictine liquor, the folks behind this recipe. It's also easy to make in a pitcher or punch bowl.

1 ounce of Bénédictine (herbal)
3 ounces chilled green tea
Green tea powder for garnish (optional)

Prepare green tea and let it cool. Pour Bénédictine into a stemmed glass or teacup, fill with ice, and add the green tea. Or multiply this recipe by the number of people you are serving, and add to a pitcher. In that case, keep the ice separate until ready to serve. Garnish with green tea powder and serve with a straw.

Are hosting: The Oaxacan Punch

This recipe from beverage consultant Tad Carducci makes about 30 drinks, and blends the bitterness of Averna with the smokiness of mezcal and sourness of the citrus juice to make for a tasty and refreshing punch.

37 1/2 ounces Averna Amaro (bitter orange liqueur)
22 1/2 ounces mezcal
15 ounces grapefruit juice
15 ounces lemon juice
7 1/2 ounces agave nectar
45 ounces ginger beer
7 1/2 ounces cold filter water
Grapefruit and lemon slices

Evenly split all ingredients between two punch bowls and stir gently. Add blocks of ice or provide ice on the side. Garnish with grapefruit and lemon slices.

CHAPTER 12

A Matter of Taste: A Step-by-Step Guide for Appreciating Every Type of Liquor

Now that we've covered the technical side of taste and how to work your way around a liquor store and bar menu, let's talk about how to conduct an actual tasting and how to decipher and communicate what your nose and mouth think of your subjects. This process will help ensure that you always drink something you love, or, at the very least, appreciate.

Your first reaction may be, "Whaaaaa? I can't stick my schnoz in a glass at a bar!" And the truth is, you would look kind of funny going through the following motions in public, particularly if you were all serious about it.

But I'll tell you, tasting parties are a blast to host and a comfortable way to get familiar with new liquors. Plus, you get an excuse to throw on your party dress, pull out your prettiest glassware, expose your guests to new booze, impress them with how refined you are, and learn your guests' tastes for future gift ideas and cocktail menus. Write your guests' comments about each spirit in your handy tasting log. Doing a home tasting exercise is also a great way to get a handle on a bottle you just don't know what to do with yet, or determine your preference in, say, a scotch or Demerara rum. Over time, tasting exercises will seem less like a step-by-step process and come more naturally when sipping spirits.

SETTING UP

When you're setting up for a tasting, even if it's a solo mission, avoid using plastic glasses, which greatly alter aromas and tastes of spirits (they contain all kinds of chemical compounds). Instead, opt for a tulip or cylindrical glass, which concentrates the aromas without putting forward that god-awful ethyl alcohol stink that burns your nose hairs.

Tasting involves focus, not only for your brain, but also your senses. Outside smells and heavily flavored foods taint your perception of a spirit, so avoid cooking, lighting scented candles, or placing fragrant flowers on the table during a tasting.

Keep water on the table for drinking in between sips of alcohol, and for rinsing glasses between spirits; make sure the water's filtered so no mineral or chlorine tastes affect your palate. Place an ice bucket on the table, so tasters can dump the rinsing water into it. Offer plain cracker or pretzel palate cleansers, but you'll want to avoid most other snacks during the actual tasting because their flavors and spices will tire out your tongue. That's why you also want to limit the number of spirits you try— three is ideal, definitely no more than four. Otherwise, your brain will get exhausted and start making up aromas your nose can't truly confirm. Ensure that this is a blind tasting, so that your guests' perception of the liquors are not tainted by the brand's ads they have seen or what they may deduce about the taste from the bottle's label. Arrange tasting glasses from left to right, using some order suggestions below based on the spirit. Serve them at room temperature, as over-chilled or warmed spirits mask some of their pure essences. Do the tasting before dinner, so that you and your boozin' buddies have clean and focused palates. Pour your first spirit and read on!

ONE STEP AT A TIME: GENERAL TASTING GUIDELINES

1. *Bring the glass to eye-level and tilt it.* Look at the spirit's glow, color, and clarity, which could indicate the age of the spirit and how well it is filtered. The darker it is, the older it may be. Is it translucent or slightly opaque? The latter means it was probably not filtered properly after coloring was added. If the spirit is completely clear, it is unaged but could still lack translucence from proper filtering.

2. *Swirl the glass in order to observe the viscosity of the product.* How are the legs? Are they runny or slow? Is the liquid thick or thin? The slower the liquid trickles down the side of the glass, the more full bodied the spirit (it also indicates a higher alcohol content). As with wine, this action also helps aerate the liquor, which means letting in oxygen that releases aroma compounds.

3. *Unlike with wine, there's no need to put your face inside the glass.* Besides, you can't fit your face in a tulip glass anyway! Instead, tilt the glass and sniff slowly from a couple of

inches away; keeping your eyes closed to focus your brain and your mouth slightly open to eliminate the harsh, nasal alcohol burn. Encourage tasters to say what they smell out loud.

4. *Take a small sip, swish, and spit it out into the bucket.* This action gets your mouth accustomed to the flavor and intensity of the spirit because initially, your mouth will send wild signals to your brain like, "Hey, this stuff tastes crazy!"

5. *Take another sip so that a small amount of spirit is on your tongue's tip.* Roll it around in your mouth to expose it to all of your taste buds. Pay attention to its texture. How does it feel? Do you detect sweet, salty, sour, and bitter?

6. *Next, take a sip and let the booze go straight to the back of your mouth so that it hits each sensor.* What types of flavors do you notice? Use free association to immediately voice specific notes without restraint. See if you can be specific. Instead of saying "sweet," you might realize the spirit reminds you of crème brulée or hazelnut pudding. In addition to describing a spirit with jazzy, pointed adjectives, be sure to say not only whether you like or don't like it, but also why or why not. Does it remind you of floor cleaner? Does it taste too much like rubbing alcohol? Be creative. No answer is wrong.

7. *Swallow another taste and observe the finish.* Does your mouth feel velvety or gritty? Does the taste linger or instantly dissipate?

8. *Now add a few drops of distilled or filtered, room tempera-ture water to the spirit.* This opens up the spirit and changes the entire dynamic of the drink. Keeping the water at room temperature will ensure that it doesn't alter the spirit's essences. See if you can uncover any hidden flavors you didn't notice before. Water will also make the spirit easier to drink if it was harsh on your palate initially.

9. *Nose the glass again.* You can sometimes pick up additional or different flavors after having added water.

10. *Cleanse the palate.* Take a sip of water and press the crackers with your tongue against your palate in the roof of your mouth to thoroughly cleanse the taste buds and give them a break.

11. *Rinse the glass and repeat with the next spirit.*

Now, on to more specific suggestions for tasting each individual spirit!

TASTING GIN

Because gins are made with a range of botanicals and ingredients and each recipe is different, it's especially important to pay attention to subtle essences to truly learn the characteristics that differentiate them.

Here are three suggestions for setting up a gin tasting:

Foreign-Distilled Brand vs. American-Distilled: Since many gin brands originated in Europe but were then licensed to an American producer for distilling in the U.S., one way to conduct a tasting is to try an American-distilled label against a similar foreign distilled brand of the same style. This indication is on a bottle's label (it will say "Distilled in . . ."). You may notice very subtle differences, and it's fun to point them out.

Different Styles: Arrange no more than four glasses of different styles in an escalating row of juniper taste to show how this principal botanical influences the gin's character. For example, you arrange from left to right beginning with a floral or herbal American gin because it will most likely be lightest, then London Dry, Dutch or Genever, and finally Old Tom gin, which would be the most distinctive.

Four Brands of the Same Style: To get a handle on a certain style of gin, work with no more than four brands of gins in the same style (i.e a London dry) and try to guess what each distiller may have done differently in the process, and which you like best.

Tasting Tips

- Spicy and salty snacks can work with gin since they counter its bitter taste, but try to save them for the end of the tasting.

- Pay special attention to the gin's finish. An awesome gin will finish clean and fresh. The juniper shouldn't linger too long. Over time, you'll start to discern subtle differences from gin to gin, so don't fret if it seems daunting at first.

TASTING WHISKEY

New whiskey drinkers may find any whiskey's smoky, wood, and/
or aromatic flavors intense, so don't worry if it takes you a while to
find your stride.

Because of the vast array of whiskey products out there, you
can arrange a tasting many ways. Here are a few ideas:

Four Brands of the Same Style: This means four bourbons,
four scotches, four moonshines – you get the idea. Since various
brands may finish them in different casks or age them differently,
this way provides some insight into what makes a particular bottle unique.

Same Style, Different Ages: Older isn't always better, contrary to
popular belief. Or for you, maybe it is! This is how you find out. Try
scotches, bourbons, or ryes of different ages to find out which one
you like best and to figure out why. Arrange from youngest to oldest.

Four Different Styles of Similar Characteristics: Perhaps all of
the spirits you choose are made predominantly with rye, are all
about 10 years old, or were all finished in sherry casks. This way of
tasting is excellent for a newbie whiskey drinker, because the subjects are likely to be the very different, but on a fair playing field
because of their shared characteristic.

Same Style, Different Regions: This works best with scotches because their region of origin heavily influences their flavors (think
tones of seaweed, iodine, and brine, sweet sherry, or charred/
smokiness). Avoid wearing out your palate by arranging scotches

with increasing intensity; perhaps start with a Speyside and end with an Islay, or start with blended scotches and work your way up to the peaty single malts.

Tasting Tip

- There are special and beautiful glasses for tasting whiskeys made by Riedel, a renowned stemware company, and others, but a dessert wine glass, tulip, fluted—heck, even a rocks glass will do.

TASTING RUM

If you like rum but aren't sure which type is your go-to yet, go crazy by tasting them to find out!

When tasting rums in a flight, you can arrange them two ways:

From youngest to oldest: Choose several ages or styles of rum, arranging them from light to dark. The white rum will offer the purest expression of the sugarcane or molasses. If you want to get very specific, choose a selection of four ages or styles by the same brand for the best apples-to-apples comparison. Or try it both ways: one tasting of ages amongst various brands, and one of the same brand.

The same class, by country or distillery: Though rum is not affected by climate quite as much as some other spirits, each country and distillery employs its own techniques to leverage the heat's effect on fermented mash, to account for the variances in sugarcane crop that year, and when finishing or tweaking the rum. Arrange four rums of the same style (such as white, amber, dark, spiced, or añejo) made by four different distilleries in various places. Try to discern their distinguishing qualities and guess why. It's a fun game to play with guests and an interesting display of your geographic savvy.

Tasting Tips

- Look for balance. The rum should not be so sweet that it is syrupy or like biting into a sugar cube. If you are tasting an aged rum, tannins should not be present. It must be easy to drink, but show complexity.

- If there is any doubt, trust your nose on whether it is good or not.

TASTING MEZCAL AND TEQUILA

If you suspect your friends have never actually tasted a good tequila or mezcal, it's time to offer everyone a bit of enlightenment. Set up a tequila or mezcal tasting the following ways:

Different Styles, Same Brand: Choose a silver, reposado, and añejo (always 100 percent agave, rather than a mixto) from one distillery to demonstrate the difference in the ages, aromas, and complexities. Because tequila and mezcal can be harsh on a newbie's palate, this method might be an easier way to identify differences and gradually ease your guests' mouths from the most robust to the least.

One Style, Different brands: Choose one style, such as silver or reposado, from three different distilleries to demonstrate the nuances between house styles. Since every distillery may use a slightly different production process, you will notice subtle differences in smokiness, earthiness and sweetness.

Tasting Tip

- Keep it authentic. Incorporate the spirit's heritage into the festivities. When the tasting is over and you've poured the first glass of your guests' new favorite mezcal, for example, encourage them to practice the Oaxacan tradition of spilling a little bit of mezcal on the earth before finishing. It signals thanks to nature for the drink. Or serve the first pour in a glass rimmed with worm salt (recipe below) and a few slices of orange, as Oaxacans do.

HOW TO MAKE WORM SALT

Worm salt—or sal de gusano—is a popular condiment in Oaxaca and Guadalajara. Made from salt, ground chiles, and powdered worm, worm salt is usually eaten with mangoes, citrus, melons, and peaches. A mezcal glass is often rimmed in sal de gusano—a salty and spicy twist on the traditional salt rim. Since a powdered worm can sound a little scary to guests (not to mention a tad hard to get in the U.S.), make it sin-worm by grinding 1 tablespoon sea salt and 1 tablespoon Mexican chile powder (available at Latin markets) together.

TASTING BRANDY

There are so many different kinds of brandies that it can be difficult to narrow them down in a tasting. But there are several ways to do it:

Same category, different ages. See whether that VSOP cognac is actually worth the extra moolah over a VS Cognac; you'll also be able to understand how aging imparts certain characteristics in a brandy.

Same age, different categories. If you want to learn the nuances between, say, a cognac, a Calvados, and an Armagnac, make sure they're all around the same age. For example, you could pit a VS cognac and VS Armagnac against a Vieux or Reserve Calvados; as you sip them, see if you can taste how the different type of wood used for aging (or other parts of the production process) differentiates them.

Same category and age, different distiller. This is a good way to understand the difference between brand styles. For example, you could taste three plum brandies or three XO Cognacs made by three different companies.

Tasting Tips
- Brandy doesn't have to be served or tasted in a huge balloon snifter to be respectable (though it certainly is fun). A tulip or fluted glass will do.
- During the tasting, dab some of the liquid on the back of one hand. The warmth of your hand will cause the alcohol to evaporate, and leave behind the essences of its flavor, such as chocolate, wood, vanilla, or fruit. Then sip, and your palate will confirm what your nose told you, thereby allowing you to appreciate its true character even more.
- When you taste, you may notice sweetness, lightness, or fruitiness. Think about whether the body is soft and smooth,

or bitter and harsh. The finish is the way brandy makes your mouth feel after swallowing, and the length refers to how long the sensation lasts. The best brandies will have a long finish. Younger brandies have a stronger taste while the finest brandies will be so smooth you won't believe they are high proof.

TASTING VODKA

Vodka is the most difficult spirit to taste because many times, the taste has been purposely distilled out of it. Still, it is a good exercise. To get the most out of a vodka tasting, line no more than three vodkas up in one of two ways:

Same style, different brands: Tasting different brands of the same style (say, three Polish vodkas) allows you to hone in on what you like and don't like about a certain type, as opposed to swearing it off because you had one brand you didn't care for.

Different styles (i.e. a Polish, domestic, and Finnish brand): Trying a Polish vodka next to a domestic and Finnish one will help you learn about the characteristics that might make a Polish vodka better with a certain mixer, or a Russian vodka better with fish. This type of tasting is best for a novice, particularly because the different styles will be made from different matter, such as potato, wheat, or rye.

Tasting Tips
- To avoid tainting the flavors during your introduction to the spirit, do not taste the vodka ice cold (though I realize that may make this mostly tasteless spirit easier to drink. The point is

to train your palate here!).

- Pay special attention to the grain or base on the nose. It's very likely the smell will be neutral if unflavored, so watch for congeners that may make it smell a little off—like nail polish remover, rotten eggs, or wet hay. If the vodka has any of these—even subtle—aromas, it's likely poor quality.

- Heed texture. The matter from which vodka is made can affect its texture. Vodkas made from wheat may give you a crisp taste, while those made from potatoes will offer a more creamy mouthfeel. Describe these qualities freely while tasting. Other adjectives that might be useful are grainy, buttery, or beady. If the vodka feels heavy or oily, it may have been rounded with water and sugar, which is no good.

TASTING LIQUEURS

Because liqueurs come in a range of variations that include seemingly everything under the sun, the only way to truly compare liqueurs in a tasting is to lump them into flavors, which may contain different spirit bases or a different type of the fruit. For example, you can do an orange liqueur tasting with Grand Marnier, Solerno, Bols Triple Sec, Mandarin Napoleon, and Cointreau; or you can do a cherry liqueur tasting with Luxardo, Cherry Heering, and Kirsch. You can throw some cheapy brands in between to really taste the difference and drive home that you get what you pay for.

In particular, you'll want to observe a few things:

Smoothness: How does the liqueur go down and how does it feel in your mouth? Is it silky and natural or is it cloyingly sweet, almost sticky? You'll want it to be the former.

Flavor: Is the predominant flavor subtle or overpowering? Like with other spirits and in cocktails, you're looking for balance. What other flavors and spices can you identify? How close does the flavor taste to its origins? For example, a banana liqueur should have a fresh banana taste and smell.

Tasting Tip

- Once you've finished the tasting and have determined your favorite and why, research some fast facts about how that liqueur is made. Perhaps it is made from a certain type of fruit that is grown in a certain type of climate, or perhaps it has a rum base you like. Doing this will help you hone your tastes. You can also identify characteristics in each liqueur that you think would make it pair well with certain other ingredients. Catalog this information for future cocktailing at home!

CHAPTER 13

Party On:
Everything You Need to Know
to Shine at your Shindig

Hosting a party is the most fun when you've got your bar dialed,. For one, having a captive audience in your home allows you to share your most bangin' boozy beverages and, real talk –gives you a chance to show off your new bartending skills! It's also an opportunity to show your besties the best possible time, on your own terms. Once they get a taste of the gorgeous cocktails you've prepared, your friends will never settle for a whiskey and Coke or vodka tonic again! Show them how to enjoy themselves more by drinking well and no one will deny your reign as the hostess with the mostest (this phrase, by the way, was coined to describe Perle Mesta, a Washington, D.C. feminist, socialite and ambassador to Luxembourg during the Truman administration). Her keys to a successful party? Cool guests, hot food and a warm hostess.

But of course, you don't want to be so busy mixing drinks for your guests that you have no time to enjoy their company. Having a party is a lot like cooking. If you spend time preparing in advance, all you'll have to do is sit back and put it on the stove, so to speak. To relieve some of your party duties, don't be afraid to pre-make drinks or have guests mix their own. It's only crucial that the drinks taste good and the ingredients are high quality. If your guests learn something in the process, bonus! Here are a few go-to party drink ideas that will have you living it up as much as your party goers:

BOWL' EM OVER: PERFECT PUNCHES

Punch comes from the Hindi word panch, which means five (as in the rule for putting the perfect punch ingredients together: one of sour, two of sweet, three of strong, one of weak). East Indian punch was made with a sugarcane distillate called arrack, plus spices, lemon juice, water or tea, and sugar in the 16th century. Punches, which eventually made their way to the Americas in the late 17th century and became a must-have at sophisticated parties, can be made with all kinds of spirits.

Punch may give you flashbacks to your jungle-juice-in-Igloo-coolers college days, but today's concoctions are much classier. Since a punch can be prepared in advance, it'll keep you from being chained to the bar. Plus, a punch allows guests to drink as much or as little as they like. They don't have to wait for you to ask, "Can I get you another?" Show your guests how much care went into a punch by placing an ingredient sign next to the bowl: "Fresh squeezed juice from 10 oranges, 1 teaspoon of homemade aromatic bitters . . ."

HELPFUL PARTY PUNCH TIPS

- One quart of punch will yield eight four-ounce servings. Each guest will probably have two or three servings over the course of a three hour party.

MAKE A PUNCH

Harvest Punch

This recipe from bartender Lynnette Marrero has enough high quality ingredients to impress guests, but is low maintenance enough that you won't break a sweat. It yields 30 servings.

45 ounces Zacapa 23 rum (you can substitute this for a
    younger aged rum to save on cost)
30 dashes Angostura bitters
2 1/2 ounces fresh-pressed apple juice
15 ounces lemon juice (from seven to eight lemons)
5 ounces pomegranate molasses
15 ounces star anise syrup*
Sparkling apple cider (optional)

Combine all ingredients (but sparkling apple cider) in a large pitcher with ice. Stir well and pour into a punch bowl, straining out the ice. Top with sparkling apple cider immediately before serving.
*To make star anise syrup, simmer 1 part sugar with 1 part water and 2 star anise until the sugar dissolves. Remove the anise and let cool.

Double Orchard Punch

From Meaghan Dorman, a bartender at Raines Law Room in New York City, this recipe makes about 20 servings and is not too boozy, making it easy to drink.

32 ounces fresh peach tea
24 ounces Laird's Applejack
12 ounces simple syrup
8 ounces lemon juice

Combine ingredients in a punch bowl, and add a block of ice. Garnish by floating the lemon wheels and apple slices in the bowl.

- Don't top off the bowl when your punch is getting low. Always replace it entirely so you get rid of the dregs and the watered down remains, which taint the flavors of the drink.

- Don't use ice cubes in punch bowls because they'll only water it down. Instead, set out a separate ice bucket so guests can add their own when served. If you want to chill the punch itself, you can thoroughly rinse a half gallon of milk or orange juice carton, fill it with filtered water and freeze it to create a large, slowly melting block of ice you can place in the bowl.

- Always strain all ingredients before adding them to the bowl. There's nothing grosser than seeing lots of fruit and herb dregs floating around in your delicious punch.

- If the recipe calls for soda or champagne, add it to the punch just before serving so the fizz will last as long as possible.

- Don't let your guests see a dry bowl unless the party's over. No excuses!

KEEP IT CLASSIC: DIY OLD-FASHIONED BAR

The old-fashioned is my go-to cocktail. Why? Because it's versatile, classy, and best of all, can be made with any spirit just about everywhere. Originally created in the 1800s with whiskey, this drink preserves the flavor of a spirit more than most cocktails because of its simplicity, so you can use quality booze without feeling guilty. This classic cocktail is also a great way for guests to find out if they like a particular spirit, so encourage them to play bartender and hone their tastes. A traditional old-fashioned goes something like this:

2 ounces spirit of choice

3 dashes of bitters

$1/_2$ ounce of sweetener, depending on your taste; or one sugar cube

Dash of club soda (optional)

Pitted cherry and orange slice (optional)

If working with a sugar cube and/or an orange slice and cherry, place these in a rocks glass, add bitters, and, if desired, a splash of soda. Crush them with a muddler or spoon, add an ice cube, and then the spirit. If you are working with a syrup sweetener, add all ingredients to the glass (still muddling the fruit) and top with ice.

Serving your guests old-fashioneds is a great way to show off your good taste and keep the bar fuss to a minimum. Consider putting out an old-fashioned bar with five interchangeable ingredients stations; guests can create their own desired combos, as long as they have the ratios down (put out an instructions sign or recipe cards to be sure). Replenish the bar throughout your party, and watch your guests get creative!

Spirits	Sweeteners	Bitters	Water	Garnish
Rye, scotch or bourbon whiskey	Simple syrup	Angostura	Oversized square cubes	Lemon twists

Spirits	Sweeteners	Bitters	Water	Garnish
100 percent agave tequila, either blanco, reposado or añejo	Agave syrup	Peychaud's	Regular ice cubes	Orange slices
Aged rum	Honey syrup	Flavored bitters, such as orange, chocolate, lavender, or whiskey	Soda water	Pitted cherries

FIGURING OUT HOW MUCH TO SERVE

The general rule of thumb is to plan for more than you think you'll need. That means to assume each guest will indulge in about two drinks the first hour and one per hour after that. Always buy extra garnish. They make nice displays and then you'll have it on hand if necessary. Some liquor stores have buyback policies for unopened bottles, which is especially helpful if you're only serving a couple of spirits. Always buy a little more than you think you need, and either return unopened bottles for a refund or save them for the next party.

Plan for about one pound of ice per person for the party. Be sure that the ice you use is made of filtered or distilled water, as tap water has minerals and chemicals that can taint the flavor of a drink.

ARE YOU BEING SERVED?:
GUIDELINES FOR WHEN TO OFFER WHAT

Throwing a spirit-acular party is all about showing guests a good time. Here are a few guidelines for deciding what to serve:

ARE YOU SERVING ONE COCKTAIL AT A TIME?

YES	NO
Don't switch back and forth between spirits. Switching every other drink's base between gin and scotch, for example, could be a recipe for Tums, not to mention an unpleasant mix of flavors that will detract from your guests' full enjoyment of each cocktail.	Have two different spirits available. If you are serving two types of drinks simultaneously throughout the night, offer one with a light spirit (blanco tequila or gin), and one with a dark spirit (like aged rum or whiskey), so that everyone's preference is met.
And	And
If you decide to serve just one signature cocktail, make sure it's not overwhelmingly bitter, sour, or sweet.	Offer at least two taste options. To satisfy everyone's palate, offer two types of cocktails, like a bitter and sweet drink or one sweet and one sour drink.

DO YOUR GUESTS NEED TO DRIVE?

YES

Opt for drinks that are not too boozy. You want your guests to remember how fun the party was, after all. Choose drinks with ratios that consist of no more than a third of alcohol. They will still be delicious, but your guests will thank you later.

NO

Bring on the shots, people! (Just kidding.)

WILL THERE BE MORE THAN 10 PEOPLE?

YES

It's okay to serve your drinks in high-quality plastic glasses with a nice shape, but no plastic cups!

NO

Always serve drinks in your best glassware. These guests are probably your closest friends and family, so make drinking your cocktail an experience by letting it shine in a nice glass.

And always garnish, garnish, garnish. Present the drinks well. Go to the farmers' market and experiment with fruits and vegetables to incorporate into your cocktails and to display.

BOTTLE MEASURING CHEAT SHEET

Each serving of spirit is about 1 to $1^1/_2$ ounces, give or take, so that is the guideline I've used to come up with serving estimates based on the size of the bottle you buy.

- Fifth = Roughly 25 ounces, about 15 drinks
- Liter = Roughly 34 ounces, about 22 drinks
- Half bottle = Roughly 13 ounces, about 8 drinks

PAIRING COCKTAILS WITH FOOD

You wouldn't think there'd be such a dilemma in pairing a drink with a dish. After all, we do it with wine, right? But there are a few challenges with spirits. For one, many bartenders believe that the cocktail is not meant to be paired with food. Not only is savoring a cocktail meant to be its own ritual, but their characteristics do not always mesh well with foods the way wines do. Others believe that to be a bunch of malarkey and that cocktails have the same potential to pair harmoniously with that beef bourguignon as a merlot. The only way to know for sure is if you try it yourself. When you do, try a few simple tips to get the most of your experience:

Go low on the sugar. Sugary drinks can overwhelm the tastes in food (after all, it is often used as a masking agent).

Mind the temperature of your booze. If a spirit is served too cold when paired with a dish, it will bring forward the food's acidic, salty, and bitter flavors, while calming the syrupy sweetness of sugars. If a spirit is served at a warmer temperature, the dish should be low in sugar, or the combo will be too heavy.

MEET THE GOODETIME GALS

According to their website, Cameron Cooper and Lindsey Reynolds have many loves in life: 1950s housewives, pastel Pyrex bowls, the perfect polka-dot dress, Southern hospitality, picnic foods, and a well-dressed cocktail (and man). They combined those interests with the creation of their event bartending service, which offers vintage flare and impeccable taste, and began out of a love for fresh drinks, like muddled watermelon basil margaritas during the sweltering Texas summer. These two libation-loving ladies adore scotch and retro cocktails and they bring the Betty Draper and Joan Holloway act with them to gatherings

all over Austin. They also know how to throw a bitchin' party. Planning the details of an event seem overwhelming when you're throwing together several different elements that don't quite synch. So what is the Goodetime Gals' best tip for entertaining?

Follow a theme. Decide on an overarching idea like Mexican, speakeasy, cowboy BBQ, carnival—whatever theme you'll have the most fun with. Then choose colors, drinks, and décor accordingly. And just because it's a theme, doesn't mean you have to go overboard with it. Subtle details in the décor, and purposefully chosen drinks that match the ambience work just as well. As hostess, play the part, too! Make drinking your cocktails an event worth dressing up for.

Don't force your food and booze to compete. You want to look for complementary characteristics, and the best way to do that is to pair opposites. For example, that's why sour drinks pair well with spicy foods.

Seek inspiration from the dish's garnishes. If a recipe calls for a basil sprig, explore basil drinks, for instance.

Choose a versatile drink that could go with multiple courses. If you try to pair a cocktail for each course, you might have lots of really drunk people on your hands (including yourself). That's not to mention you don't want people to race to drink them and not have time to truly savor them.

Avoid bubbly drinks. I like a good fizz before dinner, especially, but nix them once the dinner starts. They won't stay carbonated.

Heed texture and mouthfeel. If you are eating pork, for example, you'll want to serve a cocktail that cuts the grease and which exhibits the spicy and earthy notes that you'd choose a malbec for. This promotes balance and overall enjoyment on your palate.

If it tastes right to you, it works! Pairing can be a fun and interesting lesson in flavors, so don't stress over it.

PARTY PROTOCOL: HELPFUL HOSTING HINTS

So you have an awesome drink menu and your house is ready for guests, but now it's time to talk about all of those other things a good hostess is responsible for, like etiquette. When in doubt, heed the traditions our mothers' and grandmothers' followed, 'cause boy did they know how to throw a classy shindig! Here are a few helpful tips:

→ Relax. Guests will sense stress, which affects the ambience.

→ Greet everyone as they walk in the door and immediately offer each guest a drink.

→ Walk through the party with a tray of food because people are often too shy to be the first ones to help themselves to a spread.

→ Don't take guests up on their offer to help. Make them sit down and enjoy themselves.

→ Always make sure you have enough toilet paper and napkins. These seem like simple and silly "musts," but running out could be a total bummer for your partygoers.

→ Avoid leaving cocktail messes out for an extended period of time. This is where good preparation comes in handy. If you've prepared your drinks and snacks in advance, you'll have plenty of time to make sure there are no unsightly spills or dirty dishes lying around.

→ Stay sober (mostly). Your goal is to have a good time as host, but you've also got to be on top of your game, helping guests mingle with each other, conversing intelligently, and keeping things orderly.

GROUNDS FOR DELICIOUSNESS: COFFEE COCKTAILS

I adore hosting brunch for several reasons, including that people rarely have other commitments during this time, and because breakfast food is yummy and cheap to make. Plus, you can have a ball with a Bloody Mary bar (see instructions on page 248) or flavored champagnes (think various syrups and fruit purees). And while an evening shindig can be kickin' till the wee hours of the night whether you want it to or not, a brunch party often lasts two or three hours, which leaves the rest of the day for other activities.

Best of all, you can give your guests an unexpected treat by pairing coffee with booze. And though coffee cocktails go best with brunch, you can really serve them any time, including late afternoon events (when you may need a pick-me-up), or after dinner. Great coffee cocktails are not only a novelty, they're also crazy delicious. To put together a memorable coffee concoction, it's important to know how much the quality of the coffee matters.

Like wine and spirits, coffee can contain notes like pomegranate, jasmine, citrus, almonds, or chocolate, which enhances cocktails (we're talking beyond the usual Baileys Irish Coffee here). But because coffee is complex, coffee cocktails are hard to do well. There are acids, sugars, and bitter tastes that must be factored into the formula, plus various brew methods and bean qualities.

Concocting a dynamic and tasty creation that perfectly marries seemingly odd ingredients requires trial and error. But a great coffee cocktail always starts with great coffee.

Trevor Corlett, owner and barista of MadCap Coffee in Grand Rapids, Michigan; Michael Philips, 2010 United States and World Barista Champion; and New York City coffee gurus Cora Lambert of RBC Bar and Troy Sidle of Alchemy Consulting reveal seven tips for better coffee—and therefore better coffee cocktails, here:

Freshness is key. In this case, coffee is *not* like a fine wine—it doesn't get better with age. From the time a bean is plucked from a tree to the time it lands in your cup, its flavor and quality have deteriorated quite a bit. The more a bean is exposed to oxygen, the more CO_2 gases release and the more rapidly flavors escape from it. Coffee is freshest within four to six days of roasting. Once coffee is ground, oils begin to go rancid and push to the surface of your cup (always grind beans at home immediately before use). The fresher your coffee, the better the coffee cocktail.

Buy your beans from a local roaster. Sometimes flavors in the brew are actually determined more by the roast process than the bean itself. Befriend a local roaster who is knowledgeable about the beans he carries and will guide you based on the flavor profile you'd like.

Aim for balance. Caffeine and alcohol can have an interesting result when mixed together, so use caution when experimenting with cocktails. The drink should be balanced and the flavors should complement each other, without one element dominating the other. Fortified wines, rums, and cognacs tend to pair naturally with coffee, while the earthiness of whiskey and tequila might make for a wet hay taste. But maybe not—it can depend on your brew method, so . . .

Experiment with brew methods to get your desired taste. Different brew methods result in different flavor profiles. For example, the immersion method, which involves fully immersing ground coffee in cold or room temperature water for a day, eliminates bitter qualities that usually arise in hot coffee. The French press method achieves great body in a coffee but can sometimes over-extract flavors. The Chemex or pour-over method produces balanced brews but is slow, and espresso offers a more concentrated brew but requires more time and expensive equipment. Each method will result in a different taste—even with the same bean—so experiment to see which works best with the base spirit you've chosen.

Use good, clean water at the right temperature. Just as fresh, pure water is important when distilling a quality spirit, it's also important when making good, flavorful coffee (minerals in unfiltered water taint the beans' flavor). Water that is too hot will turn the coffee bitter while water too cool will turn it sour. Let the coffee cool to the touch before mixing. Otherwise, the alcohol will burn when mixed with the coffee, smell like a distillery, and cause imbalance in the cocktail.

Brew at the proper ratio. Aim for a ratio of one-third ounces coffee to one-half ounces water for optimal brew strength.

Sugar and cream are your friends, but so are many other ingredients. Taste the coffee on its own and determine its subtle notes, which will guide your mixing flavors. Do you taste hints of pomegranate? Then grenadine, which is derived from pomegranate, may complement it. Allow the marriage of flavors even if they seem off the wall. You'll never know if you don't try!

Coffee doesn't go with only Baileys. Here are two recipes that combine tequila with espresso and fruity notes in unique ways you wouldn't expect.

Created by Justin Trevor Winters for CBTL
(The Coffee Bean & Tea Leaf Company)

Santa's Secret
1/2 ounce premium espresso
1/2 ounce silver tequila
1/4 ounce grenadine
Serrano chili
Cherry for garnish (optional)

Place 2 thin slices of Serrano chili peppers in a cocktail shaker. Add grenadine and muddle thoroughly. Pour tequila and espresso into cocktail shaker and add ice. Shake vigorously. Strain contents into a shot glass and garnish with a Serrano chili slice or cherry.

The Olifant*
2 ounces premium espresso
1 ounce vodka
1 ounce tequila
1 ounce cream liqueur
1/2 ounce Cointreau
Cherry for garnish

Place all ingredients in a cocktail shaker, add ice, and shake vigorously. Strain the contents into a martini or coupe glass. Garnish with a cherry.

*Olifant means elephant in several African languages

—▶ Remember what your guests like. Part of being hospitable is catering to their likes and recalling them later. Discreetly jot down notes. If you've hosted a guest before and are serving something he or she will enjoy, be sure to mention it (Brownie points!).

—▶ The goal is not to get your guests drunk. They will need to make it home, and you also want to be sure that everyone gets along and has a good time. Encourage guests to help themselves but keep an eye out for inebriation.

—▶ Never make a big deal out of nondrinkers, but do accommodate them. Create mocktails with fresh juices and serve them in the same glasses as the alcoholic ones, and never bring attention to their preference in front of other guests, since you may not know the circumstances.

HOLD 'EM OR FOLD 'EM: WHEN TO SERVE YOUR BEST BOOZE

There's no excuse for skimping when it comes to serving your guests. What you serve at your party is a reflection of your personality and taste. That said, there's no reason to mix your $90 bottle into a cocktail for guests who won't necessarily be able to taste the difference. I reserve tastings of my best bottles for intimate groups so that I can tell them the story of the spirit, why it is special, or to simply offer something exceptional to go with great post-dinner conversation.

HOW TO WIN OVER BEER DRINKERS

Are your guests more of a brewski crew, rather than liquor lovers? Win them over by combining the two. Yes, there is more to a "beertail" than meets the shot-in-a-pint-glass (move over, Jägerbomb). Bartenders have long known that mixing beer and liquor makes for chemically complex concoctions, but tipplers have just begun elevating beertails beyond their fraternity party reputation.

Beer cocktails—or beertails—combine the best qualities of the craft beer and craft cocktail movements: experimentation, refinement, and envelope-pushing flavors. At their best, beertails showcase the work of a brewer who tinkered with a limited, yet prized seasonal batch for months to get just the right hints of chocolate, hops, or fruit. In some cases you can even pass over the sparkling wine or flavored soda a cocktail recipe calls for in favor of an effervescent microbrew.

A proper beertail begins with a well-balanced cocktail and is topped with an equally dynamic craft beer (never shake the beer with ice, as it alters the texture and could potentially explode). The beer should either complement or contrast with the cocktail's flavors. Imbibers may initially taste only the brew but the cocktail's distinctive aromas rise through the head. By the middle of the glass, both beer and cocktail dance together on the palate like old friends.

Here, beertail revolutionaries share four recipes that pass, rather than bomb the beertail test:

SMOKIN' HOPS

From Ashley Routson, "director of awesomeness" at Bison Brewing in Berkeley, California, and founder of BeerMixology.com.

1 ounce mezcal
$1/2$ ounce lemon juice
$1/2$ ounce agave nectar
2 dashes hot sauces
4 $1/2$ ounces American IPA
Lemon peel

Shake all ingredients except for the beer with ice. Strain into
a pint glass filled with ice, top with the beer, and garnish with
lemon peel.

RUB & RYE
From Francesco Lafranconi, executive director of mixology and
spirits education for Southern Wine and Spirits of Nevada in Las
Vegas.

1 $1/2$ ounces rye whiskey
$3/4$ ounce maple syrup
$3/4$ ounce lemon juice
1 ounce egg white
5 ounces peach, apricot, or fruit beer
Mesquite salt or dry rub
BBQ bitters (available at specialty stores, TheBostonShaker.com,
    Kegworks.com, and Amazon.com)

Rim a double rocks glass with mesquite salt or your favorite dry
rub. Fill halfway with ice. Vigorously shake the rye, maple syrup,
lemon juice, and egg white; strain into glass. Top with the beer
and finish with five drops of bitters.

BEE'S NEST
From Timothy Faulkner, archivist at the H&F Bottle Shop and
former bartender for Restaurant Eugene and Sauced in Atlanta

1 ounce London Dry gin
$3/4$ ounce lemon juice

3/4 ounce honey syrup
  (see recipe below)
4 ounces white ale

Shake all ingredients except the beer and strain into an ice-filled Collins glass. Top with white ale.

HONEY SYRUP
Mix 2 parts honey with 1 part hot water until dissolved.

DARK & STOUTLY
From Adam Seger, a Chicago-based consulting mixologist, advanced sommelier, certified culinary professional, and creator of hum, a botanical liqueur.

1 1/2 ounces ginger habanero syrup (see recipe below)
1 1/2 ounces 15-year rum
1/2 ounce fresh lime juice
5 ounces stout beer
Lime wedge

Shake all ingredients except the beer in a shaker with ice and strain into a goblet filled halfway with fresh ice. Top with beer and garnish with lime wedge.

GINGER HABANERO SYRUP
Combine 1 quart turbinado or raw sugar; 1 fresh habanero pepper, seeded and chopped; 1 pound fresh ginger, sliced with skin on; and 3 cups water and boil for about three minutes to dissolve sugar. Cool, strain, and refrigerate up to three weeks.

WHAT CAN I BRING?

I asked Meaghan Dorman, a bartender at Raines Law Room in New York City, what her favorite entertaining tradition is and she did not disappoint. "If guests ask what they can bring, ask them to bring a special bottle they've been waiting to open. We all have one of these, and never seem to be able to justify opening it," she says. "All the guests then share a taste with the other guests, all of whom will appreciate it." This helps everyone learn about a new brand or spirit, and creates fun memories about opening a "special bottle." When guests gift you a bottle, post a sticky note to the bottom with the date, occasion, and the name of the giver. When you finally open it, send a note to the giver saying thanks, telling them what you liked about it, and what the occasion was, for a thoughtful touch.

WELL-READ:
CLASSIC COCKTAIL BOOK RECOMMENDATIONS

Want to learn more about entertaining and mixing up drinks at home? Get your feet wet with fine spirits and ingredients by making cocktails our mothers, grandmothers, and great-grandmothers drank. Here are a few vintage books that you may be lucky to find and want to keep handy for practice and parties. Plus, they just look cool on your bar. Dozens more can be found if you just keep your eye out at thrift stores and on Ebay and Etsy.

- *Jerry Thomas' Bartenders Guide: How to Mix Drinks* (1862) by the father of the American bar

- *The Savoy Cocktail Book* (1930) by hotel bar cocktail pioneer Henry Craddock of London's Savoy Hotel

- *Prohibition Punches* (1930) by Roxana B. Doran, which features concoctions by the wives of United States politicians

- *The Fine Art of Mixing Drinks* (1948) by David A. Embury, a lawyer and consumer-turned-drinks-guru whose wisdom is still lauded by bartenders today

Acknowledgements

I'd like to thank my mom, who came up with the fun and catchy title for this book and encouraged me to write it when the thought had not even crossed my mind. I guess that's what moms do. And then there is my dad, who encouraged me from a young age to follow my bliss and not to worry about money, hence why I decided to take on the laborious but rewarding task of writing this book. Members of the spirits industry have been unduly enthusiastic as well, which also encouraged me to pursue the project with vigor.

It goes without saying that my friends, Grandma Horne, and the Kulp and Munch families, have been great supporters of this work and I appreciate them tremendously. This project was a labor of love not only for me, but for my husband, Jay, who from the beginning believed in me, read the draft line by line, and never complained when I needed to taste a new product or test dozens of cocktail recipes...

Thanks to Lisa Butterworth and Patricia Mariani, the eagle eye editors of this book, as well as Lan Truong, my designer, and

Rebecca Pry, my illustrator. I wrote the following pieces first for TheLatinKitchen.com, where they can still be found: How to Make the Perfect G&T, Cachaça 101, How to Make the Perfect Mojito, 'On Sipping Tequila' with Bertha González Nieves, Infuse Tequila: Four Tips for Creating Tasty, Naturally Flavored Tequila, Pisco's New Day in the USA with Diego Loret de Mola, Grounds for Deliciousness, and How to Win Over Beer Drinkers.

Bibliography

Abercrombie, Paul. *Organic, shaken and stirred : hip highballs, modern martinis, and other totally green cocktails.* Harvard Common Press, 2009.

Abou-Ganim, Tony. *Modern mixologist : contemporary classic cocktails.* Agate Surrey, 2010.

Altaraz, I. M. *Factors motivating American social drinkers in accepting vodka.* 1958.

Ayala, Luis K. *Rum experience : the complete rum reference.* Rum Runner Press, 2001.

Axelrod, Alan and the Players. *Complete idiot's guide to mixing drinks.* ALPHA, 1997.

Bergeron, Victor J. *Trader Vic's rum cookery and*

drinkery. Doubleday, 1974.

Blue, Anthony Dias. *The Complete Book of Spirits.* William Morrow Cookbooks, 2004.

Bovis, Natalie. *Edible Cocktails: From Garden to Glass - Seasonal Cocktails with a Fresh Twist.* Adams Media, 2012.

Broom, Dave. *Rum.* Octopus Publishing Group, 2003.

Calabrese, Salvatore. *Cognac : a liquid history.* Cassell, 2005.

Carter, Youngman. *Drinking Champagne & Brandy.* Hamish Hamilton, 1968.

Chartier, François. *Taste buds and molecules : the art and science of food, wine, and flavor.* Houghton Mifflin Harcourt, 2012.

Chunder, Huey. *The Hangover Companion: A Guide to the Morning After.* Michael O'Mara, 2007.

Cunningham, Brian. *Liquid art : a practical guide to common liqueurs.* Roaring River Publishing Company, 1990.

Curtis, Wayne. *And a bottle of rum : a history of the New World in ten cocktails.* Broadway, 2007.

Cutler, Lance. *Tequila lover's guide to Mexico and Mezcal:*

everything there is to know about Tequila and Mezcal ... including how to get there. Wine Patrol Press, 2000.

de Barrios, Virginia B. *Guide to tequila, mezcal and pulque.* Mexics, 1999.

DeGroff, Dale. Craft of *the cocktail : everything you need to know to be a master bartender, with 500 recipes.* Clarkson Potter, 2002.

Elliott, Virginia. *Quiet drinking; a book of beer, wines & cocktails and what to serve with them.* Harcourt Brace, 1933.

Esquire magazine. *Handbook for hosts.* 1953.

Felten, Eric. *How's your drink? : cocktails, culture, and the art of drinking well.* Agate Surrey, 2009.

Fisher, Mary Isabel. *Liqueurs, a dictionary and survey; with sections on dry spirits, aperitifs, and bitters.* Meyer, 1951.

Foley, Ray. *Tequila 1000 : the ultimate collection of tequila cocktails, recipes, facts and resources.* Sourcebooks, 2008.

Gaige, Crosby. *Crosby Gaige's Cocktail Guide and Ladies Companion.* M. Barrows and Co., 1941.

G.L. *Science of taste: being a treatise on its principles.*

Hamlyn. *Little book of brandy cocktails.* 2001.

Haralson, Carol. *Kindred spirits : tending bar, entertaining friends, toasting life.* Council Oaks, 1992.

Herlihy, Patricia. *Vodka : a global history.* Reaktion Books, 2012.

Irving, Andrew. *How to cure a hangover.* Little Books, 2011.

Kaye, Jordan and Marshall Altier. *How to booze : Exquisite Cocktails and Unsound Advice.* Harper Perennial, 2010.

Knorr, Paul. *Vodka bible.* Sterling Innovation, 2010.

Mautone, Nick and Marah Stets. *Raising the bar : better drinks better entertaining.* Artisan, 2004.

Meehan, Jim. *PDT cocktail book : the complete bartender's guide from the celebrated speakeasy.* Sterling Epicure, 2011.

Meilach, Dona and Mel. *Homemade Liqueurs.* Contemporary Books, 1979.

Moore, Victoria. *How to Drink.* Andrews McMeel Publishing, 2009.

Murdock, Catherine Gilbert. *Domesticating Drink: Women, Men, and Alcohol in America, 1870-1940.* The John Hopkins University Press, 2001.

National Federation of Women's Institutes. *Home made wines, syrups, and cordials; recipes of Women's Institute members.* 1956.

Pacult, F. Paul. *Kindred spirits 2 : 2,400 reviews of whiskey, brandy, vodka, tequila, rum, gin, and liqueurs from F. Paul Pacult's spirit journal 2000-2007.* Spirit Journal, Inc., 2008.

Pogash, Jonathan and Rick Rodgers. *Mr. Boston Official Bartender's Guide.* Wiley, 2011.

Pringle, Laurence. *Taste.* Benchmark Books, 2000.

Purcell, Lauren and Anne Purcell Grissinger. *Cocktail parties, straight up! : easy hors d'oeuvres, delicious drinks, and inspired ideas for entertaining with style.* John Wiley & Sons: 2005.

Rathbun, A.J. *Ginger bliss and the violet fizz : a cocktail lover's guide to mixing drinks using new and classic liqueurs.* Boston: The Harvard Common Press, 2011.

Regan, Gary. *The Joy of Mixology.* Clarkson Potter, 2003.

Regan, Gaz. *The Bartender's Gin Compendium.* Xlibris Corp., 2009.

Rouseff, Russell L. *Bitterness in foods and beverages.* Elsevier Science Ltd., 1990

Rowley, Matthew B. *Joy of moonshine : recipes, knee slappers, tall tales, songs, how to make it, how to drink it, pleasin' the law, recoverin' the next day.* Sterling Publishing Company, 2007.

Siegelman, Steve. *Trader Vic's tiki party! : cocktails & food to share with friends.* Ten Speed Press, 2005.

Simmons, Marcia and Halpren, Jonas. *DIY cocktails : a simple guide to creating your own signature drinks.* Adams Media, 2011.

Sperandeo, Victor. *Trader Vic's book of food & drink.* Doubleday & Company, 1946.

Stuckey, Barb. *Taste what you're missing : the passionate eater's guide to why good food tastes good.* Free Press, 2012.

Watkins, Christine. *Alcohol abuse.* Greenhaven Press, 2012.

White, Francesca. *Cheers! : A spirited guide to liquors and liqueurs / distilled, blended and bottled.* New York: Paddington Press, 1977.

Weir, Joanne. *Tequila : a guide to types, flights, cocktails, and bites.* Ten Speed Press, 2009.

Wisniewski, Ian. *Vodka : discovering, exploring, enjoying.* Ryland Peters & Small, 2003.

Wondrich, David. *Killer cocktails : an intoxicating guide to sophisticated drinking : a hands-free step-by-step guide.* Collins, 2005.

Wondrich, David. *Punch : the delights (and dangers) of the flowing bowl.* Perigee Trade, 2010.

Index